D1130855

BUSINESS PRACTICES IN EMERGING AND RE-EMERGING MARKETS

Business Practices in Emerging and Re-Emerging Markets

Satyendra Singh

HD
70
.D44
S56
2008

BUSINESS PRACTICES IN EMERGING AND RE-EMERGING MARKETS
Copyright © Satyendra Singh, 2008.

All rights reserved. No part of this book may be used or reproduced in any manner whatsoever without written permission except in the case of brief quotations embodied in critical articles or reviews.

First published in 2008 by
PALGRAVE MACMILLAN™
175 Fifth Avenue, New York, N.Y. 10010 and
Houndmills, Basingstoke, Hampshire, England RG21 6XS
Companies and representatives throughout the world.

PALGRAVE MACMILLAN is the global academic imprint of the Palgrave Macmillan division of St. Martin's Press, LLC and of Palgrave Macmillan Ltd. Macmillan® is a registered trademark in the United States, United Kingdom and other countries. Palgrave is a registered trademark in the European Union and other countries.

ISBN-13: 978–1–4039–7622–2
ISBN-10: 1–4039–7622–8

Library of Congress Cataloging-in-Publication Data

Singh, Satyendra, 1966–
    Business practices in emerging and re-emerging markets / edited and authored by Satyendra Singh.
        p. cm.
    Includes bibliographical references and index.
    ISBN 1–4039–7622–8
    1. Industrial management—Developing countries. 2. Competition—Developing countries. I. Title.

HD70.D44S56 2008
65809172'4—dc22   2007030426

A catalogue record for this book is available from the British Library.

Design by Newgen Imaging Systems (P) Ltd., Chennai, India.

First edition: March 2008

10 9 8 7 6 5 4 3 2 1

Printed in the United States of America.

Contents

Part II   Business and Ethical Orientations

3 **Business Orientation, Brand Image, and
    Business Performance**   **45**
    Satyendra Singh

List of Figures and Tables

Figures

Tables

List of Abbreviations

BAN	Bain Capability Center
BCG	Boston Consultancy Group
BPO	Business Process Outsourcing
CEO	Chief Executive Officer
CFO	Chief Finance Officer
FPIS	Firm Practice Information System
GRC	Global Research Center
EFCC	Economic and Financial Crimes Commissions
ICPC	Independent Corrupt Practices and Other Related Offences Commission
KAM	Kenya Association of Manufacturers
KRD	Knowledge Resource Directory
KPO	Knowledge Process Outsourcing
MKC	MAC & Co. Knowledge Center
NAFDAC	National Agency for Food and Drug Administration Commission
NCC	National Copyright Commission
NDLEA	Nigerian Drug Law Enforcement Agency
NIPC	National Investment Promotion Commission
NPM	New Public Management
OML	Oil Mining License
OPL	Oil Property License
PDNet	Product Development Network
R&D	Research & Development
R&I	Research and Information
SIC	Standard Industrial Classification Code
SAL	Structural Adjustment Loan
SAP	Structural Adjustment Program
SD	Standard Deviation
SON	Standard Organization of Nigeria

UAE	United Arab Emirates
UNCTD	United Nations Conference on Trade and Development
UK	United Kingdom
VIF	Variation Inflation Factor

Acknowledgments

I gratefully acknowledge the support of University of Winnipeg in providing the Major Research Grant (# 0–60–7380–61020–000) and Discretionary Grant (# 0–60–7122–61020–000) for the research contained in this book. I am particularly thankful to Prof. Dr. Fung-Yee Chan, head of the department for making the office available to me during my sabbatical. It was a great resource. I would also like to thank Ms. Jenna Buckley for taking the time to proofread the chapters, and Dr. Meera Kaur, my wife, for being supportive of the project. Finally, it was my good fortune to work with the editor Anthony Wahl at Palgrave MacMillan Publishing, New York, United States—many thanks to him.

Preface

It appears that most Western firms, particularly giant blue-chips firms, prefer to mechanically translate their business practices and marketing methods to emerging markets in other parts of the world. True, why bother, if they have significant economies of scale and brand recognition. But often this strategy fails to yield desired results because what business practices worked well in the West could not work so well in emerging markets elsewhere. This book is designed to highlight some of the prevailing business practices that you can use to your advantage in the emerging markets of China, Ghana, India, Kenya, Nigeria, and UAE.

Based on the research conducted for this book, it is evident that these markets are undergoing significant economic growth. This growth coupled with a growing class of young professionals and the increasing number of middle-income households has created a demand for internationally recognized brands and products as well as for services of global standards. The arrival of foreign firms in the emerging markets has set a culture of competition and consumerism and has thus changed consumer behavior and lifestyle. Goods are now competitively priced and may also be purchased on credit. Clearly, a better understanding of the competition, business, economy, and social dynamics is needed. The business experience and academic expertise of the contributors of this book will provide the reader with the necessary information to make informed decisions when dealing with the emerging markets.

I urge you to recognize the benefits associated with the business practices highlighted in this book. The comparative nature of some of the chapters will further enlighten you about marketing areas where foreign firms can learn from local firms—and vice-versa—to achieve a sustainable competitive advantage in the global marketplace.

It is my sincere hope that you will find this book interesting and meaningful. Please do send me your comments at s.singh@ uwinnipeg.ca. I promise to respond.

SATYENDRA SINGH
Winnipeg, Canada
May 30, 2007

Notes on Contributors

Dr. J.T. Akinmayowa is Associate Professor in the Department of Business Administration at the University of Benin, Lagos, Nigeria. Before joining academics, he worked as HRD Manager in Nigerian Telecommunications. He is a founding member of the Management Academy of Nigeria. He was the editor of *Benin Journal of Social Sciences* (from 2001 to 2004) and an external examiner and a visiting scholar to the University of Ghana. He has published three books: *Man-in-Organization: A Practical Approach to the Study of Human Behaviour in Organizations* (Benin City, Nigeria: Nigerian Management Consultancy Forum, 1996), *Business Management Foundation* (Benin City, Nigeria: Nigerian Management Consultancy Forum, 2003), and *Human Resources: Critical Issues in Management and Organizational Development* (Benin City, Nigeria: Nigerian Management Consultancy Forum, 2006), and twenty articles in academic journals in Nigeria and overseas.

Prof. Dr. Kwaku Appiah-Adu is currently Head of Policy Coordination, Monitoring, and Evaluation at the Office of the President, and Ghanaian Project Director of the Central Governance Project. He previously was a Consultant with PricewaterhouseCoopers and lectured at Cardiff, Southampton, and Portsmouth Business Schools. He has been elected to the ANBAR Hall of Excellence for Outstanding Contribution to the Literature and Body of Knowledge. Kwaku has served on the boards of several blue-chip companies and is a member of the president's Ghana Investors' Advisory Council, and Coeditor-in-Chief of the *Ghana Management Review*.

Dr. Ajay Bhalla is an Associate Professor at Cass Business School, London, United Kingdom. His research involves studying offshoring forms, vendor relationships, and vendor learning strategies of *Fortune* Global 500 firms. He has published on the subject in leading journals such as *Journal of Operations Management*, and *European Management*

Journal. He actively works as an industry specialist in the area and has consulted large multinational firms.

Dr. Gin Chong is Associate Professor of Accounting at College of Business, Prairie View A&M University (Texas), he has published and presented over 80 academic papers on materiality, corporate governance, and performance measurements. A qualified accountant, he was invited as a visiting scholar to five European and Asian countries. Dr. Chong has received three best paper awards and the Greatest Research Contributions Award from Southampton Solent University (United Kingdom).

Prof. Dr. Peter M. Lewa is a social scientist with extensive working experience in both the public and private sectors. He has been in research, teaching, and consultancy for 16 years, 12 at university level. He has worked for the Government of Kenya for a total of 17 years. He is an established management specialist in Kenya and the region and consults widely in various areas of management, finance, and development.

Dr. Satyendra Singh is Associate Professor in the Department of Business and Administration at the University of Winnipeg, Canada. Dr. Singh has designed and taught courses at all levels in India, the United Kingdom, and Canada, widely published in such journals as *Industrial Marketing Management, Journal of Global Marketing, Journal of Services Marketing,* and *Services Industries Journal,* among others, and presented several papers at international conferences such as AMA, AMS, BAM, EMAC, and NACRA, among others. He is the author of *Market Orientation, Corporate Culture and Business Performance* (Aldershot, UK: Ashgate Publishing Limited, 2004), and editor-in-chief of the *International Journal of Business and Emerging Markets* (Olney, UK: Inderscience Publisher, 2008).

Chapter 1

Introduction

Satyendra Singh

In the last decade or so, several developing countries have been adjusting their economies through economic reform policies whose impact on the markets and consumers are significant. For example, the rapid changes in the international markets and their ever growing importance to firms of all sizes mean that local firms are now forced to compete with the foreign firms that take advantage of relatively low investment costs and to increase their global presence through strategic international alliances. Firms make decisions to enter foreign markets on the basis of the market development prospects and expansion of local economies. Falling trade barriers and the advent of new technologies suggest that local firms have to work harder and smarter to stay ahead of growing competition. In response to such changes taking place in markets, it is logical to expect that the arrival of foreign firms forces local firms to either adopt foreign business paradigm or face the prospect of extinction. For instance, local firms now have to resort to innovation, technology upgrades, and customer service in addition to paying attention to activities such as market orientation, ethical issues, changing lifestyle, and consumer behavior, and so forth.

The reason for adopting the business paradigm is simple: now consumers in the emerging markets are able to compare products and services between local and foreign firms. As a result, local firms have become competitive by being market oriented, that is, being able to meet the needs of customers. But satisfying the needs of customers is not sufficient, because some demanding customers have a desire to know the production process as well. They want to ensure that firms do not exploit the environment, experiment on animals, or engage in unethical practices. The sources for such education were Internet technology, mass communication, and the strong positioning of foreign brands that were perceived as *pure*, *natural*, and free from *unethical practices*—either during the production process or while marketing. Further, the economic reform policies designed to increase the purchasing power of consumers contributed to an increase in their spending that gave birth to consumerism. Because marketing is the core discipline of consumption, it is uniquely empowered and positioned to influence consumer behavior. This book is designed to highlight current business practices in the emerging markets by tracking business and ethical orientation of firms, monitoring lifestyle and consumer behavior, and reporting business performance measurement and standards.

Aims and Objectives of the Book

The aims and objectives of this book are to provide (1) a text in international business that is applicable to both business students and practicing managers in emerging markets of transitional economies; (2) a coverage of business orientations such as market, social, economical, and ethical orientations as strategies to achieve competitive advantages; (3) a coverage of changing lifestyle and consumer behavior in the emerging markets; and (4) an assessment of resultant business practices and performance measures adopted by International Joint Ventures.

Definition of Emerging Markets

Definition of emerging market is controversial and inconsistent (Batra, 1999; Peng, 2000). Organizations such as International Monetary Fund, United Nations, and the World Bank, among others differ in their definitions. Thus, there is no worldwide agreement on how to categorize countries based on development. A common wisdom is that developing and emerging markets have traditionally been defined not by what they are but by what they are not. For example, Hong Kong has a well-developed local economy, but its domestic market is miniscule given the size of its economy. Its economic prosperity is based on import and export to China. So, Hong Kong may be a developed country in a narrow-definition sense but it suffers from a risk exposure equivalent to any emerging market. Most business and investment managers agree with this line of argument. In general, emerging markets of particular interest to international investors and business managers are those tracked by the International Finance Corporation (IFC) and the Morgan Stanley Capital International (MSCI). The IFC definition of emerging market has four characteristics: (1) growth,

(2) change (economic, financial, and political), (3) ability to invest, and (4) size and liquidity. MSCI distinguishes between emerging markets and developed countries using three criteria. To be classified as a developed country, (1) the country's per capita income must exceed $10,000; (2) the country should have stable macroeconomic policies; and (3) the market capitalization of publicly traded companies and the volume of shares traded on the stock exchange should be sufficient. Failure to meet any of the above criteria will classify the country as an emerging market. Thus, Israel or South Korea would pass the income criterion and yet belong to emerging markets. The World Trade Organization (WTO) does not have definitions for developed or developing country. It distinguishes between the two sets based on self-selection. Two-thirds of the WTO's 149 member countries are designated as developing countries, of which 50 are designated as least-developed countries. The United Nations Development Program (2005) classifies countries based on a human development index for each country that takes into account factors such as life expectancy at birth, adult literacy and educational attainment, and gross domestic product (GDP) per capita at Purchase Power Parity (PPP). A low to medium score on the index usually corresponds to characteristics of emerging markets. Similarly, the World Bank's (2006) classification of countries is based on gross national income per capita (GNI) adjusted for currency fluctuations. Clearly, different definitions will result in different classifications of countries, because the characteristics are country specific. Therefore, each chapter in this book gives its own definition of emerging market and follows in general what Errunza (1997) suggests: the true test for emerging status is the commitment and credibility of reforms/liberalization together with an acceptable market development and a potential for investments. The implicit or explicit barriers to the free flow of capital that segment emerging markets are the defining characteristics. Geographically, emerging markets comprise of former states of Russia, Eastern Bloc, Asia, Middle East, and a few countries in Latin America and Africa. It is also suggested that some emerging markets such as India, which once (1000 B.C) had a well-developed economy, should also be classified as re-emerging markets. For the purpose of the book, emerging markets are practically synonymous with re-emerging markets and developing countries.

The Conceptual Framework of the Book

The premise of this book is that consumer behavior is influenced by what firms offer and how they educate consumers to consume.

Figure 1.1 captures the general structure and process of consumer behavior that leads to formalizing business practices and strategies. This framework, although fairly simple, theoretically sound, and intuitively appealing, reflects our beliefs about the general nature of consumer behavior. The arrows flow in opposite direction because of the interactive nature of the factors that determine the relationship between business practices and emerging markets. Further, merit of the feedback mechanism demonstrates that emerging markets are dynamic and subject to change.

Although a competitive advantage can be achieved through several strategies (e.g., by emphasizing on superior quality products and services, attaining economies of scale, pursuing innovation, and developing technology, among others), the concept of achieving competitive advantage through developing *business* and *ethical* orientations in firms in emerging economies is relatively new and scarcely tested. Little is known about how managers decide what competitive advantages distinguish their businesses from competition and how those advantages

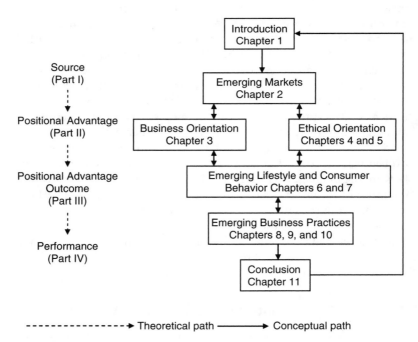

Figure 1.1 The conceptual framework

were gained. Drawing on Day and Wensley's (1988) theory of source-position-performance, we have conceptualized *emerging markets* as the source, *business and ethical orientations* as the competitive positional advantage of the firms, *lifestyle and consumer behavior* as outcome of the positional advantage, and *emerging business practices* as resulting performance of the firms. We hypothesize that emerging markets are the source of competitive advantage because these markets present opportunities to foreign firms to enter the markets and market their products and services. We assume that the foreign firms that exploit the emerging markets are business and ethically oriented. Extending the seminal work of Keith (1960) about Pillsbury's evolution through production, selling, marketing, etcetera, we define business orientation as a three-component—marketing, social, and economic—orientation that aims to achieve desired exchange outcomes (sales and profit) with target markets (Kotler, 1997).

For the definition of ethical orientation, we have drawn on two moral philosophies: deontological and teleological. Deontological philosophy is rule-based and incorporates the use of logic and code of ethics protocol to identify moral duties, whereas teleological philosophy is consequence-based and incorporates the use of cost-benefit analysis, and the evaluation of costs incurred by society as a whole. We have also assumed that foreign firms and consumers have higher moral standards and purchasing power than firms and consumers in emerging markets. Through this assumption, it is logical to expect that the presence of foreign firms in emerging markets will force local firms to be business and ethically oriented. Thus, we hypothesize that local managers will attempt to position their firms as business and ethically oriented to have competitive positions over their nonbusiness and nonethically oriented counterparts.

Then, these firms are expected to use their competitive position to influence the lifestyle of consumers, modify their behavior, and increase their spending. This is probably not news; however, the extent to which business and ethical orientation of firms contributes to lifestyle and changing consumer behavior can be surprising. To explain this, we advance the theory by adding an intermediary step that we call *positional advantage outcome* to the framework, as it is necessary in an emerging market to modify significantly the lifestyle of consumers before firms can expect to notice superior business performance. This is because of two reasons that, although less applicable to Western markets, are significant in emerging markets. First, the consumers in emerging markets are not used to foreign or foreign-style products (e.g., not accustomed to eating burgers in breakfast—cultural reason, or beef—religious reason); and, second, some consumers may not have enough purchasing power (e.g., not accustomed to taking bank loans—cultural reason, or embarrassed to apply for a credit card—psychological reason). True, with the passage of time, the lifestyle turns into behavior that generates constant needs and desires. To satisfy this, a consumer decision-making process is activated that causes business managers to adjust their business strategies to accommodate the new lifestyle.

The Pedagogy, Positioning, and Organization of the Book

This book offers a different approach to international business. One of the key intentions of this book is to provide a multidimensional analysis in multinational markets. Therefore, it is based on the recognition of diversity in the emerging markets and of the knowledge of local consumers. The book compels the reader to be an out-of-the-box thinker as much as Gorn (1997) invites us to break out of North American boxes. In this regard, it is written in a pragmatic and issue-related style germane to the markets. By researching the important business-focused projects in six countries, this book highlights the business practices and strategies of the emerging market masters. Selection of the emerging markets—China, Ghana, India, Kenya, Nigeria, and United Arab Emirates—is based on the unique market conditions and significant potential growth for both foreign investors and local exporters. Further, the concept of this book places a high value on the relatedness of themes; therefore, the contributors of the chapters have been selected with the objective to ensure that the conceptual issues raised in this introduction chapter are followed up in a logical manner in the succeeding chapters.

In addition to providing contextual relevance and novelty on emerging markets, this book differentiates itself by responding to numerous calls made for business schools to revise their curricula and introduce newer pedagogical strategies that are better suited for developing the necessary professional skills for today's students (Jenkins and Reizenstein, 1984; Buckley et al., 1989; Commission on Admission to Graduate Management Education, 1990; Elliot et al., 1994; Pfeffer and Fong, 2002). Achieving the professional skills through the pedagogical strategies—interaction in the classroom and decomposition of the chapters—is a distinct point of differentiation of this book.

Interaction in the classroom is based on the objectives stated in the beginning of each chapter that relates to a specific issue in an emerging market and facilitates two-way communication between the professor and students, and among students. Because different chapters are on different countries, the objectives of these chapters are to develop tolerance, respect, and open-mindedness in a culturally diverse world. These chapters should create an environment conducive to participating actively in the learning and teaching process, so the business students will have an increased understanding of foreign consumer behavior, different economies, languages, cultures, customs, and business practices. The objectives are designed to accommodate different perspectives on different issues. Further, the decomposition of the chapters in a group setting is another aspect of the book that allows students to take a chapter as a group project, evaluate it critically, and present their findings. This approach fosters interactivity with each other while the professor acts as a consultant or manager of the learning process. In fact, this approach is recommended for business students, as they will be required to work in small groups in real business situations.

This book is positioned as a research-based book, written by native experienced professors, and is rich in context, theory, and practice. So, it is specific to critical issues of emerging markets, exposing the readers to various specific critical issues relating to business in the context of emerging markets. This book is organized in four parts: source, positional advantage, positional advantage outcome, and performance. Part I has one chapter and relates to issues concerning transformation of economies from a planned economy to a market economy and its impact on businesses. Part II has three chapters and deals with the need for firms to be business and ethically oriented. Part III has two chapters and focuses on changes taking place in lifestyle and consumer behavior. And, Part IV has three chapters on emerging business practices and strategies. In the following section, importance, relevance, and usefulness of the chapters are briefly presented. As mentioned earlier, each chapter has objectives that serve as questions for either classroom or workshop discussion.

Summary of Chapters

Part I   The Emerging Markets

Economic reform policies in Kenya have responded to the Structural Adjustment Programs (SAP) that were implemented in the African continent to reduce the role of state and increase the participation of private sectors in the economy. Peter Lewa, in chapter two, looks at the theoretical and conceptual issues relating to the SAP in the emerging market of Kenya, a country that was quick to embrace economic development programs along with other cognate economic initiatives sponsored by Western countries. By applying a urban bias theory rather than taking a universal perspective, Lewa analyzes Kenyan firms and provides answers to two fundamental questions: What is the extent to which the SAPs have altered business practices of Kenyan firms? How will the newly emerged business paradigm determine whether the market players will succeed or fail in the global economy? In addition, he asserts that Kenyan business leaders should develop market-oriented firms and a skilled labor force, and that the slogan of the African union *democracy and economic development* must be implemented. Lewa offers a prescription for change by recommending a new approach to corporate leadership, an approach that puts emphasis on departure from the supply oriented autocratic leadership to a market-oriented democratic leadership style, one which creates competitive environment, generates information relating to customers, and develops suitable products to satisfy their needs.

Part II   Business and Ethical Orientations

In chapter three at a broader level, I examine the impact of economic reform policies, instituted by the Government of India in 1991, on the consumers, and the extent to which these policies have altered firms' marketing, social, and economic practices. The economic reform policies have propelled India to an unprecedented level of economic growth and reshaped markets by introducing new opportunities to foreign and local firms. This burgeoning consumer market has attracted international firms to promote their products and services. The rapid pace of economic development not only brought prosperity to Indian consumers but also enhanced their purchasing power and spending habits. This change in society established a culture of consumerism (Singh, 2003). I contribute to the chapter by discussing the impact of economic reform on business performance, comparing business practices of foreign and local firms, and highlighting the future of marketing in the Indian market.

In chapter four, I examine the effects of two moral philosophies—deontological and teleological—on profitability. Drawing on the source-position-performance theory, it is argued that firms that are perceived ethical are more likely to have a positive impact on profitability than firms that are not. Results indicate that ethical business practices lead firms to superior profitability through the acquisition of competitive advantage. Irrespective of the moral philosophy practiced by firms, results further suggest that the effects of ethical practices on profitability are initially negative but turn positive with higher levels of ethical orientation. Indeed, managers can command a premium price for their products if their firms are being perceived as ethical.

In chapter five, Taiwo Akinmayowa questions unethical business practices prevalent in Nigerian businesses. The selection of the emerging markets for the study could not have been better. For example, Uniliver allegedly hedged up its profits by about N1.2 billion, and African Petroleum (AP) concealed N26 billion debt during the privatization of Federal Government shares in the oil company, amounting to about N2.1 billion (Onyenankeya, 2003). Admittedly, the Western managers of firms who were once perceived to be more ethical than the rest of the world could no longer depend upon their clean corporate image, particularly given the recent scandals created by the world giants. For example, Worldcom, Xerox, Quest Communication International, Arthur Anderson, and Halliburton were involved in financial scandals. Akinmayowa suggests how Nigerian firms can have a competitive advantage by being ethical in areas relating to product adulteration and piracy, deceptive packaging and promotion, wrong labeling, tampered operating instructions, manipulated expiry dates on products including health care products, misleading advertisements, advance fee fraud, money laundering, and document racketeering. Indeed, the Nigerian government is committed to pursue a range of economic reforms to create a business-friendly environment to attract foreign investors.

Part III   Emerging Lifestyle and Consumer Behavior

Clearly, the implementation of economic reform policies has an impact on firms and consumers. Firms have become more competitive and consumers more sophisticated. And one of the ways of expressing sophistication is the willingness to drink wine—an indication of changed lifestyle. In chapter six, I focus on the lifestyle and consumer behavior of Indian consumers brought about by economic liberalization, as evidenced by a significant increase in wine consumption and wine producers in India. Due to the arrival of the Internet technology and rise in education, today, Indian consumers are more informed, discerning, and health conscious than before, so their decision-making process is more logical, rational, and personal. Taking these social and personal changes into account, I argue that the gradual rise in wine drinking in India is a sign of changing lifestyle because the majority of the consumers prior to economic reform could not afford to drink wine, and that the previous social culture was not conducive to wine drinking.

Thus, selection of wine as a product is suitable for the objective of the study because moderate use of wine is good for health (i.e., prescription-based consumption), and entertainment (i.e., for pleasure-based consumption). In other words, the attitude of consumers toward wine consumption has changed. Singh tracks the *attitude* of consumers to predict the lifestyle-based segments—prescription versus pleasure. Because wine purchasing is a behavioral process that involves individual choices and preferences based on lifestyle, I conceptualize and proposes that the emerging Indian wine market can be segmented on the basis of the *healthy lifestyle (prescription reason)* that aims to be free from cardiovascular disease, and the *happy lifestyle (pleasure reason)* that aims to seek pleasure in a social setting. As segments are related to behavior, they present a useful starting point (Kotler and Armstong, 1996) for examining differences between segments based on purchases and usages (Morris, 1996), particularly because segment-based lifestyle is more contemporary than personality and more comprehensive than personal values (Blackwell et al., 2001). Indeed, wine is a sophisticated product and requires sophisticated marketing.

In chapter seven, I, in collaboration with Kwaku Appiah-Adu, extend the focus of lifestyle in the emerging market of United Arab Emirates. Their premise is that if the lifestyle in emerging markets is becoming compatible with Western lifestyle, then the advertisements created in the West should be effective in emerging markets as well. To test the premise, they examine the effects of the emerging market of United Arab Emirates on lifestyle as evidenced by creativity in advertisements in that country, and measure the extent to which creative directors are successful in retaining creativity while transforming advertisements from the Western market to the emerging market. It is an important issue for international managers because now they have to respect the culture and traditional values of the emerging market. Straight translation of advertisements from English to Arabic is neither effective nor sufficient.

Thus, the key issues that I and Appiah-Adu address are: How do creative directors translate creative themes of lifestyle-based advertisements from the Western market to the emerging market? What happens to the creativity in advertisements during transformation? Does it remain intact or altered? The assumption is that consumers grow up in a particular culture and become accustomed to that culture's value systems, beliefs, and perception processes. Consequently, consumers respond to advertising messages that are congruent with their culture, rewarding advertisers who understand their culture. For this very reason, foreign firms must generate creative advertising ideas to convey their messages without offending consumers' value system in the emerging market. Indeed, the development of advertising campaigns can be challenging in the emerging market; therefore, an understanding of cultural differences is necessary for successful international marketing.

Part IV   Emerging Business Practices

Undoubtedly, as evident in preceding chapters, marketing is becoming increasingly relevant to emerging markets. In chapter eight, Kwaku Appiah-Adu and I argue that the increasing interest in marketing practices and its implementation stems from the important contribution of marketing to the survival of firms in today's fiercely competitive business environment. They advocate that firms should not only concentrate on the fundamental 4Ps—product, price, promotion, and place—but also focus on customer-oriented factors such as customer satisfaction, research and development, and quality management, among others.

Drawing from a sample of firms based in the emerging market of Ghana, they combine the Ps and compare the two sets of managers (foreign and local) to identify Ps that are more important and explain why. Selection of the market is ideal as Ghana is among the first sub-Sahara African countries to subscribe to the International Monetary Fund's Structural Adjustment Program and is considered by the International Monetary Fund and World Bank experts as a model for success in the Third World. Further, they investigate the underlying differences between the perceived importance and performance of marketing activities in foreign and local firms operating in Ghana, determine the role of the marketing function, and identify actual performances of marketing activities such as firms' core competencies, foreign price competitiveness, logistical practices, intermediaries network, distribution activities, personnel training, outlet surroundings, among others. True, even the most outstanding product or services needs the right positioning in the right market at the right time.

Obviously, performing well in emerging markets is good. But how good is good? It must be measured against a set target by using standard performance measurement method so that the performances of business units could be compared. However, the literature on how preference of overseas firms is measured seems to be limited. This could be due to the fact that the process of locating part of the Western business activities to emerging markets has only emerged recently. In chapter nine, Gin Chong identifies two major factors—internal (i.e., agency, control, strategy, technology, and transaction costs) and external (i.e., culture and society, economy and market size, government and politics, industry structure, and resource-based supports)—and suggests an appropriate method for performance measurement of firms operating in the emerging market of China.

Chong notes that several firms tend to rely solely on the financial perspective, whereas others such as Kaplan and Norton (1996) use a combination of both financial and nonfinancial indicators for the measurement of business performance. Laitinen (2002), however, suggests that performance should be measured and evaluated by a matching process, for example, the costs or investments should be matched with results or benefits. Chong proposes to test the validity of the model in China and compares it with the United States. Specifically, he reports on (1) how performance is being measured and assessed; (2) which approach and process are practiced; and (3) which measurement is deemed fair and appropriate. Findings and discussion from this chapter will help international managers understand Chinese and U.S. practices on performance measurement and set appropriate level of targets for both the parents and overseas firms alike.

Over the last decade, we have also observed firms transferring their business processes such as information technology (IT), customer service, transaction processing, and research and development to emerging markets such as India and China. Termed as offshoring, this practice is defined as a process by which firms undertake some of their business activities at offshore locations. Usually, firms shift manufacturing or menial activities to offshore locations to take advantage of low costs of wages in emerging markets; however, in the late 1990s, a new type of offshoring has emerged—information technology. Offshoring IT functions to emerging markets enables Western firms to compete globally. In fact, high-quality work and services provided by emerging markets have led Western firms to realize that offshoring may offer new opportunities to build organizational capabilities, leverage innovation processes, and enhance knowledge-driven processes.

In chapter ten, Ajay Bhalla introduces a case study that illustrates the experience of a large consulting firm called MAC & Company that set up an internal offshore research operation in India. The study suggests that successful offshoring should depend not only on how much cheaper it is to perform activities offshore versus in-house but also on developing the right offshoring option. When offshoring in emerging markets, Bhalla points out that managers can choose from partnering with a specialist provider to setting up a wholly owned offshore facility. The net benefit of offshoring need not be as high as the wage differentials between the countries, because overreliance on offshore outsourcing can damage the ability of firms to innovate products or services, develop internal capabilities, and achieve technological breakthroughs. The case illustrates how offshoring the research function in an emerging market can lead to the transformation of MAC & Company.

In the same chapter, Peter Lewa, through a case study, discusses the emerging business practices in Kenya in the automobile industry. This case describes the evolution and operations of MAST East Africa Limited as a result of economic liberalization. The liberalization increased competition in the marketplace and forced the company to address the issue of change management. The case demonstrates how MAST managed change.

Chapter eleven draws conclusion. It is clear from the text of the book that the key characteristics of an emerging market are (1) the shift in the market constellation from a seller's to a buyer's market and (2) the ability of formerly state-owned firms to transform themselves into market-oriented competitive firms. Consumers are changing their behavior rapidly and applying a rather rational buying behavior, causing tension for international business managers. The chapter addresses the persistent question as to what can viably be promoted in the emerging markets and the appropriate form of business practices through which such possibilities can be pursued.

References

Batra, R. "Marketing Issues and Challenges in Transitional Economies." In *Marketing Issues in Transitional Issues*, ed. Batra, R., 3–35. Norwell, MA: Kluwer Academic Press, 1999.

Blackwell, R.D., Miniard, P.W., and Engel, J.F. *Consumer Behaviour.* Orlando: Harcourt, 2001.

Buckley, M.R., Peach, E.B., and Weitzel, W. "Are Collegiate Programs Adequately Preparing Students for the Business World?" *Journal of Education for Business* 65, no. 3 (1989): 101–105.

Commission on Admission to Graduate Management Education. *Leadership for a Changing World Los Angeles*, Graduate Management Admission Council, 1990.

Day, G.S., and Wensley, R. "A Framework for Diagnosing Competitive Superiority." *Journal of Marketing* 52, no. 2 (1988): 1–20.

Elliot, C., Goodwin, J.S., and Goodwin, J.C. "MBA Program and Business Needs: Is There a Mismatch?" *Business Horizon* 37, no. 4 (1994): 55–60.

Errunza, V.R. "Research on Emerging Markets: Past, Present, and Future." *Emerging Markets Quarterly* 1, no. 3 (1997): 5–14.

Gorn, G. "Breaking Out of the North American Box." In *Advances in Consumer Research*, ed. Brucks, M., and McInnis, D. Vol. 24, 6–7, Provo, UT: Association for Consumer Research, 1997.

Jenkins, R.L., and Reizenstein, R.C. "Insights into the MBAs: Its Contents, Output, and Relevance." *Selections* 1 (1984): 19–24.

Kaplan, R.S., and Norton, D.P. *Balanced Scorecard.* Boston: Harvard Business School Press, 1996.

Keith, R.J. "The Marketing Revolution." *Journal of Marketing* 24, no. 1 (1960): 35–38.

Kotler, P. *Marketing Management.* Englewood-Cliffs, NJ: Prentice Hall, 1997.

Kotler, P., and Armstrong, G. *Principles of Marketing.* London: Prentice-Hall, 1996.

Laitinen, E.K. "A Dynamic Performance Measurement System: Evidence from Small Finnish Technology Companies." *Scandinavian Journal of Management* 18, no. 1 (2002): 65–99.

Morris, J. "Segment Your Market to Survive." *Communications International* 23 (1996): 131.

Onyenankeya, K. "Financial Crimes: The Nigerian Experience." *Nigerian Stock Market Annual* (2003): 25–33.

Peng, M.W. *Business Strategies in Transition Economies.* Thousand Oaks, CA: Sage Publications, 2000.

Pfeffer, J., and Fong, C.T. "The End of Business Schools? Less Success than Meets the Eye." *Academy of Management Learning and Education* 1 (2002): 78–95.

Singh, S. "Effects of Transition Economy on the Market Orientation-Business Performance Link: The Empirical Evidence from Indian Industrial Firms." *Journal of Global Marketing* 16, no. 4 (2003): 73–96.

United Nations Development Program. *Human Development Report.* New York: Oxford University Press, 2005.

World Bank. *World Development Report 2006: Equity and Development.* New York: Oxford University Press, 2006.

Part I

The Emerging Markets

Chapter 2

Market Liberalization in Emerging Economies: Changing Business Practices

Peter M. Lewa

This chapter demonstrates how economic reform in Kenya has been shaped by the influence of politically powerful vested interests. The reform can, therefore, be largely explained in a political sense. In the wisdom of urban bias that underlines Structural Adjustment Programs (SAP), it was observed that the poor performance of Kenya's economy was due to political motivations, yet politics was a neglected dimension in the reform process right from the beginning of SAPs. Politics should have been better understood and better managed in reform in order to improve reform outcomes. Using the urban bias theory, the chapter provides a useful explanation as to why African governments had formulated and implemented policies that were antirural, thereby undermining agriculture—the most important sector in their economies. The specific objectives of the chapter are to (1) understand the key features of a state-controlled economy; (2) appreciate how liberalization of Kenya's economy changed business practices; (3) appreciate the value of politics and political interest groups in the economy; (4) understand the emerging economy of Kenya; and (5) appreciate the critical factors affecting the emerging markets of Kenya.

Introduction

Kenya is a large country situated in Eastern Africa. Its total land area is estimated at over 580,000 square kilometers (Downing et al., 1989). Its land mass stretches from the Indian ocean in the east to Lake Victoria in the west and from the Serengeti plains in the south bordering Tanzania to Ethiopia in the north. Sudan and Uganda border Kenya to the west, while Somalia is to the east. The country straddles the equator with the natural environment ranging from the coastal monsoon belt through arid and semiarid lands to temperate highland zones suited to farming pattern to that of Europe (Hunt, 1984). These zones provide the bulk of the crops for home consumption and export. In between are the large areas of semiarid agricultural land where pastoralism and subsistence farming are carried on simultaneously. The western part of the country consists of well-watered tropical uplands.

Kenya is divided by administrative boundaries mostly laid down during the colonial time for ease of administration. There are eight provinces including the metropolitan city of Nairobi. A province comprises several districts. Within each district there are divisions, and each division has several locations that in turn have several sublocations. A sublocation is made up of several villages. In many ways, Kenya is a microcosm of Africa. Most of the important African ethnic groups are found in Kenya (Anker and Knowles, 1983). They include Bantu, Nilotic, Nilo-Hamitic, Arab, Asian, and European peoples. The indigenous people have consumption habits and lifestyles that are found elsewhere in Africa. Many of them consume local as well as foreign-produced goods and services. Due to increased urbanization, foreign-produced goods and services have gained prominence even among people who have traditionally depended on locally produced goods and services.

Several years of colonial rule in Kenya that ended in 1963 have had immense influence on the development of the country's economy, politics, and people in general. Mosley et al. (1991) summarize the central features of Kenya's political economy before liberalization as the domination of the economy by large agrarian interests that also dominated policymaking, a patchy and politically weak industrial sector, and the dominance of racial issues in economic policymaking. These political factors are important to understand Kenya's experience with reform measures implemented in the early 1980s. The first factor explains why so much was expected of Kenya when she embarked on SAPs, and the last two factors why she delivered so little initially from the World Bank's viewpoint.

A crucial legacy of the colonial period was the use of key sectors of the economy for patronage purposes. The basic features of the paternalistic, bureaucratic, colonial state became the model for the independent state of Kenya. At independence in 1963, the state was left as the dominant source of power and used the hitherto generally centralized institutions for exercising that power. Local rule quickly assumed the same structures as existed before independence. The existing ideology of the time supported the idea of a strong state and as such the new state of Kenya became an important player in the economy.

The new state exercised its control through creation of state enterprises in nearly all sectors and also continued a system of controls and licensing of businesses. No business could engage in any activity without obtaining numerous licenses including those for marketing and movement of goods. Reforms within the SAPs agenda aimed to challenge this arrangement. In Kenya, as in many other countries, public enterprise has been the principal feature of official policy for many years and before the call for reforms was sounded in the early 1980s, private enterprise in nearly all sectors had been completely overshadowed by public enterprise. Those holding official positions in public enterprises wielded immense power and in many ways determined how marketing developed in Kenya.

Kenya never had serious deep ideological differences. As Arnold (1981) observes, "The political elite wants to maintain the broad status quo of a reasonably capitalist-oriented society whose state interventions are geared to ensuring maximum Kenyan participation in this process." The civil servants use their offices to create power bases for themselves and their collaborators. Some use their power bases to launch themselves into politics. They must keep active rural and urban support through the client-patronage system of Kenya. They must pay the farmers well, please the elite, and provide them with services in order to get their support (Lewa, 1995).

Methodology

Because of a dearth of secondary data, the researcher relied on primary data. Because the agricultural sector is the mainstay of Kenya's economy, much of the available literature relates to agriculture, and agricultural firms, particularly state enterprises and organizations in the distributive trade. Use of in-depth interviewing techniques and anecdotal evidence were critical in this study. Use of structured surveys was avoided, as these were not found appropriate for this highly politicized area of investigation, where information is traditionally secretly guarded. Data collection methods used for the study were in-depth interviews, focus group interviews, and rapid rural appraisal.

In-depth individual interviews were guided by a detailed checklist that contained the issues of interest. The researcher, through the visits to each of the industrial firms, selected respondents for the interview and administered the checklist. This technique is well suited to obtaining information of a sensitive or complex nature (Magrath, 1992); however, it suffers from elite bias (Lipton and More, 1972). To overcome the bias, the responses of each of the firms interviewed were checked against each other and the matters that could not be clarified that way were crosschecked during a focus group interview. To qualify for inclusion in the focus group, respondents (all 35 years or more of age) must have had at least (1) ten years of work experience at senior levels; (2) a first degree or equivalent; and (3) a direct involvement in the relevant products or services. There was a gender balance in the group. We obtained the sample frame from the list of members provided by The Kenya Association of Manufacturers (KAM, 2006).

During the earlier period of the pilot study, we realized that the questions were sensitive and thus the use of direct interviewing technique was not feasible. This led to the choice of indirect interviewing method; however, the need to crosscheck information on the actual operations, attitudes, and perceptions of selected firms necessitated the use of the focus group interview technique. This technique is useful and appropriate in the context of marketing policy studies in finding out information about industrial (milling) facilities and other local facilities (Magrath, 1992). It may also be used in eliciting views about a subsector's performance, constraints and opportunities for development, and government policies (Holtzman, 1986). The selected group consisted of representatives from the large industrial concerns such as maize and wheat milling firms, automobile industry players, grain marketing and distribution firms, and agricultural enterprises (some of which have substantial state interest). Also private traders and some consumers had been invited because of their interests in the research.

Rapid appraisal was used during the period of the pilot survey. The aim was to test the checklist to be used for the main field research. At the same time, this researcher wished to get a feel of the broad change in the reform process and gauge the sensitivity of the issues in question. Quick responses were needed and, therefore, this method deemed appropriate. By examining various market factors, officials from major manufacturers, government officers, and donor agencies, the reform issues requiring in-depth interviews were brought to the surface. Interviews were followed up by telephone calls and visits to enhance feedbacks from the respondents. This was necessary to facilitate and explore areas of interest with specific information in specific areas.

The Theoretical Framework

Later in the reform process, calls for democracy were made (Mosley et al., 1991; Toye, 1992). We realized that the power in developing countries was diffused, fragmented, and not competitive. There was a need for democracy so that everyone could get a chance to enjoy universal suffrage, citizen rights, and basic freedoms, ensuring poor people enjoyed increased opportunities (World Bank, 1986). By implication, because of the lack of democracy, the citizenry was disadvantaged and only those interest groups with power were able to benefit from the state-controlled marketing activities. The groups that benefited were the politically well-connected and included industrialists, bureaucrats, and urban workers who formed a coalition that captured governments for their own interests (Lipton, 1977; Bates, 1981). Politics had thus assumed a new dimension in the reform agenda.

Omission of Politics in SAPs

SAPs emphasized, among other changes, the withdrawal of the state, privatization of state enterprises, reduction of the role of marketing boards in marketing and distribution activities, increased role of the private sector and the markets, decontrol of the price regime, increased role for the voluntary sector—all at the expense of the political aspects of reform. This was a serious omission in the reform process. As Toye (1992) observes, "When at the very beginning of the 1980s, international agencies such as the IMF and the World Bank suddenly started to advocate policies of structural adjustment to the governments of developing countries, discussions of the political aspects of structural adjustment were very much *sub rosa*. They were not on the formal agenda of debate."

Yet politics was a key factor in the reform process. In fact, it became the point of reference for politicians in Kenya when they commented on the reforms. At the height of reforms, politicians in Kenya described them as suicidal (*Weekly Review*, 1994a, b, 1995). The government of Kenya pursued reform measures only when it had been considered politically prudent to do so (Mosley et al., 1991). Yet the politics of the reform program and how it had affected the marketing function remained largely unexplored. Private companies in Kenya faced particular difficulties arising mainly from the failure of the government to reform the existing institutional arrangements when reforms were instituted. This was particularly so in terms of the marketing arrangements and price controls. There had been failure to understand how Kenyan politics and particular interest groups operated in Kenya. One reason is that reforms initially were seen from the point of view of economics, and politics became an agenda item only much later.

Political Interest Groups

Interests both within and outside Kenya had influence on Kenya's reform. External interests express themselves through donors such as the World Bank, International Monetary Fund, and European Commission, among others. Individual donors also have their own vested interests in reform. Several types of vested interests that had influence in Kenya's major sectors, especially agriculture, exist (Heyer et al., 1976; Cowen, 1985; Bates, 1981, 1989; Lofchie, 1989). For example, Toye (1992) observed that the arrangements of maize and maize products' marketing in Kenya constituted a well-established vested interest of large maize farmers, including the president. Mosley et al. (1991), commenting on the delay of the World Bank structural adjustment loan to Kenya due to the government's failure to decontrol maize and maize products' movement and delay in land reform, observed that "it was scarcely in the interest of the large farmers who made up the bulk of the President's agricultural power base. More dramatically, it was also the case with maize decontrol." The bureaucracy, allegedly manipulated as a direct instrument of presidential power (Toye, 1992), is yet another group. Politicians, ruling party supporters in both rural and urban areas, and producers and distributors in the various sectors comprised the other beneficiaries of government intervention in the economy.

The influence of politics in the reform process has been recognized in the case of other developing countries as well (Toye, 1992; Bates and Krueger, 1993; Krueger, 1993). In their study of eight countries, Bates and Krueger observed that it was very often political factors that influenced the authorities negatively in their adoption of reforms. In other words, the pressure of political interest groups had an important bearing on reform. Disagreement with the donors on key aspects of reform, such as sequencing and timetabling of key aspects as well as withdrawal of donor funds in 1991 to force the government of Kenya to adopt multiparty democracy, contributed to government's initial slow response to reform (Mosley et al., 1991). The nature of government reaction to reform therefore can at best be described as uncertain and very slow indeed in the initial stages. This is in spite of the fact that some of the reform measures such as lifting of controls had immediate, certain, and positive results (Lewa, 1995; KAM, 2006). However, it should be observed that once reform measures became entrenched, Kenya accelerated its move to reform its economy.

Mainly because of the previous government's controlled trading regime, manufacturers of goods and services had undeveloped marketing, distribution, and transportation systems. Thus, their marketing and business systems remained largely underdeveloped. In addition, the private sector initially did not take up the challenge of reform because of problems of finance, underdeveloped markets, poor infrastructure, and confusing legislation. Despite agreeing in principle to liberalize all sectors of the economy and thus to allow the development of the private sector, the Kenyan government has generally adopted a slow and phased approach that it considered more politically feasible (Duncan, 1992).

Reforms led to changes in the way business and marketing functions used to be carried out. Old coalitions became irrelevant and new ones emerged. In the postliberalization phase, particularly after 1992, new coalitions formed, and this altered the way transactions and relations in the marketing system used to be. The nature of competition also changed.

The old coalition of mostly large urban interests, large farmers, state marketing boards, politicians, and key industrialists used to be tied together through a system of regulatory frameworks, notably controls and permits. Even though they captured government policies for their own benefits, their way of operation, their impact, and their constitution disagreed with the conventional view of the theory of urban bias.

Original business arrangements as explained above were disturbed by the introduction of market liberalization measures, and new ways of transacting business started forming in the marketing system. Many market actors increased their activities and started doing business in innovative ways. They started developing sources of supply and new markets. The resultant coalitions benefited both the rural and urban areas. Previously, because of controls, consumers had to accept whatever producers offered. They had almost no choices.

If the urban bias theory has relevance to the reform of the key economic sectors including the industrial sector, the expectation is that those interests that used to benefit from the previous marketing arrangements would oppose the reform. There would be negative effects on the urban interests through reduction of rents accruing to them. However, all the interest groups supported the reforms that led to the liberalization of the economy. They were so enthusiastic that they surprised the politicians and bureaucrats who used to argue that the different interests would not support reform (KAM, 2006). The Kenyan experience of reform goes beyond the simplistic approach of an urban coalition, benefiting only the urban centers at the expense of the rural areas. In Kenya, the interests are both rural and urban, and the various groups are linked in intricate ways. The situation is much more complex than the urban bias theory would seem to suggest. It would appear that the institutional arrangements that existed before reform determined what happened after reform. History also seems to explain some aspects. Some exogenous factors such as donor pressure also contribute to the explanation. In other words, a combination of factors explains the reform process in Kenya. The power of politics is, however, the key persuasive factor.

Emerging Economy of Kenya

To be able to determine whether an African economy is emerging, it is important to establish some basic characteristics. For the purpose of this study, we define an economy as emerging if we find that it is in a process of sustainable per capita income growth. Several indicators define sustainable growth; to begin with, a healthy economy would have a fairly efficient macroeconomic framework accompanied by a fairly good level of international competitiveness (Bigsten and Kayizzi-Mugerwa, 2001). Second, the economy should have reasonably efficient and competitive domestic markets. Third, the level of human resource development, quality of infrastructure and institutions, and institutional frameworks would be consistent with an economy set for rapid expansion. Fourth, an economy must have substantial governance, political accommodation, and maturity in a democratic sense. Finally, an emerging economy is expected to become gradually less dependent on aid, thereby relying more on domestic savings and foreign private inflows for investment (Bigsten and Kayizzi-Mugerwa, 2001).

Kenya is considered to be an emerging economy because it has a sustainable per capita income growth. Several factors indicate that the growth is sustainable. Kenya has managed to achieve an impressive Gross Domestic Product (GDP) growth rate of 4–6 percent per annum. In spite of initial resistance to economic liberalization, the economy has been growing steadily. Initially, growth was achieved through improvements in the policy environment and through political liberalization that brought about multiparty politics. With liberalization, domestic private investments have increased, but mostly through the substantial inflow of foreign investments. The country has been pursuing sound fiscal and monetary policies with some degree of success. Inflation has been kept under check and revenue collection has improved through the efforts of the Kenya Revenue Authority. Kenya's international competitiveness can be said to have increased over time since trade liberalization was effected. There has been a marked growth in horticultural exports, and some manufacturing organizations have become leading regional exporters.

Following the liberalization of the economy, the minimizing of government interference in the economy provided opportunities to domestic markets to grow without inhibition. Many state enterprises have been privatized, and the monopoly on the marketing of goods, commodities, and services curtailed. Though initially scarce, competitiveness in the domestic market has increased. Today there is cutthroat competition in most industries.

Notable efforts have been exerted to enhance the financial system of Kenya. The financial system has grown in terms of product diversification and its reliability. Corruption in the system, especially in the banking sector, has been checked. One of the most notable features today is the growth of investments in the stock exchange. Recent times have witnessed oversubscription to initial public offers. Money had to be returned to the public because of oversubscription. Even though the financial sector is still somewhat fragile, it can be argued that there has been notable growth. Abuse of the system by the political elite has been checked and many other constraints are being addressed with a good degree of success.

The development of human capital is important for economic growth. Kenya has been fortunate in this area in that it has well-trained people with requisite technical, conceptual, and human relations skills. Thus, Kenya has a good supply of skilled labor and should be able to sustain economic growth.

Kenya's infrastructure is relatively more developed than its neighbors. Her trunk roads, which occupy most of the country, are good. The high energy costs and the slow restructuring of the telecommunications sector are major bottlenecks in manufacturing and other production activities. However, the policies put in place by the government should ensure major improvements. The major international agencies and donors reduced aid to Kenya from the early 1990s. This means that Kenya has been funding its development efforts with very little or no support in some years. There has been a marked reduction in aid dependence. In spite of this, the economy has been growing steadily over time. In addition, there has been a controlled level of foreign debt.

Since the advent of multiparty politics in Kenya, it can be argued that there have been major improvements in the management of the economy. Even though corruption and rent seeking in some sectors are still rampant, there has been reduced political interference in economic matters. Governance has increased and the rule of law has been addressed through legal reform measures. Privatization and decentralization have been affected with some degree of success but local capacities are still low, and public finance is still mismanaged at the district and constituency levels. The above discussion suggests that Kenya's economy is sustainable and is expected to prosper.

Economic Restructuring

The global recession of the early 1980s negatively affected emerging economies such as Kenya. Their exports collapsed, interest rates rose, private capital flows reduced, and most countries could not meet their debt obligations. The recession incited a revolution in aid policy. Major international institutions and donors to developing countries, particularly the World Bank, made the availability of aid to recipient countries subject to changes in their policies. This called for the restructuring of the economies of developing countries. SAPs were implemented in most countries as a consequence. They were meant to reduce the role of the state in the economy and to encourage the private sector to play a more significant role in the economy. This was clearly a shift from the thinking of the earlier period in which the state had a substantial role in the economy. The argument at the time was that the state should not only maintain macroeconomic balance but also undertake direct responsibility in investments and capital formation to encourage growth and development. The changes led to economic liberalization where the markets were freed from government control and private sectors were encouraged to play a significant role. The wisdom behind this was the New Public Management (NPM) thinking. The NPM came about in the early 1980s because of changes in development thinking. The NPM thinking encourages increasing efficiency in operations and accountability in economic management. Nowadays, new pressures confront governments in every part of the world. Central values relating to the role of the state, markets, and citizenship began to be contested. Questions were raised to determine the role of the various actors in improving service delivery. How public administration should change to take on the new roles of working in partnership with the private sector and communities is the question. The common slogan these days is that governments should *enable* and *regulate* the private and community sectors rather than directly engage in the provision of goods and services. With the NPM wisdom, the state began to be reinvented (Osborne and Gaebler, 1992).

A major feature of the NPM is the introduction of market mechanisms in the running of public service organizations, also known as the marketization of public services. The earliest form of marketization of public services was the introduction and implementation of competitive bidding or tendering for public services (Ascher, 1987). Other forms of marketization such as the use of internal markets and privatization have also been developed and used increasingly since the 1980s. They impacted directly on how the private sector began to play increased roles in the economy and how this affected the marketing functions of most organizations. NPM has two strands. The first strand is called managerialism. According to Pollit (1990), managerialism involves the following elements: (1) continuous increases in efficiency; (2) the use of ever more sophisticated technologies; (3) a labor force disciplined to productivity; (4) a clear implementation of the professional management role; and (5) managers being given the right and freedom to manage. The overall aim of management is to gain more effective control of work practices so that effectiveness and efficiency can be enhanced.

The second strand of NPM is based upon indirect control rather than direct authority. The characteristics of the second strand of the NPM are (1) continual improvements in quality; (2) emphasis upon devolution and delegation; (3) appropriate information systems; (4) emphasis upon contracts and markets; (5) measuring performance; and (6) increased emphasis on audit and inspection. The NPM system of governance has accountability and transparency components. Accountability requires putting the interests of *consumers* (citizens) ahead of self-interested groups, whereas transparency requires *openness* in the conduct of public service business. It is argued that accountability and transparency improve service provisions.

A variety of market mechanisms have been proposed and adopted under NPM. While *deregulation* and *privatization* are the main vehicles for improving private goods and service provisions, *corporatization* and *contracting* are the main means in NPM for applying market principles to spending and buying decisions in the public realm. Although the state has become smaller in terms of its role in the market, it still holds the key responsibility of creating a level playing field for all market actors. Market actors are expected to develop to the extent that they are able to improve the delivery of goods and services to consumers. Liberalization challenged marketing practices, leading to the development of new marketing practices. How the new marketing practices develop in emerging economies would determine whether market players succeeded or failed in a globalize economy.

At the time of Kenya's independence, it was imperative for the new nation to decide on its development priorities and policies. Decisions had to be taken with regard to the to-be-created institutions and to-be-created policies for economic growth and development. Following the great depression in the 1930s, belief in markets began to be questioned. Also, the belief that Russia had achieved success through state intervention and industrialization provided further impetus for the Kenyan state to intervene in the economy. Industrialization through import substitution was consistent with economic thought in the 1960s. However, this was given more weight by the fact that investments in Kenya's industries were in the hands of Kenyan Asians and foreigners. Further, indigenous Kenyans were encouraged to invest in industries. The government encouraged industrialization by being an investor itself. Thus, government intervention, controls, and ownership were encouraged. Once the government entrenched itself this way in the economy, politicians, bureaucrats, and other interest groups got an opportunity to create wealth, employment for their relatives, and a channel for acquiring political power. Many bureaucrats eventually used their former positions to launch themselves into politics.

Since independence in 1963 to the late 1980s, Kenya had a state-controlled economy in which major decisions that affected the operations of firms were made by the state without much regard to what the firms felt. This state of affairs insulated many firms that had direct access to politicians and key decision-makers. Their operating environment was certain and predictable at the time. Most businesses operated on the basis of traditional management styles, with historically entrenched company values, attitudes, and beliefs. Under such circumstances, most firms had a ready market. In fact, the automobile industry could not satisfy the demand for vehicles as was evident from the long waiting lists of their customers.

Logic of Reform

The call for reform has its basis in the change in the development - orthodoxy in the 1980s. In the 1950s, 1960s, and 1970s, donors, particularly the World Bank, supported state intervention in the economy by encouraging significant development schemes in which the state had interests (Bates, 1989; Gibbon, 1992). Aid to African countries emphasized the transfer of high-level technology (Bates, 1988). The thinking of the time was that the government was supposed to be the key player in development (Brett, 1987). Governments invested in state enterprises and supported development of industries that established strong ties with these state enterprises. In Kenya, large-scale industrial concerns such as maize, wheat, barley, cement, and rice milling plants were encouraged through the policy of import substitution.

The change from the 1980s questioned particularly the role of the state in the economy (Berg, 1981; Sandbrook, 1986). The heavy involvement of the state in the economy is argued to have led to a slow development because it had interfered with the free working of the market. In the case of emerging economies, evidence emerged that state intervention had in many cases resulted in inefficient industries, requiring enterprises to be on permanent subsidization (Wade, 1990; Nellis, 1992). Rent seeking tended to arise from excessive government intervention (Krueger, 1974). SAPs strongly influenced by the works of Lipton (1977), Berg (1981), and Bates (1981) were designed to deal with the stagnating and deteriorating economic conditions brought about by inappropriate government economic policy interventions. SAPs thus have their basis in the thinking that government intervention had been harmful and had slowed the development in developing countries (Berg, 1981; World Bank, 1986). The argument in favor of SAPs was that state control must be rolled back and the private sector be given a chance (World Bank, 1991).

Dramatic changes occurred since the late 1980s when the government of Kenya, following the pressure from Bretton Woods institutions and other agencies, agreed to liberalize the economy. Liberalization effectively opened the floodgates in most industries leading to increased competition. Goods and services began to move freely into and within Kenya. Protected industries were exposed to unprecedented level of competition.

Initial Responses to Market Liberalization

Many firms began to face significant changes as imported goods and services challenged the locally produced ones. Industry analysts labeled the 1990s as the era of economic uncertainty for most industrial organizations. Many were negatively affected by increased competition, sluggish consumer spending, and the slower-than-anticipated economic growth underpinned by inflationary pressures. Many consumers reduced or deferred spending on anything other than the bare essentials. Because imported goods were generally cheaper, many customers shifted their loyalties to imported goods. Fierce competition resulted in lower margins for most organizations. Many producers confronted the intense competitive pressure by restructuring. Traditional organizational structures, with their hierarchical, top-down approaches and historically entrenched values of stability and security, proved unworkable under a liberalized environment. Little, inadequate, or no marketing, as well as traditional structures, systems, and values that formed the bedrock of past successes in times of government control and certainty, began to threaten the very existence of many industries (KAM, 2006). To survive, firms had to respond strategically to these challenges by institutionalizing change.

In most sectors, big companies dominated most industries in Kenya during the controlled period. For example, the automobile industry included household names such as Coopers Motor Corporation Limited, Lonhro Motors East Africa Limited, DT Dobie Limited, and Marshalls East Africa Limited. There were also other medium-sized companies such as Kenya Motor Corporation, Colt Motors, Simba Motors, Ryce Motors, Mashariki Motors, and Amazon Motors Limited. Following the liberalization of the economy, the automobile industry, like other industries, started to experience a major decline in sales, though the impact of the liberalization was not felt immediately due to the large number of outstanding orders (Mutuku S., 2003).

The early 1990s saw a buildup in pressure and the creation of opportunities for most industries as a result of pressures that had been emerging for several years. Before 1980, most state-protected firms were very successful; they enjoyed the protection and a close relationship with the government. In such an environment, firms needed to maintain a presence in government decision-making circles and have expertise in their work; they did not need to have a strong marketing focus (Mutuku M., 2004; Lewa, 2006). The traditional management style tended to be paternalistic and bureaucratic; the organizations were conservative with a compliant middle management. The focus of most organizations was on government patronage for survival.

Strategic planning that existed in many firms during the controlled-trading regime was mainly restricted at the corporate level. Planning is about making decisions about survival for future. The planning at the time of the controlled-economy was what a key manufacturer of tires called bad planning. It was meant to sustain organizations in such a way that their status quo was maintained (e.g., Firestone East Africa (1969) Ltd.). It was good under the assumption that the economy of Kenya would remain under government control.

Product and market development activities were not pronounced during the controlled regime. Companies hardly looked for new product development opportunities to sustain their growth, and they hardly cared for margins, as they were content with the status quo. Indeed, new product launches were very few. Pricing strategy followed the dictates of the monopolies and price control commission. Pricing was a gamble as the commission determined pricing limits. Some politically well-connected companies, of course, influenced the government to set up prices as per their whims. Promotional budgets were kept at the bare minimum during the controlled trading regime. Promotion was meant to provide basic information and not to fight for increased market share.

During the controlled trading regime, many companies in general relied on small groups of carefully selected distributors. In most cases, such groups did not develop alliances with manufacturers. When liberalization was effected, many producers lost their most trusted distributors and agents. For example, following liberalization in 1994, Firestone East Africa, the only producer of tires, was abandoned by its key distributors. The firm realized that it had never built sustainable strategic alliances with its distributors who abandoned its tires and tubes for cheaply imported ones (Lewa and Mayaka, 2005). Research and development expenditures were kept at a bare minimum in most organizations. Expenditures in this area were aimed at product modifications and expenditures for new product development were quite rare during the controlled trading regime.

By the 1990s, it became necessary to take stock and affect significant changes to the organizational structures of most organizations (KAM, 2006). The new structures emphasized the customer divisions as the *drivers of the business* while functional divisions such as system design, engineering, and supply divisions now operated in support of the different customer divisions. The focus was no longer solely on engineering and production but on serving the customer better. Many firms began to move away from the traditional focus on the 4Ps (product, price, promotion, and place) of marketing, to managing relationships with customers, suppliers, and retailers. They started to look at people, processes, and organizations. Most manufacturing organizations obviously felt a need for change. The overriding imperative was to create a *felt need for change* for everybody. Management needed to instill dissatisfaction with the status quo in order to rally an organizational change toward customer focus.

Anecdotal evidence suggests that most organizations found out that this was easier said than done. Even when a crisis threatened the very survival of the organizations, it was not enough of a compelling motivator. The change was not widely understood or appreciated; therefore, most firms decided to carry out a *medical treatment* that identified the internal problems and external threats and opportunities (Mutuku S., 2003). Strategic planning seemed to find its way into organizations in Kenya. This was an effective means of focusing the stakeholders' attention on issues central to the future of most organizations. This succeeded in highlighting the gap between the present reality and potential future state; hence, a tension that was the first stage in moving toward customer focus was created.

Most organizations significantly reduced their workforce. The aim of this restructuring was to create an organization that was more responsive, more competitive, less internally focused, and more attuned to the needs of the marketplace. However, the rapidly changing external environment saw most organizations unprepared for the change. There was a lack of understanding on how to move this new *customer first* philosophy into the very competitive environment in which the government could no longer offer protection (Mutuku M., 2004). The top management in most organizations sought to use the marketing imperative as a catalyst for change (KAM, 2006). They reformulated their mission statements and established strategic plans at the same time. Strategic planning suddenly became important for most organizations in Kenya. The benefits of adopting the new ways of learning and working together were clearly outlined by changing the process and by developing new mental tools that challenged the traditional mindset. Most firms' traditional, internal engineering/product focus was shifted to viewing the customers as partners and providing them with the value-added solutions. Most organizations also started plans to redesign their work processes, systems, and structures to foster environments that encouraged participation and information sharing and pushed decision-making further down the organizations' hierarchy. Eventually, organizational attitudes and assumptions were challenged and, in most organizations, everyone was encouraged to consider new ways of thinking (KAM, 2006). The culture of most organizations began to change but the competition did not relent. This led to a better appreciation of marketing among Kenyan organizations.

Marketing Practices before Liberalization

Marketing is responsible for more than sales. It is a key function for ensuring that every aspect of the business is focused on delivering superior value to customers. It must ensure that networks of strategic partners are developed to help deliver lifetime value to customers. Companies have to allocate their resources in proportion to what customers want. This helps get the customer for life. In addition, firms must plan strategically and train their people to equip them with the right skills, knowledge, and attitudes necessary in a liberalized trading environment. Marketing may be defined as an organizational function and a set of processes for creating, communicating, and delivering value to customers and for managing customer relationships in ways that benefit the organization and its stakeholders (AMA, 2004). To deliver value to customers, marketers devise marketing activities traditionally described as the marketing mix or the four Ps.

Market-oriented organizations tend to operate on the basis of the marketing concept that holds that an organization must organize its activities around the primary goal of satisfying its customers in the best way possible. Market-oriented organizations develop marketing strategies to manage themselves in advantageous ways. Marketing strategy refers to the position that a company takes with regard to its marketing functions of pricing, promotion, advertising, product design, and distribution. In a perfectly competitive market, these functions of marketing enable firms to find and stimulate buyers to increase the firm's output. Under the circumstances, a firm is able to engage in product development, pricing, distribution, and promotion without major external inhibitions. Moreover, a firm is able to continually seek innovative ways of meeting changing customer needs.

Government Interference in Perfectly Competitive Markets

Aims of the reforms in Kenya were to reduce the role of the government and to encourage the private sector to play a greater role in the economy. To encourage private sectors to play a greater role in markets, marketing had to be liberalized or freed from state control. Controlling the workings of the market was meant to correct failures that rose in the workings of the free or perfectly competitive market.

A perfectly competitive market is assumed to have certain characteristics. For example, it is expected that in such a market, (1) there are a large number of firms competing with each other; (2) the products offered to the market are homogeneous; (3) each product or firm has a small share of the market; (4) firms pursue profit maximization; (5) consumers and producers possess all the necessary information about prices and markets; (6) the factors of production are perfectly mobile so that they can be easily switched from the production of one type of good to another; and (7) there is possibility of free entry and exit from the market.

The perfect market does not take into account social costs and benefits in most cases. Such a market is unable to ensure the supply of both public and merit goods. Public goods such as police protection and defense benefit all, and people cannot be excluded from consuming them. Those benefiting from their consumption have no economic incentive to pay for them. Merit goods such as education and health care are worth providing in greater volume than would be purchased in a free market. Higher consumption of such goods is in the public interest in the long run and hence government intervention is to take care of these deficiencies.

Government intervention in Kenya was exercised through controls. The controls were exercised in a variety of ways including control on pricing, foreign exchange, movement of goods and services, interest rates, licensing, imports of raw materials, and industry location considerations. Government intervention in the market created distortions. Monopolies, particularly in the case of state enterprises, were also created through government intervention. Competitors were prevented from entering the markets where the state had interests. State interests ranged from hotel business to milling to distribution to transport to mining, among other sectors. The government was indeed a major player in the economy. Under the circumstances, such protected firms charged higher prices than normal. They also restricted supplies to mark up prices without any fear, as there was hardly any competition to sell at a lower price. Artificial shortages were created.

Under the controlled marketing regime, consumers lacked essential information. They therefore ended up spending more on products and services than needed with full information. Price controls guaranteed certain prices to producers. No incentives improved the quality of goods or added to the value. Research and development activities were limited. Growth of market share was limited by legislation and controls. Distribution channels did not develop beyond a list of friendly businesses (Lewa, 1995). Innovation lacked in most cases as there was no incentive to be innovative. Consumer choice was limited to a few goods and services. Promotional activities were limited to providing very basic consumer information, with increased promotional activities occurring where there was some competition brought about by the existence of substitute products or by competing products of multinational organizations.

Initially the fledging private sector of Kenya did not take the challenge of reform as was expected (Lewa, 1995). In addition to the problems of underdeveloped private trade, there was strong competition that new market entrants from overseas posed. They flooded the Kenyan market with imported goods. The nature of competition changed. This led to the creation of marketing departments in most firms.

Changing Marketing Dynamics

The market liberalization gave rise to certain changes. Kenya Motor Institute and Kenya Association of Manufacturers identified the following apparent changes relating to marketing practices.

Market Share

Unlike before liberalization, growth in market share became an important factor in most industries. Industries became highly dynamic with ever-increasing competition brought about by new global entrants. Firms that did not command a significant market share or were not firmly entrenched in a particular segment of the market could not survive the competition.

Product Quality

The consumers began to look for quality products at competitive prices. For companies manufacturing and selling goods, this meant looking for better quality raw materials, superior engineering, durability, and energy efficiency.

Production Differentiation

Firms that became highly successful in their industries were those that managed to segment the market and offered different products for different segments. Consumers had become aware of different sizes and other dimensions of the products they needed. This was also the case with those companies that considered themselves as producers for one business segment only; even for a company such as Firestone East

Africa (1969) Limited, which had a monopoly and which before liberalization manufactured and sold tires and tubes through wholly owned subsidiaries in Uganda and Tanzania, product differentiation strategy became important in the liberalized tire market. The company had to start thinking of different tires and tubes to suit different market needs.

Economic Performance

The performance of the economy was the key determinant of success in a liberalized marketing regime. Critical factors included rate of inflation; the strength of the local currency; cost of energy; performances of the tourism, agriculture, and financial sectors; and donor conditionality, among others. High inflation rates, high costs of electricity, reduced food supplies, fewer tourists, and devaluation of the shilling soon after liberalization were the problems that led to falling consumer purchasing power and sales of most products in some industries. However, improvements occurred following liberalization.

Price and Low-Cost Production

In the liberalized marketing environment of Kenya, the low-cost producers became usually the most successful. Thus, firms were forced to invest in cost-saving measures and technology to deliver quality goods. Because of the availability of inexpensive and low-quality imported goods in the Kenyan market, the only way to long-term survival was through the low-priced quality goods. Total Quality Management (TQM) assumed a new meaning.

Effective Distribution System

After liberalization of the market, most industries realized that they must have well-established distribution systems to meet customer needs. Important factors in distribution were availability of quality goods, delivery reliability, and effective customer service.

Research and Development

In a liberalized global economy, modern manufacturing methods and technical product developments became important to remain competitive. Therefore, most firms engaged in both process and product research and development. This meant use of the latest production techniques and application of modern processes in the whole arena of manufacturing, sales and marketing, distribution, and management.

Raw Materials

In most Kenyan industries, producers and sellers of goods began to bargain with suppliers of raw materials over costs and availability. Strategic planning became more prominent than ever.

Financial Strength

Adequate financial strength is required for companies to remain competitive and to respond to possible strategic moves by competitors. Financial support is necessary for quality assurance programs, distribution system needs, and research and development requirements. Central Bank's regulations and financial markets' movements affected the availability of money. Following liberalization, most firms became sensitive to changes in the money market and their effects on business operations.

The Future of Marketing in Kenya's Emerging Economy

The future marketing depends on adjustments to global practices. Postliberalization made firms realize that certain adjustments to business operations were necessary. Evidence from industries suggests that firms moved away from production focus to customer focus. They began to redefine customer value and embrace the concept of TQM in their marketing activities. Innovativeness increased and strategic planning played a significant role in most organizations (KAM, 2006).

Customer focus requires building superior customer responsiveness. A company cannot be responsive to its customers' needs unless it knows what those needs are. The first step to building superior customer responsiveness is to get the whole company to focus on the customer. All employees must be trained to see the customer as the focus of their activities. Once employees are trained to be customer oriented, they are in a better position to identify ways of improving the quality of customer service. Once a focus on the customer has been achieved, the next step is to satisfy the identified needs of the customers. This requires efficiency, effectiveness, quality, and innovation. Further, the company can best satisfy its customers if it customizes the product to the requirements of the individual customer and cuts down the response time. Customization involves varying the features of goods or services to tailor it to the unique needs of the groups of customers. In addition, satisfying customer needs requires being responsive to customer demands. Improved responsiveness can improve margins as companies can charge premium prices. Reducing response time increases competitiveness. It requires that the marketing functions communicate customers' requests to manufacturing, and that manufacturing and materials management functions quickly adjust their production plans and schedules to meet customer demands in a flexible manner.

It is apparent that companies must define their businesses in terms of their customers and not in terms of products, services, factories, and offices. Focus of firms shifted from transactions to relationship. Customers become key allies, and thus firms must make long-term commitments to maintain their relationships with customers. Businesses are increasingly likely to be a network of strategic partnerships among various specialized areas such as design, technology, distribution, and information specialists. These measures would increase responsiveness to customers.

Given the increased importance of long-term, strategic relationships, firms must place increased emphasis on strategic planning and relationship management skills. Strategic market planning can no longer be the sole responsibility of a few specialists or just the top management team. Rather, everybody in the firm must be charged with the responsibility for delivering value to customers. This will increase responsiveness to customer needs. In addition to customer responsiveness, organizations must continue to focus on the other building blocks of competitive advantage—efficiency, quality, and innovation. Efficiency is measured by the costs of inputs required to produce a given output. Increased efficiency thus means lower costs in producing a given output. Increasing employee productivity is a significant way of increasing efficiency. Employee training and development must therefore be given attention if sustainable competitiveness is desired.

Firms must identify what quality means in the perspective of the customer. Quality can be improved through the TQM technique. TQM is based on the following premises: (1) improved quality means that costs decrease because of fewer mistakes, less rework, fewer delays, and better use of time and materials in the productive process; (2) as a consequence of the above, productivity increases; (3) better quality leads to a higher market share and this gives opportunity to a company to increase prices; (4) profitability increases as a consequence of the above; and (5) more jobs are created as a consequence.

TQM requires firms' commitment to quality, customer focus, quality assurance, goal setting, incentives, performance, defect identification and correction, relationships with suppliers. Over a period of time, competition can be viewed as a process driven by innovation. Innovation is the process by which organizations use their skills, resources, and new technologies to produce reliable products at a low cost. Through innovation, organizations can respond better to the needs of their customers. However, innovation is a risky process as it can result in inefficient technologies and products unwanted by customers. One of the ways to minimize risk to organizations is to adopt flexible structures that give workers the freedom to experiment and be creative. However, successful innovation can revolutionize industry structure in positive ways. One of the most common consequences of innovation nowadays has been to lower the fixed costs of production; thereby, reducing barriers to entry and allowing new smaller, innovative, and entrepreneurial firms to compete with the large established ones.

In future, firms must step outside their traditional systems of operation and become more market oriented. They must involve their employees more in company affairs, train them more in quality control and assurance, and benchmark their performance to remain relevant.

Conclusion

The chapter has provided indicators of the extent to which political interest groups have shaped policy through their immense influence. Government actions in the economy have not been consistent with economic theory. Kenya, since the colonial times, has gone beyond market economics into the realm of the economics of organization. It has extended beyond the economics of organization into the political arena. Economic policy determination in the marketing system in Kenya has been influenced by factors that have led to the initial policy choices to suit the existing political situation.

Institutions were created in Kenya for the common good of vested interests. These interests were used as the point of reference when making important decisions affecting the economy. The colonial government created a politicized economic system for the benefit of the powerful interest groups. The independent Kenyan government continued the policies of the past and the economy was captured for the benefit of powerful political interest groups, which included politicians, bureaucrats, and large African farmers. Thus, politics became an important element in the creation of institutions. Politics became the overriding factor in the distribution of the national cake. It became the channel for climbing to the top and using the position to accumulate.

Creation of institutions in the economy, state appointments to positions of influence, and the conferring of political power were used to secure the benefits from exchanges in the market. Thus, politics has been used to generate, protect, and redistribute wealth through the patron-client system of Kenya to reward those supporting the political regime and to punish those who do not support it.

To understand the reform of Kenya's economy, one must move beyond the theory of institutions to politics. Government control of marketing activities intended to correct market failure resulted in marketing inefficiencies. The marketing function was constrained and many organizations failed to explore the function fully. Production activities, pricing, promotion, and distribution functions were affected negatively. Following liberalization, firms took the challenge and began to exercise marketing functions in a professional way. Increased competition led to the discovery of what marketing could do for organizations. Organizations began to innovate, develop products and markets, and pursue quality in a bid to deliver value to customers.

The future appears bright for marketing-oriented firms. They must, however, train their personnel, apply modern technology, be quality conscious, and apply strategic planning in their operations.

References

AMA. American Marketing Association, www.ama.org, 2004.

Anker, R., and Knowles, J.C. *Population Growth, Employment and Economic-Demographic Interactions in Kenya*. Aldershot, UK: Gower Publishing Company Ltd., 1983.

Arnold, G. *Modern Kenya*. London: Longman Group Limited, 1981.

Ascher, K. *The Politics of Privatisation: Contracting out Public Services*. London: Mac Millan, 1987.

Bates, R.H. *Markets and States in Tropical Africa: The Political Basis of Agricultural Policies*. Berkley: University of California Press. 1981.

———. *Toward a Political Economy of Development: A Rational Choice Perspective*. Berkley: University of California Press, 1988.

———. *Beyond the Miracle of the Market: The Political Economy of Agrarian Development in Kenya*. Cambridge: Cambridge University Press, 1989.

Bates, R.H., and Krueger, A.O. *Political & Economic Interactions In Economic Policy Reform: Evidence from Eight Countries*. Oxford: Blackwell, 1993.

Berg Report. *Accelerated Development in Sub-Saharan Africa: An Agenda for Action*. World Bank, 1981.

Bigsten, A., and Kayizzi-Mugerwa S. *Is Uganda an Emerging Economy?* A report for OECD's Emerging Africa project, 2001.

Brett, E.A. "States, Markets and Private Power in the Developing World: Problems and Possibilities." *IDS Bulletin* 18, no. 3 (1987).

Cowen, M. "Change in State Power, International Conditions and Peasant Producers: The Case of Kenya." *Journal of Development Studies* 22, no. 2 (1985): 355–84.

Downing, T.E., Gitu, K.W., and Kamau, C.M. *Coping with Drought in Kenya: National and Local Strategies*. Boulder: Lynne Reinner, 1989.

Duncan, A. "The Reform of Agricultural Prices and Markets: Comparative Experience from Kenya, Tanzania and Zimbabwe," paper presented at a workshop on maize market liberalization and private sector response in eastern and southern Africa, Harare, October 2–4, 1992.

Gibbon, P. "A Failed Agenda? African Agriculture under Structural Adjustment with Special Reference to Kenya and Ghana." *The Journal of Peasant Studies* 20, no. 1 (1992): 50–96.

Heyer, J., Maitha, T.K., and Senga, W.M. *Agricultural Development in Kenya: An Economic Assessment*. Oxford: Oxford University Press, 1976.

Holtzman, J.S. "Rapid Reconnaissance and Food System Research in Developing Countries." *MSU International Development Working Paper* no. 30 (1986).

Hunt, D. (1984), *The Impending Crisis in Kenya: The Case for Land Reform*. Aldershot: Gover Publishing Limited, 1984.

KAM. Kenya Association of Manufacturers. *Business Symposium*. Nairobi: CAM Training Center, 2006.

Krueger, A.O. "The Political Economy of the Rent-Seeking Society." *American Economic Review* 64 (1974): 291–303.

———. *Political Economy of Policy Reform in Developing Countries*. Cambridge: MIT Press, 1993.

Lewa, P.M. "Kenya's Cereals Sector Reform Programme: Managing the Politics of Reform," paper presented at the workshop on the changing public role in services to food and agriculture at the School of Public Policy. University of Birmingham, 1995.

———. "Winning Strategies," paper presented at a workshop organized by the Kenya Association of Manufacturers for its stakeholders, 2006.

Lewa P.M., and Mayaka C. "A Case Study on Firestone East Africa (1969) Ltd: Liberalization of the Tire Industry." *Global Business School Network*, 2005.

Lipton, M. *Why People Stay Poor: Urban Bias in World Development*. London: Maurice Temple Smith, 1977.

Lipton, M., and Moore, M. "The Methodology of Village Studies in Less Developed Countries." *IDS Paper* no. 10 (1972).

Lofchie, M. *The Policy Factor: Agricultural Performance in Kenya and Tanzania*. Boulder: Lynne Rienner Publishers, 1989.

Magrath, P. "Methodologies for Studying Agricultural Markets in Developing Countries." *Natural Resources Institute Marketing Series* no. 2 (1992).

Mutuku, M. "Change Management in Kenya's Automobile Industry," unpublished MBA student paper, Alliant International University, California, 2004.

Mutuku, S. "Change Management in Marshalls East Africa Limited," unpublished MBA student paper, Alliant International University, California, 2003.

Mosley, P., Harrigan, J., and Toye, J. *AID and POWER: The World Bank and Policy Based Lending in the 1980s.* London: Routledge, 1991.

Nellis, J.R. *Contract Plans and Public Enterprise Performance.* Washington DC: World Bank, 1992.

Osborne, D., and Gaebler T. *Reinventing Government: How the Entrepreneurial Spirit Is Transforming the Public Sector.* Reading: Wesley, 1992.

Pollit, C. *Managerialism and the Public Service: The Anglo-American Experience.* Oxford, UK: Blackwell, 1990.

Sandbrook, R. "The State and Economic Stagnation in Tropical Africa." *World Development* 14, no. 3 (1986): 319–32.

Toye, J. "Interest Group Politics and Implementation of Adjustment Policies in Sub-Saharan Africa." *Journal of International Development, Policy, Economics and International Relations* 4, no. 2 (1992): 183–99.

The Weekly Review, (December 2, 1994a), Nairobi.

———. (December 16, 1994b), Nairobi.

———. (January 6, 1995), Nairobi.

Wade, R. *Governing the Market: Economic Theory and the Role of Government in East Asian Industrialisation.* Princeton: Princeton University Press, 1990.

World Bank. *Financing Adjustment with Growth in Sub-Saharan Africa 1986–1990.* Washington DC: World Bank, 1986.

———. *World Development Report.* Oxford: Oxford University Press, 1991.

Part II

Business and Ethical Orientations

Chapter 3

Business Orientation, Brand Image, and Business Performance

Satyendra Singh

The transformation of a planned economy to a market economy has attracted a multitude of foreign firms, forcing local firms to compete against the foreign firms for the same customers. This chapter explains the importance of various types of business orientations such as marketing, social, and economic, as practiced by both foreign and local firms. Further I discuss the efficacy of brand image to mediate the relationship between the components of business orientation and business performance. Results based on data from foreign and local firms in India indicate that marketing orientation in the foreign group has an indirect positive impact on business performance via brand image, whereas economic orientation has a direct impact on business performance. In local firms, none of the components of business orientation contribute significantly to brand image; however, a significant positive association between brand image and business performance was observed. The chapter discusses the results and proposes implications for the managers and researchers.

Introduction

Environments previously characterized by high political risk, poor infrastructure, high trade barriers, and low growth rates are now disappearing (Kolde, 1992; Singh, 2003). The economic reform policies initiated by the Government of India in 1991 have propelled the nation to an unprecedented level of economic growth and reshaped markets by introducing new opportunities to multinational and local firms alike. This burgeoning market has attracted firms worldwide to promote their products and services in India. The rapid pace of economic development brought prosperity to Indian consumers that enhanced their purchasing power significantly. This purchasing power over a period of time changed the habits of consumers and established a culture of consumerism. This very culture of consumerism provides grounds for testing the impact of the new business orientation on business performance. For the purpose of the chapter, business orientation comprises of marketing, social, and economic orientations. This chapter responds to the call by Cova and Svanfeldt (1992) that there has been very little research into the actual use of new marketing. Will successful firms employ these new types of marketing and management methods, or are they just textbook utopian ideas?

Importance of marketing has been recognized since the 1960s; however, it is marked by differences of opinions among academic researchers over the nature and utility of present marketing. For example, theorists (Gummeson, 1991; Hulbert and Pitt, 1996) predict a demise of marketing as a function, therefore, creating a need to transform whole organizations to be market oriented. On the other hand, Kotler (1994) insists on retaining marketing as a separate function but working in harmony with other departments. Others (Venkatesh, 1989; Firat, 1991; Cova, 1996) have gone the extra mile to assert the philosophy of postmodernism on the premise that present marketing models and logical concepts such as SWOT (strength, weakness, opportunity, and threats) analysis, 4P's (product, price, promotion, and place), Ansoff Matrices or BCG (Boston Consultancy Group) are often too simplistic. These concepts do not seem to fit the present conditions of the markets, because markets tend to become more fragmented and global, society more individualistic and educated, and consumers more economical and demanding. These changes in society have forced the local consumers to imitate behavior of foreign consumers, which is often individualistic in nature and based on images. In other words, today's customers consume products that are consistent with their perceived identity. For example, while piercing of body and coloring of hairs may represent individualistic identity, eating fast food frequently and following fashion rapidly may signify a change in society. Demanding excessively personalized services may represent an example of customization, whereas browsing Web sites on cellular phones may suggest the need for access to global communications at all times. This very change in society and consumer behavior has led to consumption of image-oriented products. This chapter aims to discover the role of such image-oriented products in achieving business performance.

The purpose of the chapter is to investigate how managers of foreign and local firms perceive Indian society as an exemplar of emerging market and how they orient the components of business orientation—marketing, social, and economical. Further, the chapter investigates the main factors that contribute to these orientations both positively and negatively during the post-1991 period. The implication for managers is that they will learn, given India depends on overseas markets (exports), how economic orientation is more important than social orientation, and how marketing plays a role in influencing brand image of a product and performance of a firm. In the following section, the chapter presents background to the study, defines business orientation, discusses the direct and indirect role of brand image between business orientation and business performance, tests the hypotheses, and reports the results. Then, the chapter addresses the managerial implications of the results and suggests the directions for future research.

Background to the Study

India is a vast country with over one billion consumers. Since 1991, the economic reform policies ranked India's growth performance amongst the top six in the world growth league, along with China, Korea, Thailand, Singapore, and Vietnam. In 2006, India ranked second in terms of GDP growth rate, just behind China. Further, it is predicted that the Indian growth rate can exceed China's during the first two decades of the twenty-first century (Swamy, 2002), making India's prospects quite favorable. In fact, the globalization process during the past decade has forced companies to adopt a global outlook through which the world has become their markets. This globalization has also increased purchasing power parity of Indian consumers, putting them among the top four in the world. Naturally, now Indian consumers have relatively more disposable income. The polarization between rich and poor within the society that existed before appears to be disappearing. Society is becoming more egalitarian, which has influenced consumers to be more individualistic, informed, and demanding.

In light of the above changes experienced by the consumers in their lifestyle, there is a greater need for analysis of the role and the effectiveness of business strategies in emerging markets. Such an analysis requires an examination of whether particular strategies are associated with particular market characteristics and with particular kinds and levels of business performance (Manu, 1992). In the context of evolving

markets in India, we expect marketing, social, and economic orientations of firms to influence business performance. The premise for such
expectation is that the characteristics of the orientations are unlikely to
have similar influence across all markets. The orientations are primarily
Western and largely suited to the societies that are affluent and have a
high rate of consumption. Because the Western model is being applied
to the emerging market, it is logical to expect a difference in business
orientation between foreign and local managers toward Indian consumers. Further, we expect differences in attitude of foreign and local
firms toward the orientations for the following reasons: first, foreign
firms have advanced knowledge of business and marketing models;
second, now local firms have to learn how marketing orientation
enters into the picture of overall business, considering that the competitive environment in India is a recent phenomenon and that capital
markets have not been accessible to many firms except in the recent
years. Now that local managers have to compete with foreign managers who also have the advantage of achieving economies of scale,
local firms will have to find *new* ways to survive and serve customers;
third, having lived under a highly protected economy, local firms
rooted in local geographies and histories need to change to the business
orientation swiftly; and finally, local managers may have less marketing
knowledge and expertise but more intimate knowledge of the market
than foreign managers. Specifically, I investigate how local firms fare
vis-à-vis foreign firms in light of these reasons.

The Conceptual Model

Consistent with the conceptual framework proposed in the book,
we adopt Day and Wensley's (1988) source-position-performance
model, in which business orientation is the source, brand image a
positional mediator, and business performance an outcome (see also
Han et al., 1998). Figure 3.1 presents these relationships and
hypotheses graphically. To investigate the effects of business orientation, we hypothesize two routes: peripheral and central. The peripheral
pathway involves direct impact of business orientation on business
performance, whereas the central pathway is posited to occur indirectly
through the brand image associated with business orientation or
performance. The questions of interests here are *whether* business
orientation contributes to business performance and *how* (i.e., through
which pathway).

Extending the seminal work of Keith (1960) about Pillsbury's
evolution through production, selling, marketing, etcetera, we define

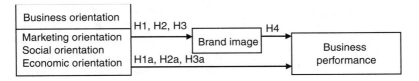

Figure 3.1 The theoretical link between business orientation, brand image, and business performance

business orientation as a three-component—marketing, social, and economic—orientation that aims to achieve desired exchange outcomes (sales and profit) with target markets (Kotler, 1997). The three-component conceptualization makes it possible to focus on the analysis of these orientations and study their direct impact on business performance and indirect impact on business performance via brand image. In the next section, we discuss each component and the role of brand image and develop hypotheses.

Marketing Orientation

It relates to the changes taking place in marketing practices in businesses, changes that tend to be more overt—markets and communications becoming more global, marketing and products more customized, and media usages more fragmented (Venketesh et al., 1993). As the social structure of society tends to disintegrate and consumers become more active, it is expected that business managers will be candid about how they conduct their businesses and about the way they manufacture products. For example, a customer who would like to have an image of being a green customer may like to know if the end product is green (e.g., biodegradable), and if the product-making process was green (e.g., environments were not polluted or rivers were not contaminated during the manufacturing process). Consumers buy brands because of the image connected to the brand. The notion of creating image reminds business managers that the action in the marketplace is based upon impressions and interpretations that consumers derive from their previous experiences (Levy, 1973).

Another characteristic of this orientation is that the markets tend to be fragmented, and, therefore, a fragmented media is needed for effective marketing communications. The consumers in the emerging market have more access to global communications than they had before economic liberalization and, therefore, have a clear idea as to what features they wish to have in their products. It is expected that marketing managers would cultivate the knowledge possessed by the customers and provide them with the customized products and services, which would lead to establishing a favorable brand image of their firms. Firms that make an effort to understand the needs of customers develop better products or services with few defects and thus reduce operational cost and enhance performance. Although the majority of studies found support for a positive relationship between market orientation and business performance (Caruna et al., 1995; Pitt et al., 1996), some researchers have identified a weak association between market orientation and business performance (Diamantopoulos and Hart, 1993; Appiah-Adu and Singh, 1998). Based on the discussion above and empirical evidence, we propose to test the following hypotheses:

H1: Marketing orientation is positively related to brand image.
H1a: Marketing orientation is positively related to business performance.

Social Orientation

It relates to the changes in the structure of modern society that are caused by the economic reform policies. It is defined as the extent to which firms demonstrate their willingness to be socially oriented by determining the extent to which social structure has become egalitarian, the society has become multicultural, and consumers have become active, educated, and individualistic (Lannon, 1996). This change in society calls for the introduction of new products and services to match the evolving needs and expectations of consumers (Jaworski and Kohli, 1990). Further, as society makes strides toward an egalitarian society, products that were previously categorized as luxury products have now become utility items. A good example of this is the telephone, which was a luxury service in many developing nations. The changes in the social fabric have made the telephone a utility item, a necessity for those wishing to pursue a Western lifestyle. True, a few customers may choose the product as a symbol through which they may form a self-image of being Western even if they are not in a financial position to afford the product. Nguyen and LeBlanc (1998) describe image as a hierarchical network of meanings stored in memory that range from holistic general impressions to very elaborate evaluations of objects that are linked to the individual's values. As society's values change continuously, it is expected that socially oriented managers will pay special attention to existing values in emerging markets as they affect the size of segments (Blackwell et al.,

2001). Buzzle et al. (1975) have shown that the size of segments is positively correlated to profitability. Therefore, focusing on consumers' values and images while staying abreast of the evolving society's needs is the approach that is most likely to lead to success. Hence we propose to test the following hypotheses.

H2: Social orientation is positively related to brand image.
H2a: Social orientation is positively related to business performance.

Economic Orientation

It relates to achieving desired exchange outcomes (sales and profit) with target markets (Kotler, 1997) while being economic. As the primary objective of any organization is to be profitable, it is becoming increasingly difficult to rely on the traditional way of marketing of mass-produced items for the creation of wealth. With the growth of the Internet and information technology, mass-customization is likely to be a significant force in the present economy as managers try to understand the individual needs of the customers (Arnold et al., 2002). Moving away from mass production to mass customization as a major source of wealth creation is in conformity with the practices that give consumers a sense of individuality and, therefore, enables them to enjoy subjective and personal experiences. For example, Hallmark Cards and American Greetings installed electronic kiosks in stores and other public places to enable people to create their own greeting cards. Although, these systems have not fully exploited the potential of mass-customization, it does suggest that the trend is present in today's society. Further, there is a rapid growth in the movement of people, thereby creating opportunities for marketers to develop markets for such segments, which could not be justified previously because of economic reasons. For example, historical sites have been promoted as images of regional cultural identity to maintain the sites' uniqueness and to retain its tourist value (Firat and Venkatesh, 1995). The globalization of information has created tourist interests in different cultures, mobilizing people and capital from one place to another. Based on personal interviews with managers, it appears that managers expect better performance (e.g., achieving economies of scale, to improve business performance) from their firms as a result of pursuing activities relating to building brand image and attaining cost efficiency.

Based on the preceding discussion, we propose the following hypotheses.

H3: Economic orientation is positively related to brand image.
H3a: Economic orientation is positively related to business performance.

Brand Image and Business Performance

Brand image is defined as a firm's ability to take advantage of image-enhancing efforts by positioning brands as global in their communications using messages such as brand name, logo, visuals, themes, and the like (Alden et al., 1999). If a firm's objective is to build a competitive advantage by creating a brand image, the symbolic consumption of products, and therefore brands, becomes an ongoing interaction between the firm and its consumers. The effectiveness of this strategy depends on the extent to which it is successful in enhancing the brand image and, therefore, acquiring new customers or retaining existing consumers. As brand image is linked with brand equity, Aaker and Jacobson (1994) find that increases in brand equity are associated with positive market returns. Changes in brand equities also produce a stock market reaction that may have a positive or negative impact on the business performance of firms. Further, Keller (1993) notes that financial valuation issues have little relevance if no underlying value for the brand has been created or if managers do not know how to exploit that value by developing profitable brand strategies. It is not surprising that mega brand firms are market share leaders too. Indeed, a large market share of firms produces large revenues for firms (Buzzle et al., 1975). Therefore, we expect firms committed to building brand image to have a positive impact on business performance. To test this assertion, we propose to test the final hypothesis.

H4: Brand image of a firm is positively related to business performance.

Methodology

Research Design

Data Collection

The convenience sample consisted of foreign and local firms operating in India. Two criteria were used to classify foreign firms: some ownership of these firms was held overseas and their parent firms' headquarters were located abroad. A two-stage sampling process was followed. The initial list comprised of firms listed in the Kompass business directory for New Delhi, Bombay, Calcutta, and Madras. These four cities are highly populated and developed compared to other cities in India, so it is expected that consumers of these cities are more likely to exhibit a more Western trend, if any, than the rest of India. From this initial list, 200 foreign and 200 local firms were randomly selected in the four cities. Following pretests for clarity, in

New Delhi, data-collection questionnaires were administered in person to the managers. Some of the initial items were dropped from the questionnaire for the reasons of relevancy and redundancy. To increase the response rate, personally administered questionnaires were preferred to postal survey. Managers were asked to complete a questionnaire that sought information on their perceptions of the business orientation. The items of the questionnaire are presented in table 3.1. The meaning of the business orientation was explained to managers and they were made aware of the purpose of the study. A total response of 308 was received; 21 questionnaires were found incomplete so they could not be utilized in our analysis, leaving an effective sample size of only 287. If the interviewer could not find a qualified manager to fill the questionnaire, a deputy manager was approached; 28 foreign and 64 Indian managers declined to participate in the study. The major reason for not being able to take part in the study was the lack of time to complete the questionnaire. Of the 308 managers, 251 requested a copy of the summary of the results. The fact that a large proportion of managers was interested in this research study explains the timeliness and essence of the study. All respondents were assured of their anonymity.

Characteristics of the Sample
The sample comprised of approximately 51 percent of local firms. The remainder of the sample consisted of foreign firms with headquarters in the United States (17 percent), the United Kingdom (13 percent), Germany (7 percent), France (4 percent), and others (8 percent). The combined sample for both foreign and local firms represented 47 percent of manufacturing and 53 percent of the service industry. Firms manufacturing durable and nondurable consumer products accounted for approximately 58 percent, whereas industrial product manufacturers represented 42 percent. Firms, having turnover of less than Rs. 50m, between Rs. 50m and Rs. 100m, and more than Rs.100m constituted 46 percent, 37 percent, and 17 percent of the sample, respectively. Similarly, firms with less than 99 employees, between 100 and 199 employees, and more than 200 employees represented 69 percent, 22 percent, and 9 percent of the sample, respectively. The questionnaires completed by a CEO/ MD/proprietor, board-level directors, and either senior managers or middle managers were 61 percent, 27 percent, and 12 percent, respectively. Based on the number of employees employed in firms in developing countries, the majority of the firms could be classified as medium-sized firms (Liedholm and Mead, 1987).

Operationalization of the Measures

Business Orientation

The scale was designed to reflect business-oriented activities practiced by managers relating to marketing, social, and economic orientations. The items on the scale were adapted from Venkatesh et al. (1993) and Lannon (1996) and personal interviews with marketing managers. These interviews were rooted in the concept of grounded theory. Strauss and Corbin (1998) state that grounded theory is driven by data systematically gathered and analyzed through the research process. In this method, data collection, analysis, and eventual theory stand in close relationship to one another. Accordingly, care was taken to examine the domain of each orientation as closely as possible while selecting the items for the scale. Criterion of uniqueness and ability to convey different shades of meaning to informants were also used (Churchill, 1979). The managers were requested to provide responses pertaining to these activities on a seven-point Likert-type scale, where one and seven formed continuum of adjectives that were diametrically opposite.

The principal component analysis was used to extract orthogonal factors that were subject to Eigen value more than one. Three factors were identified which extracted 63 percent of the total variance in the model. Results of the analysis containing the scores of α and standard α for the orientations are presented in table 3.1. The Cronbach α coefficient scores, which are above .70, confirm the reliability of these orientations. As the values of standard α, which takes into account standard deviations of items in the scale, are close to α, it lends further credence to reliability. A minimum score of .72 was recorded on each of the dimensions, which is above the score suggested by Nunnally (1978) for the scales to be reliable.

Brand Image

It was operationalized by measuring the extent to which managers were successful in promoting their products as image-oriented brands. Based on the literature review and personal interviews, seven items were initially identified that represented the extra efforts exerted by the managers to manage the image of the brand. Of the seven items, only four items were retained for the purpose of analysis. The factor analysis confirmed its unidimensionality and positive correlation among these items. To test the reliability of the scale, an internal consistency analysis (Cronbach α) was performed (Nunnally, 1978; Churchill, 1979). The reliability score for the scale is .76, which is above the acceptable cutoff score suggested by Cronbach for the scale to be reliable. The items and related statistics are presented in table 3.1.

Table 3.1   Reliability analysis for the multi-item scales

Scale items		Item-to-total correlation	α, if item deleted
Marketing orientation: α = .76, standard α = .73, variance explained by the factor = 30.1%			
X_1	Business activities: covert versus overt	.41	.74
X_2	Media usage: mass versus fragmented	.39	.75
X_3	Markets: national versus global	.42	.78
X_4	Marketing: mass versus customized/relationship	.40	.73
X_5	Communications: local versus global	.41	.76
X_6	Products: standardized versus customized	.42	.77
Social orientation: α = .75, standard α = .72, variance explained by the factor = 21.7%			
X_7	Social order: hierarchical versus Egalitarian	.41	.74
X_8	Markets: general versus multicultural	.39	.73
X_9	Nature of society: inherited versus individualistic	.41	.76
X_{10}	Media: controlled versus free access	.40	.74
X_{11}	Consumers: passive versus active/Educated	.42	.78
Economic orientation: α = .73, standard α = .72, variance explained by the factor = 11.1%			
X_{12}	Wealth creation: manufacturing versus Information/Service	.39	.72
X_{13}	Movement of people: restricted versus unrestricted	.40	.74
X_{14}	Production: mass versus customized	.38	.72
Brand image: α = .73, standard α = .73, standard α = .72			
Y_1	We try to sell the image of the product	.43	.74
Y_2	We try to make our product distinct	.40	.73
Y_3	We try to make our product desirable	.42	.72
Y_4	Our advertisements are image-oriented	.41	.72
Business performance: α = .72, standard α = .72			
Y_5	Our return on investment on image-oriented brands	.72	NA
Y_6	Our overall performance from the marketing	.72	NA

Business Performance

Return on image-oriented (ROI) brand and overall performance (OP) of firms were measured on a seven-point Likert-type scale (−3 = low performance, 0 = no difference in performance, and +3 = high performance). The ROI, adapted from the definition of Kohli and Jeworski (1990), refers to the extent to which a firm is successful in maximizing its profit on a given brand. For firms with multiple brands, only brands that were being positioned as image oriented were considered for data collection. Due to firms' reluctance to divulge performance-related data, the study employed a subjective measure of performance measurement that was primarily concerned with firms' individual performances relative to that of the largest competitor (Golden, 1992). The subjective measures of performance are frequently used in marketing research and have been found to be reliable and valid (Dess and Robinson, 1984; Pearce et al., 1987).

Analysis

The assessment of the measurement properties and the test of the hypothesized relationships presented in the conceptual model were undertaken using maximum-likelihood estimation, the observed variance, and covariance matrix. In accordance with Gerbing and Anderson's (1988) two-step approach, the measurement model was first assessed by employing factor analysis in which each orientation was assessed for internal consistency within each set of items. Items of the business orientation scale that either cross-loaded on more than one orientation or had low correlation with each other were eliminated. Next, the purified scales (i.e., the orientations) were used for the estimation of parameters in the structural equation model. In this study, the sample size of 287 was considered sufficient for this type of analysis (Jöreskog and Sörbom, 1984). The Structural Equation Model is presented in figure 3.2, and overall goodness-of-fit indices, standardized parameters estimates, and corresponding t-values are reported in table 3.2. These indicators suggest a strong fit of the model to the data in accordance with the criteria established by Bentler and Bonett (1980), and Browne and Cudeck (1993). To test convergent and discriminant validity, we specified a CFA model with intercorrelated factors, as recommended by Anderson and Gerbing (1988). Further, discriminant validity was tested by examining the deterioration of fit caused by setting the latent factor correlations to one. The difference in chi-square for each pair of orientations in both groups was found to be significant, the smallest being $\chi^2_{(3)} = 7.32$,

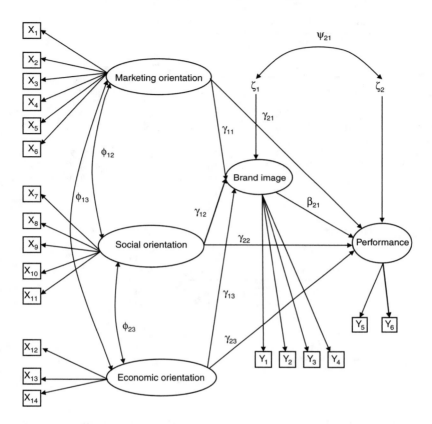

Figure 3.2 The hypothesized model

$p = .01$, suggesting that the orientations were distinct. Further, in order to have more insight into the items of the business orientation, a paired-sample t-test analysis was performed between the two sets of data: foreign and local managers. The mean scores and standard deviations for these items are presented in table 3.3. In the following section, we focus on the interpretation of the results and the emerging findings.

Results and Discussion

Marketing Orientation

Marketing orientation is positively and significantly ($\gamma_{11} = .70$, $t = 8.72$) related to the brand image in the sample of foreign managers;

Table 3.2 Parameter estimates for the structural equation models

Parameters	AMOS estimates		t-value	
	Foreign	Local	Foreign	Local
β_{21}	.71	.63	9.89	9.13
γ_{21}	.18	.16	1.83	1.80
γ_{11}	.70	.23	8.72	2.57
γ_{12}	.19	.17	1.81	1.80
γ_{22}	.19	.13	1.82	1.76
γ_{13}	.16	.14	1.83	1.77
γ_{23}	.73	.16	9.91	1.82
ϕ_{12}	.16	.15	1.84	1.79
ϕ_{13}	.14	.13	1.79	1.77
ϕ_{23}	.13	.12	1.78	1.71
ψ_{21}	.11	.13	1.68	1.78

Other model estimates	Foreign	Local
Goodness-of-fit Index (GFI)	.94	.93
Adjusted goodness-of-fit index (AGFI)	.93	.91
Root mean square residuals (RMSR)	.03	.04
Comparative fit index (CFI)	.95	.92
Chi-square (χ^2)	566	587
Degree of freedom (DF)	160	160
Coefficient of determination (R^2)	.78	.73

however, the link between marketing orientation and brand image was found to be weak ($\gamma_{11} = .23$, t = 2.57) in the sample of local managers. The result indicates that foreign managers place more importance on being marketing orientated to building brand image than their Indian counterparts. We did not find any significant correlation between marketing orientation and business performance in any of the samples. Therefore, H1 is partially supported but H1a is rejected. This indicates that activities relating to marketing orientation are not perceived by both types of managers as being important enough to have a direct impact on business performance.

Further, a paired sample t-test analyses reveal that out of six items on the orientation, both set of managers differed significantly (p < .05) on the four items. For example, there was no significant difference (4.43 versus 4.78) between the two sets of firms on the business activities. These managers appear to practice both covert and overt business activities. However, it appears that firms tend to

Table 3.3 T-test of differences between foreign and local firms

	Business orientation items	Mean (S.D.)	Mean (S. D.)	Significance
Marketing orientation				
(X_1)	Business activities: covert versus overt	4.43 (0.95)	4.78 (1.21)	n/s
(X_2)	Media usage: mass versus fragmented	6.37 (1.23)	5.13 (0.98)	.02
(X_3)	Markets: national versus global	6.36 (0.87)	5.21 (0.93)	.04
(X_4)	Marketing: mass versus customized/relationship	6.44 (1.21)	6.37 (0.98)	n/s
(X_5)	Communications: local versus global	6.24 (1.32)	4.62 (0.89)	.02
(X_6)	Products: standardized versus customized	5.91 (0.99)	4.73 (1.11)	.04
Social orientation				
(X_7)	Social structure/order: hierarchical versus Egalitarian	3.98 (1.12)	3.87 (0.94)	n/s
(X_8)	Markets: general versus multicultural	6.23 (1.23)	6.27 (0.91)	n/s
(X_9)	Nature of society: inherited versus individualistic	4.22 (0.98)	4.41 (1.13)	n/s
(X_{10})	Media: controlled versus free access	5.00 (0.89)	4.88 (0.34)	n/s
(X_{11})	Consumers: passive versus active/educated	4.74 (0.94)	4.89 (1.00)	n/s
Economic orientation				
(X_{12})	Wealth creation: manufacturing versus Information/Service	6.92 (1.11)	4.67 (1.13)	.01
(X_{13})	Movement of people: restricted versus unrestricted	5.51 (0.96)	4.21 (1.19)	.02
(X_{14})	Production: mass versus customized	6.45 (1.01)	4.54 (1.23)	.02

transform to an overt mode of business as consumers become more educated and demanding. Firms have incentives to be overt as it promotes good image and goodwill for firms among consumers. On the media usage practice, foreign firms scored a significantly higher mean than local firms.

In the present business environment, foreign managers (6.37 versus 5.13) view the fragmented use of media as being more important than their local counterparts. In the fragmented market, it appears to be difficult to achieve marketing communication objectives through conventional marketing communication tools. However, by utilizing multimedia technology, it may be possible for managers to target smaller and fragmented segments. Further, foreign managers appeared to have significantly high (6.36 versus 5.21) expectations from global markets compared to their Indian counterparts. This result is not surprising because the recent developments in the field of telecommunications and transportation, and the saturation of Western markets, have forced firms to explore emerging markets in the pursuit of business opportunities. Findings of the study reflected this trend among managers. It appears that even if Indian managers attach importance to the national market, they are in favor of global markets, too. It is interesting to learn that local firms were seeking to diversify into foreign markets as reported by Vachani (1989); however, as the local markets are yet to reach saturation, small- and medium-sized firms may be discouraged from venturing abroad on a short-term basis. On the item of marketing, there was no significant difference between foreign (6.44 versus 6.37) and local managers. It appears that the trend was considered Western for both types of firms. In the present context, mass customization and relationship marketing take a lead over mass marketing, as marketing seeks closeness to consumers and commitment to their needs, values, and individual identity. Undoubtedly, both types of managers were in favor of pursuing customized and relationship marketing strategy to reach their consumers.

With reference to a local versus global forms of communication, foreign managers scored a significantly high score (6.24 versus 4.62) compared to their local counterparts. While Indian managers took a localized approach to marketing communications, foreign managers preferred the global approach to communications. Foreign managers perceived the global market as a homogenous market, so there was little need for a change in the communications strategy. Finally, there was a significant difference between the views of foreign (5.91 versus 4.73) and local managers on the standardization of products. Foreign managers were more in favor of customizing products than their local counterparts. Given that the market in India is still a mass market and that it is largely homogenous because it consists of mainly middle and lower income groups of the society, it appears that Indian managers perceive little need for making any significant changes to their product lines. However, as the society becomes more fragmented, and consumers become more educated and active—in terms of selecting products that are consistent with their values—Indian managers would probably become more responsive to serving the needs of the small distinct group.

Social Orientation

Social orientation is not significantly (foreign: $\gamma_{12} = .19$, t = 1.81; local: $\gamma_{12} = .17$, t = 1.80) related to brand image in both samples; therefore, hypothesis H2 is rejected. This result indicates that although both types of managers perceive changes taking place in society, they do not perceive social orientation to have any significant impact on brand image. We did not find a significant positive relationship between social orientation and business performance in any groups. We reject H2a. This finding may indicate that managers do not perceive changes in society to be Western enough to have an effect on business performance. Further, paired-sample t-test statistics revealed that there were no significant differences between the two groups of firms on any of the items on the social dimension. Both sets of firms were not significantly socially oriented. However, managers of both foreign and local firms contended that social order (3.98 versus 3.87) was hierarchical and that these markets (6.23 versus 6.27) were multicultural.

With respect to the nature of society, managers (4.22 versus 4.41) observed that the society had not yet become purely individualistic; consumers had to discover their own values and beliefs. This result is inconsistent with Firat and Venkatesh's (1995) view in that consumerism has become a culture in itself and that as the society becomes more fragmented, consumers would identify themselves more with what they consume. It appears that consumers need more time to discover their individual values that would assist them in shaping their own subculture. The fact that there was no major difference (5.00 versus 4.88) between controlled and free access to media signified that managers were equally at ease using both forms of media. Essentially, media is controlled when the notion of family, institution, religion, or social class is strong; however, as consumers become more inquisitive and educated as a result of experience gained by using different products and services, there may be a need for an open media for the communication of evolving culture, values, and beliefs. Therefore, the views of managers that the society was hierarchical in nature did not conform to the notion of open media in the present context. Regarding the active and passive nature of consumers, there were no significant differences between the two groups of managers (4.74 versus 4.89). Indeed, as consumers liberate themselves from the shackles of rigid social structure, they would have greater freedom to express themselves and establish their own identity rather than organize as a group based on a certain religion or social class. Further, the process of liberalization makes consumers active to find an identity and expression in what they consume through images and meanings (Lannon, 1996; Cova, 1996). It appears that there are both passive and active consumers in the Indian market.

Economic Orientation

Economic orientation does not have a significant positive correlation (foreign: $\gamma_{13} = .16$, t = 1.83; local: $\gamma_{13} = .14$, t = 1.77) with brand image in any of the samples; therefore, H3 is rejected. However, economic orientation is positively and significantly ($\gamma_{23} = .73$, t = 9.91) related to business performance in the sample of foreign managers, and positively but not significantly ($\gamma_{23} = .16$, t = 1.82) so in the sample of local managers, which lends partial support for H3a. It may be concluded that foreign managers are more geared toward enhancing business performance by paying attention to economic activities than their Indian counterparts. Clearly, Indian managers do not perceive that the costs of increasing the economic orientation in the present society outweigh the benefits derived from such orientation. One possible explanation for the reluctance may be due to the capital required to convert the mass production layout into a mass customization facility, and the demand for the customized products in the market may not be enough to justify the initial losses from such operations. As evident, the foreign firms scored a significantly higher means than did the local firms on all items relating to economic orientation. For example, to create wealth, foreign managers (6.92) tend to depend on information and services whereas local managers (4.67) adhered to manufacturing-related activities. It seems that foreign managers were in close proximity to their consumers by generating information pertaining to their needs (Kohli and Jaworski, 1990). In addition, foreign managers (5.51 versus 4.21 of local managers) perceived that there was a greater need for the mobility of capital and people than before. This result is consistent with the view that if markets become global, the movement of people and capital should become less restrictive. Further, the advances in telecommunications coupled with the liberalization of economies and the globalization of capital would increase the mobility of people worldwide.

Next, foreign managers (6.45 versus 4.54) believed customized production to be more important than did their Indian counterparts. This finding stemmed from the fact that advances in flexible manufacturing systems, information technology, and efficient management techniques have enabled foreign firms to provide consumers with customized products and services at competitive prices. Foreign managers appearing to be equipped with production techniques that accommodate the consumers' needs probably improve the performance of their firms. Certainly, given consumers' assertion for self-identity and their quest for distinctiveness, it is expected that Indian managers would take into account the consumers' identity and distinct nature while designing products for them, which may lead to superior performance.

Brand Image

Brand image is positively and significantly (foreign: $\beta_{21} = .71$, $t = 9.89$; local: $\beta_{21} = .63$, $t = 9.13$) related to business performance in both samples; therefore, hypothesis H4 is supported. As evidenced by the parameter estimates, it appears that both sets of managers perceive that brand image improves business performance. To test further if the link between brand image and business performance contributed to the explained variance in the hypothesized model above and beyond the variance explained by the links between marketing orientation and business performance, social orientation and brand image, social orientation and business performance, and economic orientation and brand image, it was discovered that the presence of these links made little ($b \leq .02$, not significant in both samples) or no contribution to the explanation of variance in the model beyond the straight contributions of marketing orientation and brand image, and economic orientation and business performance. Therefore it may be deduced in the foreign sample that economic orientation has a direct impact on the performance of firms, whereas marketing orientation has an indirect positive impact on business performance via brand image. In the sample of local firms, we did not find any significant contribution from any of the orientations on brand image; however, evidence of a link between brand image and business performance was detected.

Implications for Managers

Findings of this chapter have direct managerial implications. The results indicate that Indian managers do not fully appreciate the benefits of being business oriented, as indicated by low scores on certain activities such as wealth creation by manufacturing, restricted movement of people, mass production, mass usage of media, and standardized products. These practices can be resolved by providing training on the relevance of each of the practices with the consumer as the focus in new marketing techniques. It is apparent that there is a need for transfer of market-oriented knowledge to the Indian economy. This new form of marketing can be achieved by modifying the Western techniques, particularly in communications, to suit the growing consumerism. To have a competitive advantage, there is a greater need than ever to follow the society's Western trend.

Further, managers need to understand the extent to which there is a Western trend present in society. The practices provided in this chapter can be utilized for the assessment of existing trends. Managers should track the nature of evolving markets closely to be able to adapt and implement a suitable business strategy. For example, as perceived by both sets of managers, our study found that India's markets were multicultural and that its consumers were more relationship oriented. So, it may be recommended that managers understand the structure of the culture that calls for being more interactive with consumers, perhaps on a one-to-one basis. Managers may like to develop a very personal form of marketing that recognizes, acknowledges, appreciates, and serves consumers through conscious and planned marketing practices. In order to get a feel for the evolving characteristics of the markets, managers should have a supple mind and be able to respond quickly to those developments.

From an investment point of view, the Indian economy indicates that numerous opportunities are available for both foreign and local managers. For example, establishing subsidiaries can be cost-effective due to inexpensive labor and a segmented market. Western firms that are skilled at performing business activities effectively are likely to be viewed as attractive joint venture partners for local firms that recognize the importance of effective business practices but somehow are underperforming in certain areas.

Future Research Directions

Despite the research contributions, the study has a few limitations, for example, utilization of the subjective measurement of business views could lead to a view that may not be consistent with actual prevailing practices. Additionally, the convenience sample the study utilized may not be a true representation of the population. However, replication of the study with a national sample would provide more confidence in the findings of the study.

From an academic viewpoint, a couple of pointers for future research arise from this study: first, to have more confidence in the acceptability of the concept and the generalizability of the findings, it is recommended to replicate the study in other emerging markets; and, as firms adapt in response to changing business environments, scholars should examine the impact of business orientation on corporate culture (Deshpande et al., 1993), and on ethnoconsumerism (Venkatesh, 1995). These areas of research may provide another perspective that may be of benefit to both researchers and practitioners.

Conclusion

The purpose of the study was to examine if the business-oriented practices adopted by foreign and local firms contributed to brand image and business performance. In this context, the chapter contributes to existing knowledge by facilitating the identification of items relating to business orientation. A domain of business orientation scale was empirically tested. From a theoretical point of view, the chapter recognizes the central role of image-oriented consumers in the business orientation-performance link. Further, the findings of the study extend our knowledge of current business practices in emerging markets on which much of the scholarly and commercial interests have been focused in recent years.

We found that the links between marketing orientation and brand image, economic orientation and business performance, and brand image and business performance are positive and significant in the sample of foreign firms; however, in the sample of local firms, only the link between brand image and business performance was found to be positive and significant. Further, findings of the study revealed that foreign managers are more likely to practice business-oriented activities than their Indian counterparts on items such as creation of wealth by generating information and offering services and customization of products and production. However, both sets of managers were significantly business oriented in treating their markets as multicultural and in targeting their consumers via relationship marketing. Surprisingly, despite the arrival of the information highway, both sets of managers still perceive Indian society as hierarchical. Most importantly, both sets of managers were almost neutral on the following four items: nature of society (inherited/individualistic); media (controlled/free access); consumers (passive/active); and business activities (covert/overt).

In general, it can be concluded that the key to success is an image-oriented product, a factor that would compel firms to offer products beyond its functional values. As the society takes a new turn and becomes more individualistic, consumers would seek self-identity through the consumption of products or services that would offer them self-expression through different images associated with brands.

References

Aaker, D.A., and Jacobson, R. "The Financial Information Content of Perceived Quality." *Journal of Marketing Research* 31, no. 2 (1994): 191–201.

Anderson, J.C., and Gerbing, D.W. "Structural Equation Modeling in Practice: A Review and Recommended Two-Step Approach." *Psychological Bulletin* 12 (Spring 1988): 411–23.

Alden, D.L., Steenkamp, J-B.E.M., and Batra, R. "Brand Positioning Through Advertising in Asia, North America, and Europe: The Role of Global Consumer Culture." *Journal of Marketing* 63, no. 1 (1999): 75–87.

Appiah-Adu, K., and Singh, S. "Market Orientation and Performance: An Empirical Study of British SMEs." *Journal of Entrepreneurship* 7, no. 1 (1998): 27–47.

Arnold, E.J., Price, L., and Zinkhan, G.M. *Consumer.* New York: McGraw-Hill, 2002.

Bentler, P.M., and Bonett, D. "Significance Tests and Goodness of Fit in the Analysis of Covariance Structures." *Psychological Bulletin* 88, no. 3 (1980): 588–606.

Blackwell, R.D., Miniard, P.W., and Engel, J.F. *Consumer Behavior.* Orlando: Harcourt College Publishers, 2001.

Browne, M.W., and Cudeck, R. "Alternative Ways of Assessing Model Fit." In *Testing Structural Equation Models,* ed. Bollen, K.A., and Long, J.S., 136–62. California: Sage Publications, 1993.

Buzzle, R.D., Gale, T.B., and Sultan, G.M. "Market Share: A Key to Profitability." *Harvard Business Review* 53 (January 1975): 97–106.

Caruna, A., Gauci, S., and Ferry, M. "Market Orientation and Business Performance: Some Evidence from Malta." In *Making Marketing Work,* ed. Jobber, D., and Uncles, M., 123–32. Bradford: Marketing Education Group, 1995.

Churchill, G.A., Jr. "A Paradigm for Developing Better Measures of Marketing Constructs." *Journal of Marketing Research* 16, no. 1 (1979): 64–73.

Cova, B. "What Postmodernism Means to Marketing Managers." *European Management Journal* 14, no. 5 (1996): 494–99.

Cova, B., and Svanfeldt, C. "Marketing Beyond Marketing in a Postmodern Europe: The Creation of Societal Innovations." In *Marketing for Europe: Marketing for the Future,* ed. Grunert, K.G., and Fuglede, D., 155–71. Aarhus: EMAC, 1992.

Day, G.S., and Wensley, R. "Marketing Theory with a Strategic Orientation." *Journal of Marketing* 47 (Fall 1988): 79–89.

Deshpande, R., Farley, J.U., and Webster, F.E. "Corporate Culture, Customer Orientation, and Innovation in Japanese Firms: A Quadrad Analysis." *Journal of Marketing* 57 (January 1993): 23–27.

Dess, G.G., and Robinson, R.B., Jr. "Measuring Organizational Performance in the Absence of Objective Measure: The Case of Privately Held Firm and Conglomerate Business Unit." *Strategic Management Journal* 5, no. 3 (1984): 265–73.

Diamantopoulos, A., and Hart, S. "Linking Market Orientation and Company Performance: Preliminary Evidence on Kohli and Jaworski's Framework." *Journal of Strategic Marketing* 1, no. 1 (1993): 93–121.

Firat, A.F. "Postmodern Culture, Marketing and the Consumer: Marketing Theory and Applications," paper presented at the American Marketing Association Conference (1991): 237–42.

Firat, A.F., and Venkatesh, A. "Liberatory, Postmodernism and the Re-enchantment of Consumption." *Journal of Consumer Research* 22 (December 1995): 239–67.

Gerbing, D.W., and Anderson, J.C. "An Updated Paradigm for Scale Development Incorporating Unidimensionality and Its Assessment." *Journal of Marketing Research* 25, no. 2 (1988): 186–92.

Golden, B.R. "SBU Strategy and Performance: The Moderating Effect of the Corporate-SBU Relationship." *Strategic Management Journal* 13, no. 2 (1992): 145–58.

Gummeson, E. "Marketing Orientation Revisited: The Crucial Role of the Part-Time Marketer." *European Journal of Marketing* 25, no. 2 (1991): 60–75.

Han, J.K., Kim, N., and Srivastava, R.K. "Market Orientation and Organizational Performance: Is Innovation a Missing Link?" *Journal of Marketing* 62 (October 1998): 30–45.

Hulbert, J.M., and Pitt, L. "Exit Left Center Stage: The Future of Functional Marketing." *European Marketing Journal* 14, no. 1 (1996): 47–60.

Jaworski, B.J., and Kohli, A.K. "Market Orientation: Antecedents and Consequences." *Journal of Marketing* 57 (July 1990): 53–70.

Jöreskog, K.G., and Sörbom, D. *LISREL-VI User's Guide.* Mooresville: Scientific Software, 1984.

Keith, R.J. "The Marketing Revolution." *Journal of Marketing* 24, no. 1 (1960): 35–38.

Keller, K.L. "Conceptualizing, Measuring, and Managing Customer-Based Brand Equity." *Journal of Marketing* 57, no. 1 (1993): 1–22.

Kohli, A.K., and Jaworski, B.J. "Market Orientation: The Construct, Research and Managerial Implication." *Journal of Marketing* 54 (April 1990): 1–18.

Kolde, E. *Environment of International Business.* Boston: Kent Publishing, 1992.

Kotler, P. "Reconceptualizing Marketing." *European Management Journal* 12, no. 4 (1994): 353–61.

Kotler, P. *Marketing Management.* Englewood-Cliffs, NJ: Prentice Hall, 1997.

Lannon, J. "What Is Postmodernism and What Does It Have to Do with Brands?" *Journal of Brand Management* 4, no. 2 (1996): 83–94.

Levy, S.J. "Imaginary and Symbolism." In *Brands, Consumers, Symbols and Research*, ed. Dennis, W.R., 233–40. Thousand Oaks, CA: Sage Publications, 1973.

Liedholm, C., and Mead, M. "Small Scale Industries in Developing Countries: Empirical Evidence and Policy Implications." In *MSU International Development Paper* 9, East Lansing: Michigan State University, 1987.

Manu, F.A. "Innovation Orientation, Environment and Performance: A Comparison of US and European Markets." *Journal of International Business Studies* 23, no. 2 (1992): 332–59.

Nguyen, N., and LeBlanc, G. "The Mediating Role of Corporate Image on Customers' Retention Decisions: An Investigation in Financial Services." *International Journal of Bank Marketing* 16, no. 2 (1998): 52–65.

Nunnally, J. *Psychometric Testing.* New York: McGraw Hill, 1978.

Pearce, J., Freeman, E., and Robinson, R. "The Tenuous Link between Formal Strategic Planning and Financial Performance." *Academy of Management Review* 12, no. 4 (1987): 658–75.

Pitt, L., Caruana, A., and Berthon, P.R. "Market Orientation and Business Performance: Some European Evidence." *International Marketing Review* 13, no. 1 (1996): 5–18.

Singh, S. "Effects of Transition Economy on the Market Orientation-Business Performance Link: The Empirical Evidence from Indian Industrial Firms." *Journal of Global Marketing* 16, no. 4 (2003): 73–96.

Strauss, A., and Corbin, J. *Basics of Qualitative Research: Techniques and Procedures for Developing Grounded Theory.* Thousand Oaks, CA: Sage Publications, 1998.

Swamy, S. "Assessing India's Economic Reforms." Frontline 19, no. 2 (2002). Retrieved March 24, 2007 from *http://flonnet.com/fl*1902/19020610.*htm*

Vachani, S. "Strategic Responses of Multinationals to Competition from Developing Country Cottage Firms." *International Marketing Review* 7, no. 3 (1989): 31–47.

Venkatesh, A. "Modernity and Postmodernity: A Synthesis or Antithesis?" In *Marketing Theory and Practice*, ed. Childers, T.L., 99–104. Chicago: American Management Association, 1989.

———. "Ethnoconsumerism: A New Paradigm to Study Cultural and Cross-cultural Consumer Behavior." In *Marketing in a Multicultural World*, ed. Costa, J., and Bamossy, G., 26–67. Thousand Oaks, CA: Sage Publications, 1995.

Venkatesh, A., Sherry, J.F., and Firat, A.F. "Postmodernism and the Marketing Imaginary." *International Journal of Research in Marketing* 10, no. 3 (1993): 215–23.

Chapter 4

Ethics and Profitability: Can They Coexist?

Satyendra Singh

This chapter examines the effects of two moral ethical philosophies—deontological and teleological—on profitability. Drawing on the source-competitive advantage-performance theory, it is argued that firms that are perceived ethical are more likely to have a positive impact on profitability than firms that do not. Based on data from Indian businesses, the results of the regression models indicate that ethical business practices lead firms to a superior profitability through acquisition of the competitive advantage. However, the results also suggest that the effects of such ethical practices on profitability are initially negative but turn positive with higher levels of ethical orientation. Implication for managers is that they can command, even in emerging markets, a premium price for their products, if their firms are perceived ethical.

Introduction

Given the recent trend toward investments in emerging markets by multinational firms, local managers are forced to compete with the foreign firms or face the prospect of extinction. As a result, local firms actively seek to achieve a competitive advantage over their rivals in today's dynamic environment. Although a competitive advantage can be achieved through several strategies such as placing emphasis on superior quality products and services (Bitner, 1992), strategy (Miles and Snow, 1978; Venkatraman and Prescott, 1990), economies of scale (Agarwal and Ramaswani, 1992), innovation (Atuahene-Gima, 1996), and market orientation (Kohli and Jaworski, 1990), among others, we propose an alternative to such strategies achieving a competitive advantage through practicing Corporate Ethical Values (CEV). This study is designed to test the proposition in the emerging markets of India. Measuring CEV of Indian firms and testing its impact on profitability is relevant for at least three reasons.

First, the Indian economic reform policies, formulated in 1991, have attracted several foreign firms (Kriplani and Clifford, 2000) that appear to practice higher ethical standards than Indian firms, although a few firms (e.g., Enron, Arther and Anderson, among others) have failed to pass the litmus test of ethics. A loss of foreign managers' confidence in Indian business practices could lead them to seek an alternative country for their investments, which could adversely affect not only the reputation of India but also its economy.

Second, India appears to be perceived as a country of unethical practices (Transparency International, 2004), so it is important that Indian managers correct this image by practicing and promoting ethical values of their firms while marketing their products. Although these values are based on certain moral philosophies, it is expected that Indian managers will learn from the foreign managers about business ethics. Learning from foreign firms is particularly important because access to the Internet has prompted Indian consumers to be more educated, informed, and influenced. Undoubtedly, local firms feel pressured to be ethical in their business practices.

Finally, changes initiated by the government propelled India to an unprecedented level of economic growth and reshaped markets by introducing new opportunities to foreign and local firms alike (Singh, 2003b). Indeed, India has different markets for different products for different firms at different prices. India is home to over one billion people—all potential consumers. Given the size of the market and economy, this study on ethics should be a focal point for scholars as well as managers.

Marketing literature is replete with studies on business ethics in several countries; for example, Australia (Allmon et al., 1997), Australia and South Africa (Abratt et al., 1992), Australia and Taiwan (Fritzsche et al., 1995), Denmark and Sweden (Lysonski and Gaidis, 1991), England (Carrigan and Kirkup, 2001), Germany, England, Austria (Schlegelmilch and Robertson, 1995), Japan (Taka and Foglia, 1994), New Zealand (Alam, 1993), Mexico (Volkema, 1998), Nigeria and USA (Tsalikis and Nwachukwu, 1991), and Russia, (Sommer et al., 2000), among others. One country that is notably missing in this research stream is India, the study by Cyriac and Dharamraj (1994) being an exception. The chapter supports the call by Donaldson (1989) that researchers, practitioners, and policymakers need empirical data on ethical decision making in organizations overseas. This call is particularly relevant for emerging markets such as India.

The purpose of this chapter is to contribute to the literature by investigating the relationship between the theory of moral philosophies and CEV of firms, and by examining the impact of CEV on profitability of firms. An investigation into this relationship is important because, with the establishment of this relation, findings provide another approach to corporate training that encourages its employees to practice corporate ethics more vividly than now.

This chapter first reviews the literature pertaining to business ethics, presents the conceptual framework for the study, and develops hypotheses. The remainder of the chapter reports the findings, highlights the implications of the findings for researchers and managers, and indicates the limitations of the research along with some pointers for future research.

The Conceptual Framework and Hypotheses Development

Scholars have made considerable effort to understand the needs and wants of customers that give motivations to be in business. According to Friedman and Friedman (1981), the primary responsibility of a business is to make profit; whereas others regard it as being able to do community service, which in turn leads to profit. For example, Henry Ford developed the car to serve the community first; that is, he helped people move from point A to point B and then paid attention to profit. This sentiment suggests that firms should offer services to society in addition to serving customers. We advance the notion by suggesting that firms should ethically serve both customers and society. While it is true that firms balance their need to generate revenue with the desire to be ethically responsible, most of the managers would agree that it is the right thing to do, and that in the long term, ethical and social responsibilities should have a positive impact on the success of firms. Consumers over time will normally recognize the organizations that attempt to be responsive to various ethical and social factors in the marketplace (Laczniak and Murphy, 1993).

What is ethical and what is not is a subject of debate. That is why it received considerable attention as an area of research: for example, theory development (Ferrell and Gresham, 1985; Vitell et al., 1993), decision-making process (Mayo and Marks, 1990; Hunt and Vasquez-Parraga, 1993), ageism in advertisements (Carrigan and Szmigin,

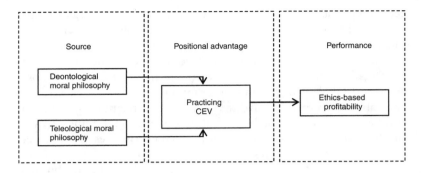

Figure 4.1 The conceptual framework
Source: The author.

2000), retailing (Carrigan and Kirkup, 2001), investments (Baker and Veit, 1996), and auditing (Cohen et al., 1996), among others. Given the importance of the subject, the globalization of businesses, and the proliferation of trade agreements designed to eliminate the trade barriers, researchers, practitioners, and policymakers will need to deal with ethical questions in an international context (Sethi and Steidlmeier, 1993). The central issue in this chapter is the extent to which CEVs are associated with moral philosophies as antecedents and profitability as a consequence. Further, this chapter offers additional insight into the study of corporate ethics by developing the theory and testing its nonlinear impact on profitability. In keeping with the view that managers should not only satisfy short-term needs of their customers but also act in the interest of society on the long-term basis, we define profitability as sustainable profit that is the outcome of firms practicing CEVs.

Drawing on the source-position-performance theory (Day and Wensley, 1988), and the ethics-based literature, a conceptual framework is proposed in figure 4.1 in which *moral philosophies* are the sources, *practicing CEV* an indicator of competitive advantage, and *profitability* the outcome at the corporate level. In the following sections, an overview of the literature relating to the variables included in the proposed framework is presented.

Moral Philosophies:
Deontological versus Teleological

To address the ethical question, several authors have drawn upon moral philosophies (Rest, 1979; Kohlberg, 1981; Reidenbach and

Robin, 1990; Smith, 1995; Dunfee et al., 1999). Given the focus of this book, this chapter limits the discussion of moral philosophies to the deontological and teleological views of philosophies. Deontological philosophy is defined as rule-based philosophy that incorporates the use of logic and code of ethics protocol to identify moral duties, whereas teleological philosophy is defined as consequence-based philosophy that incorporates the use of cost-benefit analysis and the evaluation of costs incurred by society as a whole.

Research indicates that managers who perceive an ethical problem in a given situation are more likely to have an ethical intention (Singhapakdi, 1999). Certainly, the problem of having an ethical intention was exacerbated when managers faced new competition from foreign firms following the liberalization of the economy. Because previously managers did not have to confront with such competitions, as India had a system of state-controlled industries for half a century, they could get by without paying much attention to market or CEVs. However, a recent research indicates that the competition has changed the attitude of managers toward market orientation (Singh, 2003a). Therefore, it is logical to expect that the competition should have an impact also on the attitude of Indian managers toward CEVs, and that firms are deontological while making moral decisions, given their long association with the government or state-controlled firms that are often characterized as formal, rule-based, and hierarchical.

However, Hunt and Vitell (1986) describe a marketer's ethical judgment as teleological, a process by which the marketer evaluates an evoked set of alternative actions by considering their perceived consequences as well as the probability and desirability of the consequences. Consistent with this view and chapter 3, it is expected that, as the social structure of Indian society tends to disintegrate and consumers become more active, Indian managers will be candid about how they conduct their businesses, and about the way they manufacture products. For example, a customer who would like to have an image of being a green-customer (ethically or socially responsible customer) may like to know whether the end product is green (e.g., biodegradable) and whether the product-making process too was green (e.g., whether environments were polluted or rivers contaminated during the manufacturing process) (Singh, 2003b). Indeed, managers go through the teleological evaluation process if they have knowledge of the relative importance of the alternative choices available to customers.

Although there are no known studies that suggest which of the two moral philosophies India should belong to, personal interviews with managers allow for the speculation that Indian managers are more teleological than deontological. For example, using organizational resources other than allocated for a designated purpose may not be morally acceptable to the foreign managers but may be acceptable to Indian managers, as they may see it as an opportunity to expand their business activities, or optimize the use of resources, or exercise entrepreneurial qualities. Similarly, giving a gift to a distributor as a token of building a long-term relationship may be acceptable in India but may be viewed as bribery by some foreign managers.

Given that different individuals seem to adopt different moral philosophies, perfect consensus regarding any given business practice can never be expected (Forsyth, 1992); however, based on the above anecdotal evidence that tend to be consequence-based, we test the following hypothesis:

H1: Teleological philosophy contributes more to CEV than deontological philosophy.

Link between CEV and Profitability

Generally, foreign firms possess a competitive advantage over local firms in skills (Bartlett and Ghoshal, 1995) and size (Kraft and Hage, 1989). Size is related to profitability (Kraft and Hage, 1989). We argue that local firms may compensate for the lack of these advantages by positioning their firms as ethical firms. However, such ethical positioning should be based on the issues that engage the target audience and encourage positive consumer behaviors (Carrigan and Attalla, 2001). Changing behavior of customers in favor of ethical firms requires managers to be ethically sensitive to customers' needs in order to earn their trust. We expect Indian managers to express their moral commitments as well as their conviction that ethical conduct is mandatory to establish trust. Consistent with the theory, trust is of paramount importance if exchanges have to take place (Kotler, 2003). In addition, trust is an important antecedent to relationship commitment (Morgan and Hunt, 1994) and satisfaction that results in customer loyalty (Hallowell, 1996). Loyalty leads to profitability (Reichheld and Sasser, 1990) because of reduced costs of customer acquisition, serving repeat orders, and improved mutual trust between buyers and sellers (Singh, 2004). Further, information about a firm's ethical behavior influences sales and consumers' image of the company (Mascarenhas, 1995).

Contrarily, research also indicates that consumers appear to care more about price, quality, and value than corporate ethics (Ulrich and

Sarasin, 1995; Boulstridge and Carrigan, 2000), and that consumers do not have the time to take into account the ethical aspects of their purchases while shopping (Titus and Bradford, 1996). Although Indian consumers have relatively more purchasing power and less time to spend on shopping than before economic reform, it may be conceived that some consumers may either ignore CEVs or simply will not care. If so, managers are less likely to achieve an ethical image of their firms, as there is no incentive to be ethical; the consumers still prefer inexpensive mass-produced goods to the ethically made quality premium products. Thus, profit can still be realized without being ethical.

Certainly, for firms, being perceived as ethical is costly. If managers believe that there is a significant trade-off between CEVs and profitability, successful managers are less likely to be ethically responsible. By contrast, if being ethical is identical to sustaining a competitive advantage to pursue a firm's long-term goal, managers of the firm could behave in an ethical manner. Studies also show that there is neither incentive nor sanction for being ethically responsible (Wood et al., 1986; Hunt et al., 1990).

Given the costs of orientation such as giving training to employees on the importance of practicing CEV, and possible initial diminishing returns, it is likely that practicing CEV may be detrimental to profitability in the short term but profitable in the long term when the training has generated a high level of interest in CEV among employees. This suggests that a certain level of perceived corporate ethics is consistent with organizational resources that determine its success. Based on this contingency argument, we examine the nonlinear relationship between practicing CEV and profitability by advancing the following hypothesis:

H2: There is a U-shaped relationship between practicing CEV and profitability.

Methodology

Measurements of Variables

Deontological and Teleological Variables
We measured the variables using a constant sum scale. Respondents were asked to distribute 100 points between the two scenarios that they practiced most while making moral decisions: (1) we are mostly deontological (rule-based) and incorporate the use of logic and the code of ethics protocol to identify moral duties; and (2) we are mostly teleological (consequence-based) and incorporate the use of cost-benefit

analysis, and the evaluation of costs incurred by society as a whole. The average scores for deontological and teleological philosophies are 47 (standard deviation (s.d.) = 5.6) and 53 (s.d. = 5.1), respectively.

CEV Scale

We measured the variable by using the CEV scale (Hunt et al., 1989), which reflects a composite of the individual ethical values of managers and the firm's formal and informal policies on ethics. In addition, the measure attempts to capture the broader principles of the degree to which organizations take an interest in ethical issues (and act in an ethical manner) rather than product, service, or industry-specific issues (Hunt et al., 1989). The scale has five items (table 4.1) and is measured on a seven-point Likert-type scale (α = .76). In the scale, 1 and 7 correspond to strongly disagree and strongly agree, respectively. A high score on the scale corresponds to a high presence on CEV. The factor analysis confirmed the unidimensionality of the scale (variance explained = 38 percent and Eigenvalue = 1.98); therefore, the CEV is a composite index of the sum of the items. To establish construct equivalence, we followed Berry's (1969) advice and ensured, through face-to-face interviews with the Indian managers, that the concept served the same function in India (functional equivalence), that the concept was expressed properly, and that the same classification scheme was used in India (calibration equivalence). India being a commonwealth country, businesses are conducted in English; therefore, there was no need for us to translate (Brislin, 1979) the questionnaire in Hindi. Further, the scale is well tested, so validity of the scale should not be in question.

Ethics-Based Profitability

Consistent with the approach by Singhapakdi et al. (1995), we adapted items from the organizational effectiveness menu (Kraft and Jauch, 1992) for the measurement of the ethics-based profitability. It is reasonable to expect that an ethically effective firm will have some factors contributing to profitability. Keeping this in mind, and to isolate items relating to profitability, we conducted an exploratory factor analysis. It resulted in five distinct factors. We labeled one of the factors as *ethics-based profitability* because the five items relating to profits loaded on this factor. This factor accounted for 27.3 percent variance (Eigenvalue = 1.43), out of 62 percent of the total variance. Items having a coefficient score less than .4 or that cross-loaded on factors were suppressed (Churchill, 1979). The scale finally has five items (table 4.2) and was measured on a seven-point Likert-type scale

Table 4.1 Corporate ethical value (Hunt et al., 1989)

Items	Factor loading	Mean	S.D.
1. Managers in my company often engage in behaviors that I consider to be unethical (R).	.59	2.3	.07
2. In order to succeed in my company, it is often necessary to compromise one's ethics (R).	.47	2.1	.09
3. Top management in my company has made it absolutely clear that unethical behavior will not be tolerated.	.61	5.4	.08
4. If a manager in my company is discovered to have engaged in unethical behavior that results primarily in personal gain (rather than corporate gain), he or she will be promptly reprimanded.	.54	5.8	.11
5. If a manager in my company is discovered to have engaged in unethical behavior that results primarily in corporate gain (rather than personal gain), he or she will be promptly reprimanded.	.57	5.7	.12

Notes: Variance explained = 38%, Eigenvalue = 1.98, α = .76; R = reverse−scored item. Items measured by a seven-point Likert-type scale (1 = strongly disagree, 7 = strongly agree).

Table 4.2 Ethics-based profitability (Kraft and Jauch, 1992)

Items	Factor loading	Mean	S.D.
1. The ethics and social responsibility of a firm is essential to its long-term profitability.	.63	6.2	.08
2. The overall effectiveness of a business can be determined to a great extent by the degree to which it is ethical and socially responsible.	.61	6.1	.09
3. Business ethics and social responsibility are critical to the survival of a business enterprise.	.57	6.3	.11
4. Social responsibility and profitability can be compatible.	.52	5.3	.13
5. Good ethics is often good business.	.47	5.9	.12

Notes: Variance explained = 27.3%, Eigenvalue = 1.43, α = .79. Items measured by a seven-point Likert-type scale (1 = strongly disagree, 7 = strongly agree).

(α = .79). Coefficient scores for α greater than 0.7 suggest that this scale is reliable (Nunnally, 1978). Subjective measures of performance are frequently used in business research and have been found to be reliable and valid (Dess and Robinson, 1984; Pearce et al., 1987).

Data Collection and Sample Characteristics

Data Collection

To increase response rate, we collected data by administering the questionnaires in person, following a pretest with a group of Indian managers in New Delhi and Bombay. Only indigenous, medium- to large-sized firms (i.e., with employees over 100) with a formal marketing or sales department qualified for the survey. We selected these firms because they were more susceptible than small firms to scrutiny by public and media and, therefore, expected to act relatively more in an ethically responsible manner. A convenience sample size of 200 in each city was randomly selected from the Kompass Indian Business Directory. The sample size was determined based on considerations of cost, time, and the objectives of this study. We followed the list of companies that included names of the CEOs and senior executives, we contacted them by phone to solicit their participation in the survey, informed them about the purpose of this study, and explained definitions of the variables. We obtained 248 useable responses. Although survey research often suffers from nonresponse bias, the high response rate (62 percent) and the assurance of anonymity for respondents should reduce this potential bias. Nonetheless, interpretation of the results requires some caution. One hundred and fifty-three managers requested a copy of the summary of the results, an indication that the topic was timely and interesting.

Characteristics of the Sample

The sample consisted of 61 percent manufacturing and 39 percent service firms. Firms with a turnover under Rs. 50m, between Rs. 50m and Rs. 100m, and over Rs.100m provided 47 percent, 35 percent, and 18 percent of the sample, respectively. Similarly, firms with employees between 100 and 500, and between 501 and 1000, and over 1000 represented 57 percent, 25 percent, and 18 percent of the sample, respectively. The questionnaires completed by CEOs, board directors, and senior executives were 63 percent, 24 percent, and 13 percent of the sample, respectively.

Analysis and Results

To test the hypothesis *H1* that *teleological philosophy contributes more to CEV than deontological philosophy*, we used a paired t-test. No significant differences (t-value = 2.1) between the two modes of philosophies (deontological ones coded as 1, and teleological as 0) were found on CEV of firms, suggesting that both philosophies contributed almost equally to the CEV. Therefore, in the subsequent analysis, no distinctions were made between the two philosophies. Hence, we reject the hypothesis *H1*.

To test hypothesis *H2* that there is a U-shaped relationship between practicing CEV and profitability, we employed different models of stepwise multiple regression using the CEV as an independent variable and profitability as a dependent variable. Because we have a relatively small sample size and because the power of a statistical test to reject a null hypothesis depends upon sample size, we used stepwise regression, as it searches for the set of variables that best explains variation in data (Neter et al., 1983). We controlled for a couple of variables, as previous studies suggest that they can influence profitability. To control for economies of scale, we used firm size (measured by turnover of firms). We coded industry type as manufacturing (1) and service (0). Multicollinearity was not found to influence the results of these analyses, as the Variance Inflation Factor (VIF) associated with each model was below 2, lower than the suggested cutoff (Neter et al., 1985).

Table 4.3 presents the results of the regression analyses in a hierarchical fashion to better depict the variance explained by the different sets of predictor variables. In Model 1, which contains only the control variables, the coefficient for firm size (turnover) is statistically significant and positive. Model 2 adds the main effect of the CEV, which contributes 4 percent (F = 2.97, p < .01) more than the variance explained by the control variables. As shown in the table, the coefficient for the CEV is statistically significant ($\beta = -.23$, p < .01) and negative. Model 3 adds the squared term for the CEV, which increased explained variance further by 7 percent (F = 3.15, p < .01), more than the explained variance we obtained in Model 2. As is evident, the coefficient for the CEV is still statistically significant ($\beta = -.20$, p < .05) and negative; however, the squared term for the CEV is statistically significant ($\beta = .26$, p < .01) and positive. The results suggest that the effect of CEV on profitability is initially negative but turns positive with higher levels of CEV. We accept the hypothesis *H2*.

Discussion

The purpose of the study was to examine the antecedents and conditions under which practicing CEV influences profitability. After controlling for firm size and industry type, our findings indicate that

Table 4.3　Regression analysis: Effects of CEV on profitability

Controls and direct effects Variables	Model 1		Model 2		Model 3	
Firm size (turnover)	.21*	(.07)	.20*	(.09)	.19*	(.11)
Industry dummy	.09	(.11)	.09	(.10)	.09	(.07)
CEV			−.23**	(.09)	−.20*	(.10)
CEV^2					.26**	(.08)
F	7.21		7.63		7.91	
R^2	.37		.41		.48	
$_{Adj.}$R^2	.34		.39		.46	
ΔR^2			.04		.07	
Partial F value			2.97**		3.15**	
VIF$_{max}$	1.72		1.85		1.76	
N	248		245		248	

Notes: *p <.05, **p <.01; Removal of outliers in the model 2 resulted in a smaller sample size. We report standardized regression coefficients (standard errors are in parentheses).

there are no significant differences between deontological and teleological philosophies on CEV, and that CEV is nonlinearly (U-shaped) related to profitability. Results of this chapter are relevant to business managers for several reasons. They are explained in the following sections.

Although the data did not allow for a direct comparison in India, we could draw inferences based on general responses reflected in the literature. Our finding that there is no dominant moral philosophy that contributes to CEV suggests that managers appear to adopt a combination of moral philosophies that negate the effects from each other, and that perfect consensus regarding any dominant moral philosophy has not yet crystallized in Indian corporate culture. Managers appear to take advantage of the situation before they base their decisions either on deontological or teleological philosophies; that is, in certain situations they seem to refer to rules and protocols and in others they tend to optimize outcome with available resources. Indeed, most individuals strive to be ethical in their own decision rules.

Another important finding of this chapter is the U-shaped relationship between practicing CEV and profitability. It appears that practicing CEV such as increasing awareness about ethical protocol among employees is costly. Thus, early investments in employee training may not produce substantial benefits to offset the costs. Time is required for the employees to develop ethical skills, to communicate corporate ethics to customers, and to manage the firm's other businesses. Continuing investments in the form of employees training, however, begin to reap greater benefits. These investments become less costly on average and, at the same time, produce economies and synergies such as product knowledge and ethical awareness. This valuable tactic knowledge, in turn, helps the firm provide valuable services to its client that can attract premium prices as well as more clients. Indeed, Body Shop considers cause-related marketing as a major determinant of success.

The implication for the managers is that a balanced ethical practice—a tradeoff between the two philosophies—should be a part of corporate culture and a factor in moral development of employees (Trevino, 1986). It is possible that the use of these two philosophies simultaneously could allow firms to serve their customers in valuable and unique ways that are difficult to imitate, thereby developing and sustaining a competitive advantage. There are several states in India (e.g., the South Indian states) where firms may be able to position themselves solely on moral issues and be profitable. But having an ethical platform in poor states such as Bihar, Orissa, or Uttar Pradesh may be less effective than in the rest of India. Therefore, managers in these states need to understand the appropriateness of stressing ethics to their customers because their region suffer from resource shortages, population growth, and poverty problems.

For moral development within firms, managers can make use of the differential association theory (Sutherland and Cressey, 1970), which assumes that (un)ethical behavior is learned in the process of interacting with intimate personal groups or role sets (Ferrel and Gresham, 1985). Therefore, the onus is on the managers to create an environment conducive to forming groups of employees who believe in moral philosophies. Further, employees who perceive that corporate management in their organizations support ethical behavior may also perceive their organization as being just and ethical to its employees. Regardless of moral philosophies used to practice CEV, it is important that employees have high ethical standards.

Another implication for the managers, given our finding that practicing CEV leads to high profitability, is that managers should resist their initial temptations to make short-term profit at the expense of CEV. While it is true that the long-term benefit of leveraging ethical orientation creates efficiencies and helps build tacit knowledge in a firm, it also imposes a cost. Therefore, managers must either reduce those costs or ensure that the benefit gained from practicing CEV more than offsets the costs. This can be worked out by devising richer training materials in various settings (manufacturing vs. services) and formats (printed vs. visual) so that the usefulness of the empirical reality can be translated into training the future managers. Indeed, social responsibility and profitability can be compatible (Tuleja, 1985).

Directions for Future Study

Like any other research, this study also suffers from limitations. First, generalizability of the findings is limited, as our sample may not be representative of India. It is almost impossible to collect a sample from each state of India without having substantial resources; nonetheless, having data at least from these two cities should provide a ground for comparison for further studies. To control for common method bias, we recommend that future studies should encourage respondents to seek multiple responses to the questionnaire (Podsakoff and Organ, 1986).

In addition to alleviating the limitations of this study, the research can be deepened through other related fertile avenues for future research. First, we conducted this study in the spirit of the growing interest in cross-cultural testing and in truly international generalizations of hypotheses about management in general, and marketing in particular (Aharoni and Burton, 1994; see also the special issues of *Management Science* 1994 and *Marketing Science* 1995). The replication of this study in other emerging markets would help generalize the findings. This is particularly important because our study is framed in the competing moral philosophies that are based on theoretical work from the West but the developmental work for empirical application was carried out in the emerging markets of India.

Second, it would be interesting to include the fairness heuristic of managers in the framework to determine perceptions of fairness when faced with ambiguous stimuli. The fairness heuristic postulates that perceptions of fairness in one area will influence perceptions of fairness in another area (Lind, 1992). Hence, further research should examine the determinants and outcomes of such fairness heuristic processes in practicing CEV.

Conclusion

The purpose of this study is to sensitize the managers to the moral philosophies that are crucial to practicing CEV and thereby to achieving profitability. By being perceived as ethically responsible toward customers, the managers not only earn the trust of their patrons but also generate sales. In general, society needs to build business communities of values that encourage customers to be comfortable while shopping.

References

Abratt, R., Nel, D., and Higgs, N.S. "An Examination of the Ethical Beliefs of Managers Using Selected Scenarios in a Cross-cultural Setting." *Journal of Business Ethics* 11, no. 1 (1992): 29–35.

Agarwal, S., and Ramaswani, S. "Choice of Foreign Entry Mode: Impact of Ownership, Location and Internationalization Factors." *Journal of International Business Studies* 23, no. 1 (1992): 1–27.

Aharoni, Y., and Burton, R.M. "Is Management Science International? In Search of Universal Rules." *Management Science* 40, no. 1 (1994): 1–3.

Alam, K.F. *Understanding Attitudes of Predicting Social Behavior.* Englewood Cliffs, NJ: Prentice-Hall, 1993.

Allmon, D.E., Chen, H.C.K., Pritchett, T.K., and Forrest, P. "A Multicultural Examination of Business Ethics Perceptions." *Journal of Business Ethics* 16, no. 2 (1997): 183–88.

Atuahene-Gima, K. "Market Orientation and Innovation." *Journal of Business Research* 35, no. 2 (1996): 93–103.

Baker, H.K., and Veit, T. "Ethical Attitudes and Behavior of Investment Professionals in Hong Kong and North America." *Financial Practice and Education* (Fall 1996): 21–28.

Bartlett, C., and Ghosal, S. *Transnational Management: Text, Cases and Readings in Cross-border Management.* New York: Erwin, 1995.

Berry, J.W. "On Cross-cultural Comparability." *International Journal of Psychology* 4, no. 2 (1969): 119–38.

Bitner, M.J. "Servicescapes: The Impact of Physical Surrounding on Customers and Employees." *Journal of Marketing* 56 (April 1992): 57–71.

Boulstridge, E., and Carrigan, M. "Do Consumers Really Care about Corporate Responsibility? Highlighting the Attitude-Behavior Gap." *Journal of Communication Management* 4, no. 4 (2000): 355–68.

Brislin, R.W. "Translation and Content Analysis of Oral and Written Materials." In *Handbook of Cross-cultural Psychology*, ed. Harry, T., and Berry, J.W., 389–44. Boston: Allyn and Bacon, 1979.

Carrigan, M., and Attalla, A. "The Myth of the Ethical Consumer—Do Ethics Matter in Purchase Behavior?" *Journal of Consumer Marketing* 18, no. 7 (2001): 560–77.

Carrigan, M., and Kirkup, M. "The Ethical Responsibilities of Marketers in Retail Observational Research: Protecting Stakeholders through the Ethical Research Covenant." *International Review of Retail, Distribution and Consumer Research* 11, no. 4 (2001): 415–35.

Carrigan, M., and Szmigin, I. "The Ethical Advertising Covenant: Regulating Ageism in UK Advertising." *International Journal of Advertising* 19, no. 4 (2000): 509–28.

Churchill, G.A., Jr. "A Paradigm for Developing Better Measures of Marketing Constructs." *Journal of Marketing Research* 16, no. 1 (1979): 64–73.

Cohen, J., Pant, L., and Sharp, D. "Measuring Ethical Awareness and Ethical Orientation of Canadian Auditors." *Behavioral Research in Accounting*, no. 8 (1996): 99–119.

Cyriac, K., and Dharamraj, R. "Machiavellianism in Indian Management." *Journal of Business Ethics* 13, no. 4 (1994): 281–86.

Day, G.S., and Wensley, R. "Assessing Advantage: A Framework for Diagnosing Competitive Superiority." *Journal of Marketing* 52 (April 1988): 1–20.

Dess, G.G., and Robinson, R.B., Jr. "Measuring Organizational Performance in the Absence of Objective Measures: The Case of a Privately-Held Firm and Conglomerate Business Unit." *Strategic Management Journal* 5, no. 3 (1984): 265–73.

Donaldson, T. *The Ethics of International Business*. New York: Oxford University Press, 1989.

Dunfee, T.W., Smith, N.C., and Ross, W.T., Jr. "Social Contracts and Marketing Ethics." *Journal of Marketing* 63, no. 3 (1999): 14–35.

Ferrell, O.C., and Gresham, L. "A Contingency Framework for Understanding Ethical Decision Making in Marketing." *Journal of Marketing* 49 (Summer 1985): 87–96.

Forsyth, D.R. "Judging the Morality of Business Ethics: The Influence of Personal Moral Philosophies." *Journal of Business Ethics* 11, no. 5/6 (1992): 461–70.

Friedman, M., and Friedman, R. *Free to Choose*. New York: Avon Press, 1981.

Fritzsche, D.J., Huo, Y.P., Sugai, S., Tsai, S.D.H., Kim, C.S., and Becker, H. "Exploring the Ethical Behavior of Managers: A Comparative Study of Four Countries." *Asia-Pacific Journal of Management* 12, no. 2 (1995): 37–61.

Hallowell, R. "The Relationship of Customer Satisfaction, Customer Loyalty and Profitability: An Empirical Study." *International Journal of Service Industry Management* 7, no. 4 (1996): 27–42.

Hunt, S.D., Kiecker, P.L., and Chonko, L.B. "Social Responsibility and Personal Success: A Research Note." *Journal of the Academic of Marketing Science* 18 (Summer 1990): 239–44.

Hunt, S.D., and Vasquez-Parraga, A. "Organizational Consequences, Marketing Ethics, and Sales Force Supervision." *Journal of Marketing Research* 30 (February 1993): 78–90.

Hunt, S.D., and Vitell, S. "A General Theory of Marketing Ethics." *Journal of Macromarketing* 8 (Spring 1986): 5–16.

Hunt, S.D., Wood, V.R., and Chonko, L.B. "Corporate Ethical Values and Organizational Commitment in Marketing." *Journal of Marketing* 53 (July 1989): 79–90.

Kohlberg, L. *The Meaning and Measurement of Moral Development*. Worcester: Clark University Press, 1981.

Kohli, A.K., and Jaworski, B.J. "Market Orientation: The Construct, Research Propositions, and Managerial Implications." *Journal of Marketing* 54 (April 1990): 1–8.

Kompass. *Indian Business Directory.* New Delhi, 2000. http://directory. kompass.com

Kotler, P. *Marketing Management.* Upper Saddle River: Prentice-Hall, 2003.

Kraft, K.L., and Hage, J. "Strategy, Social Responsibility and Implementation." *Journal of Business Ethics* 9, no. 1 (1989): 11–19.

Kraft, K.L., and Jauch, L.R. "The Organizational Effectiveness Menu: A Device for Stakeholder Assessment." *Mid-American Journal of Business* 7, no. 1 (1992): 18–23.

Kriplani, M., and Clifford, M.L. "India Wired." *Hyderabad Business Week*, 21 (February 2000), 82–88.

Laczniak, G.R., and Murphy, P.E. *Ethical Marketing Decisions: The High Road.* Boston: Allyn & Bacon, 1993.

Lind, E.A. "The Fairness Heuristic: Rationality and Relationally in Procedural Evaluation." *International Conference of the Society for the Advancement of Socio-Economic.* California: Irvine, 1992.

Lysonski, S., and Gaidis, W. "A Cross-cultural Comparison of Ethics of Business Students." *Journal of Business Ethics* 10, no. 2 (1991): 141–50.

Mascarenhas, O.A.J. "Exonerating Unethical Marketing Behavior: A Diagnostic Framework." *Journal of Marketing* 59, no. 2 (1995): 43–57.

Mayo, M., and Marks, L. "An Empirical Investigation of a General Theory of Marketing Ethics." *Journal of the Academy of Marketing Science* 18 (Spring 1990): 163–71.

Miles, R.E., and Snow, C.C. *Organizational Strategy, Structure and Processes.* New York: McGraw-Hill, 1978.

Morgan, R.M., and Hunt, S.D. "The Commitment-Trust Theory Relationship Marketing." *Journal of Marketing* 58 (July 1994): 20–38.

Neter, J., Wasserman, W., and Kutner, M. *Applied Linear Regression Models.* Homewood: Irwin, 1983.

———. *Applied Statistical Models.* Homewood: Irwin, 1985.

Nunnally, J.C. *Psychometric Testing.* New York: McGraw-Hill, 1978.

Pearce, J., Robinson, D., and Robinson, R. "The Impact of Grand Strategy and Planning on Financial Performance." *Strategic Management Journal* 8, no. 2 (1987): 125–34.

Podsakoff, P.M., and Organ, D.W. "Self-reports in Organizational Research: Problems and Prospectus." *Journal of Management* 12, no. 4 (1986): 531–44.

Reichheld, F., and Sasser, W. "Zero Defections Comes to Services." *Harvard Business Review* 68, no. 5 (1990): 105–11.

Reidenbach, R.E., and Robin, D.P. "Toward the Development of a Multidimensional Scale for Improving Evaluations of Business Ethics." *Journal of Business Ethics* 9, no. 8 (1990): 639–53.

Rest, J.R. *Development in Judging Moral Issues.* Minneapolis: University of Minnesota Press, 1979.

Schlegelmilch, B.B., and Robertson, D.C. "The Influence of Country and Industry on Ethical Perceptions of Senior Executives in the US and Europe." *Journal of International Business Studies* 26, no. 4 (1995): 859–81.

Sethi, S.P., and Steidlmeier, P. "Religion's Moral Compass and a Just Economic Order: Reflections on Pope John Paul II's Encyclical Centesimus Annus." *Journal of Business Ethics* 12, no. 12 (1993): 901–17.

Singh, S. *Market Orientation, Corporate Culture, and Business Performance.* Aldershot: Ashgate Publishing, 2004.

———. "Effects of Transition Economy on the Market Orientation Business Performance Link: The Empirical Evidence from Indian Industrial Firms." *Journal of Global Marketing* 6, no. 4 (2003a): 73–96.

———. "Perceptions of Post-modern Marketing Practices: The Case of Foreign and Domestic Firms," paper presented at the Academy of Marketing Science Conference at Perth, 2003b, 69.

Singhapakdi, A. "Perceived Importance of Ethics and Ethical Decisions in Marketing—A Comparison of Marketing Practitioners." *Journal of Business Research* 45, no. 1 (1999): 89–99.

Singhapakdi, A., Kraft, K.L., Vitell, S., and Rallapalli, K.C. "The Perceived Importance of Ethics and Social Responsibility on Organizational Effectiveness: A Survey of Marketers." *Journal of the Academy of Marketing Science* 23, no. 1 (1995): 49–56.

Smith, N.C. "Marketing Strategies for the Ethics Era." *Sloan Management Review* 36, no. 4 (1995): 85–98.

Sommer, S.M., Welsh, D.H.B., and Gubman, B.L. "The Ethical Orientation of Russian Entrepreneurs." *An International Review of Applied Psychology* 49, no. 4 (2000): 688–708.

Sutherland, E., and Cressey, D.R. *Principles of Criminology.* Chicago: Lippincott, 1970.

Taka, I., and Foglia, W.D. "Ethical Aspects of Japanese Leadership Style." *Journal of Business Ethics* 13, no. 2 (1994): 135–48.

Titus, P.A., and Bradford, J.L. "Reflections on Consumer Sophistication and Its Impact on Ethical Business Practice." *Journal of Consumer Affairs* 30, no. 1 (1996): 170–95.

Transparency International. *www.transparency.org* 2004.

Trevino, L.K. "Ethical Decision Making in Organizations: A Person-Situation Interactionist Model." *Academy of Management Review* 11, no. 3 (1986): 601–17.

Tsalikis, J., and Nwachukwu, O. "A Comparison of Nigerian to American Views of Bribery and Extortion in International Commerce." *Journal of Business Ethics* 10, no. 2 (1991): 85–98.

Tuleja, T. *Beyond the Bottom Line: How Business Leaders Are Managing Principles into Profits.* New York: Facts on File, 1985.

Ulrich, P., and Sarasin, C. *Facing Public Interest: The Ethical Challenge to Business Policy and Corporate Communications.* London: Kluwer, 1995.

Venkatraman, N., and Prescott, J.E. "Environment-Strategy Coalignment: An Empirical Test of Its Performance Implications." *Strategic Management Journal* 11, no. 1 (1990): 1–23.

Vitell, S., Kumar, R., and Singhapakdi, A. "Marketing Norms: The Influence of Personal Moral Philosophies and Organizational Ethical Culture." *Journal of the Academy of Marketing Science* 21 (Fall 1993): 331–37.

Volkema, R.J.A. "Comparison of Perceptions of Ethical Negotiation Behavior in Mexico and the United States." *International Journal of Conflict Management* 9, no. 3 (1998): 218–33.

Wood, V.R., Lawrence, B.C., and Hunt, S.D. "Social Responsibility and Personal Success: Are They Incompatible?" *Journal of Business Research* 14, no. 3 (1986): 193–212.

Chapter 5

Business Ethics and Marketing Practices in Nigeria

J.T. Akinmayowa

This chapter on business ethics and marketing practices in Nigeria examines some ethical issues in marketing practices. The discussion on business ethics in Nigeria, like in other countries, is crucial to development and its ramifications given the fact that businesses that are conducted ethically are more likely to create value in the society than businesses that are conducted without moral values. Therefore, in societies where business ethics do not flourish, there are bound to be problems that consumers and many organizations would have to contend with. Also, there are bound to be some problems that the nation at large and as a member of an international community would have to deal with and invest a significant amount of time, money, and energy to establish watchdog agencies. This chapter, based on events within the Nigerian context, addresses these issues.

Introduction

The motivation for this chapter is multidimensional. Nigeria as an emergent economy, like many other economies in Africa, has its problems and prospects. The nation is fast moving away from the league of dependent economies. This type of economy is noted for producing raw material often exported to the developed economies where they are processed and exported (as finished goods) back to where the raw material came from. The finished goods are often very expensive compared to the value of the raw material from which the finished goods are made. Now, Nigeria is keen to become a force in exporting finished goods, but the prospect is hampered by some business practices in the domestic market, which should be identified and discussed. There are some difficulties in exporting finished goods produced with unethical practices in Nigeria. Therefore, the need for investors to conduct their businesses ethically cannot be ignored. Also, the country has opened its door wider than ever for foreign investors. Despite the establishment of investment parameters, which the Federal Government of Nigeria often considers to be liberal to investors, foreign investors in Nigeria still face problems. Factors militating against foreign investment in Nigeria over the past twenty years include but are not necessarily limited to political instability, safety and security, infrastructural and manpower problems. Others include, advance fee fraud, nondemocratic government (or culture), international sanctions, and corruption (Yesufu, 2001).

Local and foreign investors in Nigeria ought to be reasonably sure that their investments would be safe and that businesses would be conducted ethically. They should have some idea about the potential problems that their investments are likely to face, and how to plan to deal with the constraints. Indeed, Nigeria is a benchmark for other African countries. The country has the largest population in Africa—an estimated 120 million people. Across the African continent, it is often stated that where you find ten Africans together, four are likely to be Nigerians. It is not a dispute that Nigerians are found in several African countries as well as in many other countries. Their influence cannot be ignored. For example, if one knows the problems confronting the marketing of a given commodity in Nigeria, the knowledge could be useful in dealing with the problems facing the marketing of the same commodity in several other African countries. In fact, certain business practices, ethical or unethical, found in Nigeria could be exported to other neighboring African countries, especially within the Economic Community of West African States (ECOWAS). Solving one marketing problem in Nigeria could serve as a useful guide in solving the same problem in some other African countries. This is without prejudice to the attempts made by several African countries to address peculiar problems that are sociocultural, political, economic, and technological in nature. The discussion so far points to the wide range of issues relating to business ethics that this chapter aims to deal with.

The chapter adopts an eclectic approach—integration of ideas from different perspectives. The ideas were organized systematically to achieve the objectives of this chapter. First, it is useful to define and explain the importance of business ethics because it is the cornerstone of this chapter. Second, Nigeria being the context of this chapter needs to be introduced. In particular, we need to give a clear picture of the business environment in Nigeria. Doing so is crucial. Although the business environment in Nigeria is unique, part of it is similar to some countries in Africa. Also, a small part of the Nigerian economy could also be described as developed: for example, the oil and gas and banking sectors operate using the technology and methods compara- ble to that of some developed economies. Reforms in these sectors are dynamic and are geared toward a radical change so that Nigeria would not be left behind in global competition. Nevertheless, the country still faces economic difficulties as a result of the human and environ- mental factors. Indeed, some banks collapsed. In the oil sector, the country had difficulties processing its crude oil into refined products. Sadly, it has to export the crude oil to Europe for processing and later import the refined product for domestic use. Third, some unethical business practices are identified and discussed. Fourth, the results of *The Ethics Project 2006* relevant to this chapter are presented. Fifth, government policies in mitigating the unethical practices in Nigeria and the roles of watchdog agencies are discussed. Finally, the chapter concludes with some ideas that could be useful to promote ethical business practices in Nigeria.

In sum, this chapter is divided into six sections. Section one is on business ethics. Section two is on Nigeria and its business environ- ment as an emerging market. Section three is on unethical business practices. Section four is based on the results of the *Ethics Project 2006*. Section five is on government policies and watchdog agencies. Finally, section six concludes the chapter.

Business Ethics

The term *ethics* is open to different definitions. According to Chandan (2001), ethics is probably the most difficult concept to define. It is as intangible to assess as an idea of morality or of right and wrong. It may have some facets that are universal in nature, but much of it may be defined with reference to the values established by a particular society. At least, seven broad sets of factors or forces play a role in the formation of our ethics; these are family influences, peer influences, personal experiences, values, institutional or organizational affilia- tions, law, and situational factors (Agbonifoh, 1999). Another con- tributor noted that in a general sense, ethics is the code of moral principles and values that govern the behavior of a person or group with respect to what is right or wrong. Ethics sets standards as to what is good or bad in conduct and decision-making (Shea, 1988). In *Chamber's Twentieth Century Dictionary*, the word "ethics" refers to the science of morals, a branch of philosophy that is concerned with human character and conduct: a system of morals, rules of behavior, a treatise on morals. In *Compton's Interactive Encyclopedia* (Softkey, 1997), ethics is primarily concerned with attempting to define what is good for the individual and for society. It also tries to establish the nature of obligations or duties that people owe to themselves and to each other. Also, Fry et al. (2000) observed that ethics involves a search for standards of moral conduct. Therefore, they propose that business ethics involves the search for and commitment to meet appropriate standards of moral conduct in business situations. In simplest terms, business ethics means figuring out the appropriate way to act in different business settings. In practice, business ethics is concerned with two issues. First is the difficulty of determining what actions are appropriate from situation to situation. Second is having the fortitude to carry out these ethical actions. Put together, business ethics deals with the internal values that should be at the heart of a corporate culture and should pilot business decisions and social responsibility of the organization in its immediate environment, in the larger society, and in the international community.

Therefore, it could be proposed that the practical aspect of business ethics is one of the major challenges faced by businesses in the world today. Indeed, if corporate leaders do not have difficulty in determining corporate actions that are appropriate from situation to situation and have the fortitude to apply the actions for business transactions, the world economy could have provided more value to mankind. Certainly, unethical business practices do not have political, sociocultural, technological, or economic boundaries. Unethical business practices exist worldwide in different forms (Murphy et al., 1992; Adams and Tashchian 1995; Clark and Leonard, 1998; Wulfson 1998; Wotruba et al., 2001; Somers 2001; Nikels et al., 2002). These studies suggest that the ethical behavior of business leaders is questionable. Even the Western organization leaders who were once perceived to be more ethical than the rest of the world could no longer depend on their clean corporate image, particularly given the scandal created by world giants such as Worldcom, Xerox, Qwest Communication International, ENRON, Arthur Anderson and Halliburton that collapsed under questionable circumstances. In Nigeria, Unilever allegedly hedged up its profits by ₦1.2 billion. Also, African Petroleum (AP) concealed ₦26 billion in debt during the privatization of Federal Government shares in the oil company amounting to about ₦2.1 billion (Onyenankeya, 2003). These cases demonstrate how organizations could move from grace to grass, as a result of unethical practices, especially in financial dealings.

In Nigeria, ethical behavior of human resources and its impact on development deserves empirical investigation nationwide; otherwise the nation may continue to suffer economically. Ethical behavior, which is human behavior and which we preach and/or practice to create value in a given society, is fundamental to corporate performance and economic development. Significantly, within the Nigerian context, this is more pressing given the failure of many organizations, especially financial institutions that crashed some years ago, leaving their customers in the cold. In 2006, some banks in Nigeria failed to meet the recapitalization proposed by the Central Bank of Nigeria (CBN). This reflects that part of the financial economy of Nigeria failed under the leadership of some corporate executives who were parading themselves as financial experts. Looking at the trend—from the collapse of some banks to the failure of other banks to meet recapitalization—none may be able to guarantee against the collapse of banks in Nigeria. It is as if some corporate executives are always looking for loopholes in business laws to exploit their customers. Unfortunately, they could get away with it, especially in a dull and corrupt judicial system. These may be some of the reasons why corporate executives in some countries, especially in Africa, mismanage the economy. They pursue their own hidden agenda at the expense of their organizations and the society to which they belong. Rather than creating wealth and sharing prosperity, they create business turmoil, unemployment, underemployment, high prices, poverty, and alienation. Therefore, this chapter explores practices that are not consumer friendly in Nigeria.

Nigerian Business Environment as an Emerging Market

Nigeria with a population of about 120 million people is the most populated country in Africa and consequently the largest market. The country is often regarded as the benchmark for the African continent because of its vast resources and its diverse ethnic and cultural traditions. It may even be described as the melting pot of Africa. Indeed, the nationals of virtually all the countries in the world live in Nigeria. The Nigerian business environment is currently characterized by many factors that include but are not necessarily limited to the following (Akinmayowa, 1996).

Heavy Dependence on Petroleum (Oil)

Petroleum is a major revenue earner and also the source of ethnic rivalries. In recent time, hostage taking—particularly of foreign expatriates working in the oil industry in the Niger-Delta of Nigeria—has become very problematic. Some expatriates who were kidnapped and then released left the country hurriedly and promised never to return. Thus, the oil sector in Nigeria is losing the services of expatriate managers that are desperately needed in the oil sector. Also, ethnic militia in the Niger-Delta, seeking political autonomy, is one of the biggest problems facing the country, though efforts are being made to resolve the crisis.

Low Agricultural Production

Nigeria has vast fertile arable land in many parts of the country. Given the favorable climatic conditions to agriculture, Nigeria has the potential to become the food basket of Africa and even the world. Regrettably, despite the efforts being made by the government to encourage large-scale agriculture, not much has been achieved from agriculture.

High Unemployment and Underemployment of School Leavers

Under the guise of economic reforms, many able-bodied and qualified persons cannot secure paid employment or self-employment and many have been thrown out of work as a result of retrenchment, rationalization, or downsizing. Given the large army of the employed, many are now being employed as casuals or asked to work part-time. People are doing jobs that they are not originally trained for because they have no choice in employment. And some are doing the jobs for which they are overqualified. So there is no scope for growth, learning, and self-actualization.

Inflation

Inflation in Nigeria could be compared to a jet in the air, increasing its altitude and unable to fly low. Even when the government says that inflation has fallen, it is usually not reflected in the prices of commodities, which are always rising. So, the buying power of several consumers has been diminishing; money has lost its meaning and value in the wake of rising cost of living. There is a shortage of capital as a result of high interest rates and the massive devaluation of the Naira compared to the exchange rates in the 1970s.

Underutilization of Production Capacity

Production targets in industries are no longer being met as a result of shortage of raw material and other inputs in the production process. Infrastructure supporting electricity, water, and transport is inadequate, security poor, and capacity building restricted; this creates powerlessness, hopelessness, and a lack of commitment. Within this context, it is not difficult to imagine why Nigeria has a low export potential for finished goods and has difficulties in attracting foreign investments.

Debt Burden

Given the resources of Nigeria, the nation ought to be the source of capital for other countries. On the contrary, Nigeria has been a heavy borrower and the debt has virtually strangulated the economy until recently when the money owed to the *Paris club* was paid. Yet Nigeria continues to borrow money in the midst of vast resources.

Human Burden

Above, we have identified some of the symptoms of suppression seen in Nigeria's economy, which has not succeeded in creating economic stability at home but has been attempting to be part of the global market. From the above framework, we see that the Nigerian business environment is characterized by worsening economic and social disorders. Among these are mass unemployment, underemployment, rising inflation, growing crime, individual deprivation, the collapse of the social and traditional system, and people's growing fear of the future. These conditions have reduced the ability of people to think reasonably, restricted the productive capacity of most people, and put the brakes on efficiency and the rate of development of Nigerian organizations and institutions. Putting all the above in perspective, it is not difficult to know the reasons why there are problems in Nigeria. When a nation, especially one with vast resources, cannot take care of its people, there is a tendency for people to do things that are socially unacceptable, in their desperate attempt to survive.

Unethical Business Practices

Apparently, this scenario creates the basis for the following questions: What type of marketing culture do we expect to flourish in Nigeria? What type of sales personnel and executives do we expect Nigeria to produce? What type of marketing personnel and executives do we expect to survive in the Nigerian system? Does it really matter if corporate executives are ethical or unethical within such a system? While there may be no easy answers to these questions, there is no doubt that Nigeria is characterized by several unethical marketing practices. These include but are not necessarily limited to (1) product adulteration and piracy; (2) inadequate information or misinformation of consumers by marketers; (3) deceptive packaging; (4) tampering with or manipulation of expiry dates on products including healthcare products; (5) tampering with operating instructions of manufactured products; (6) wrong labeling; (7) poor customer services in banks and insurance companies; (8) lack of guarantee for mechanical goods; (9) misleading advertisement and business promotions; (10) short-changing the customers; (11) exposing consumers to health hazards by selling expired and substandard goods; and (12) advance fee fraud, money laundering, and document racketeering. In the following section, we elaborate the unethical practices.

Product Adulteration and Piracy

Akinmayowa and Bamgboye (2000) offer a useful discussion of what product adulteration and product piracy constitute and the reasons why they exist in Nigeria. Cases of product adulteration and piracy were presented and a program of action to deal with the problems highlighted. Product adulteration and piracy constitute some of the major economic problems of both genuine manufacturers and consumers in Nigeria. Akinmayowa and Bamgboye (2000) state that product adulteration is a process whereby a product is made poorer in quality by adding something of less value to the product. Product piracy is the process whereby a person or a group steals the ideas of another person or group through illegal copying or manipulation of the work and/or trading rights of others for profit. The reasons for product adulteration and product piracy have been linked to several interrelated factors. First, the poor economic development and the failure of government agencies in preventing the exploiters from making a niche for themselves. Second, consumer negligence and the arbitrary prices fixed by retailers make consumers look for cheap products that could be fake or adulterated. Third, some manufacturers have not accepted product adulteration and piracy as a threat. Fourth, overzealous marketing strategists have been blamed for acting irresponsibly, for example, by disclosing confidential information, often on television, of what consumers should look for in genuine products, thereby giving adulterators and pirates a good lead on how to forge their products. Fifth, the fake mentality of consumers is a serious psychological problem because some of them believe that for every genuine product there is always a fake alternative.

Examples of product adulteration and piracy could be cited. The classic examples are adulterated drug and food items, which have been very problematic. It has led the Federal Government of Nigeria to establish the National Administration for Food and Drug Administration and Control (NAFDAC). Adulterated drugs that have been identified include those with no active ingredient(s): tablets containing only lactose (or even chalk) and capsules containing olive oil. Also, drugs with active ingredient(s) that are different from what is stated on the package, for example, *paracetamol* tablets packaged and labeled as *fansidar*, have been identified. Others include food and drinks contaminated with bacteria, heavy metals, trace metals, radioactive material, and banned chemicals, or those containing unapproved sweetness, color, flavors, and other additives with poor quality or/and internationally unacceptable packaging. There are also cosmetics containing harmful chemicals, and imported designer perfume that is diluted and packed locally. Also, alcoholic drinks are without information on the alcohol content. Other products illegally circulating in the market include those that are meant to be regulated only by the government, intended for restricted circulation, not registered by NAFDAC, or marked *export only*. Yet petroleum products such as kerosene, petrol, diesel, and engine oil have been adulterated with serious health, social, and economic consequences.

In a study on the social impact of the circulation of fake drugs in Benin City, Nigeria, Ojo (1991) noted that the faking and adulteration of drugs have grown and are threats to the efficacy of drugs. Data collected from 105 respondents revealed that the circulation of fake drugs is a major problem that has aggravated the troubled state of the healthcare delivery system in Nigeria. Respondents rated the circulation of fake and adulterated drugs as serious and identified Patent Medicine Stores as the major source of fake and adulterated drugs. Nigeria is noted for the problem of fake and adulterated drugs that have led to the death of many patients who consume them, especially those suffering from life-threatening diseases such as heart disease, diabetes, malaria, HIV/AIDS, and others. Indeed, it is being speculated that many countries in the West African subregion now parade fake and adulterated drugs and that some of them may have been smuggled from Nigeria.

True, the marketing of fake and adulterated drugs is usually a clandestine activity. This indicates what some managers or corporate executives may do to make illegal fast money. Such activities deprive consumers of their hard-earned money, expose them to harm and danger, aggravate their pain, and bring them and their families sorrow. It has been argued that the harm done by product adulterators is worse than the harm done by armed robbers, who may rob and leave the victim unharmed physically or, at worst, kill a few people. Regrettably, harmful drugs often kill in thousands including unborn babies. Whereas the armed robber may be arrested and prosecuted or get killed in a counterattack by law enforcement agents, product adulterators and pirates are rarely caught; even when caught, they bribe their way. On those rare occasions when they are punished, the penalties may be affordably light and so would only encourage them to continue their bad habits.

Genuine manufacturers in Nigeria, especially the major manufacturers operating with an overseas manufacturers' license and especially new investors from overseas, should allow the reality of the market situation in Nigeria to guide their investment decisions. What is obtainable through drug management in modern economies such as the United States, Canada, Europe, and other industrialized countries may not be applicable to the Nigerian society. They need to spend money on research to ensure that their products are such that they cannot be easily adulterated. Also, they should set up monitoring agents or watchdogs to supply them with information on the activities of product adulterators and pirates. The efforts of the Federal Government in Nigeria in dealing with the problems of drug adulteration and piracy and other nefarious practices in Nigeria are discussed later in this chapter.

Inadequate Information by Marketers

An honest business practice should enable consumers to have adequate information about a product or service. It is normal in modern economies to enforce consumer protection laws. To do otherwise is tantamount to withdrawal of information and may be the difference between life and death in certain circumstances. Consider the following example in Nigeria: a company manufactured a white powder that it claimed was capable of shinning the teeth. The instruction on the pack simply states, "use it to brush your teeth; it will be shinning white." The instruction did not state whether the powder is to be used *before* or *after* toothpaste is used to brush the teeth, or whether it should be used *with* toothpaste. Furthermore, the active ingredients in the white powder were not disclosed. Yet, this powder is in circulation, because some consumers believe that it shines their teeth white. However, they fail to realize the consequences of swallowing a powder whose active ingredients are unknown. Unfortunately, this type of situation is common in a predominantly illiterate society where consumers buy cheap products without labels. In such a context, some manufacturers may not provide adequate information on their products to consumers, because they may not be under any obligation to do so as there are no relevant legislation and where there is legislation, it may rarely be enforced. And when enforced, the penalty may be affordable or may not be stringent enough to serve as a deterrent.

Indeed, the practice in which sales and marketing executives provide inadequate information or misinform their consumers happens at the corporate management level. They ought to know the law or realize the ethical implications of their actions. For example, how many investors would buy shares in a company that has a ₦46 billion debt? Top officials concealed the huge debt from prospective buyers of government shares, a debt amounting to ₦2.4 billion in African Petroleum. Many investors fell into this trap of unethical business practices of those who should know the implications of their actions. Consider the case of voodoo practitioners and traditional herbal practitioners, some of them claim to have cures for the dreaded HIV/AIDS, thereby deceiving many to part with huge sums of money in search of an elusive cure. This is not surprising as voodoo practitioners and their cohorts often operate by trial and error method.

Misrepresentation of financial reports appears to be a tradition in some financial institutions. Bank customers may often be unaware that their banks are in distress and are gradually crashing until customers get to their banks one morning to see the banks under lock and key. Many customers fall victim to the banks, unaware of the banks' true financial status until the Central Bank of Nigeria or the Nigeria Deposit Insurance Commission (NDIC) takes over such banks after a short notification. In 2006, the failure of some banks to meet the ₦25 billion recapitalization requirements, as directed by the Central Bank of Nigeria, exposed their financial reality.

Clearly, there is a need for consumers to establish a nongovernmental organization to promote their interest, monitor unethical behavior in business transactions in banks, and seek constitutional redress for those who are cheated. Misinformation in business transactions, an aspect of unfair trading, is at the heart of unethical business practices and ought to be confronted.

Deceptive Packaging

In Nigeria, some retailers often provide inadequate information or misinform the consumers on product quality, quantity, contents, and the health and safety implications of some products. In addition to the unethical behavior already cited, the consumers' interest is not catered to, given the style of packaging and labeling of products.

Packaging, in addition to its primary function of protecting a product, is used to attract the customer, identify, distinguish a company's product from others, and convey a sales message. In order to sell their products, some retailers often use deceptive packaging to deceive and confuse the consumers, for example, by placing a small object in an oversized package stuffed with shredded paper, or by using flashy packages to give the impression that the product is worth its price. Other examples include toothpastes in robust tubes containing more trapped air than toothpaste. Consumers find similar tricks being used in the packaging of superglues and printing-ink cartridges.

Labeling is related to packaging as it performs both promotional and informational functions. A label, in most cases, contains the brand name, registered trademarks, the name and address of the manufacturer or distributor, the product composition, size, weight, the recommended uses of the product and, in some cases, the price of the product. An ugly practice in Nigeria is that some unscrupulous manufacturers (or in some cases product adulterators/pirates) deceitfully give the impression that a product made in Nigeria is made abroad. For example, a product made in Aba, Kaduna, or Lagos could carry a foreign label such as "Made in England" or "Made in Italy" or "Made in Paris" to give the wrong impression that the product or offer is of good quality. They do so because it is known or assumed that Nigerian consumers love foreign products more than local ones. Also, a manufacturer could affix to a product the brand name of another manufacturer's more popular brand. Examples include Italian shoe brands and exotic wine names such as Eva, Aromatic Schnapps, and Champagne; these are adulterated and sold with impunity.

Poor Customer Services in Banks and Insurance Companies

Banks and insurance companies are expected to be responsible and offer courteous service. Rather than banks seeing themselves as doing their customers a favor because the nation is underbanked, they should be levelheaded to know what their customers want and meet their needs. Given Nigeria's past record of some banks becoming hard-pressed, folding up suddenly, locking up their gates against their customers, and trapping customer deposits in their strong rooms, it is not surprising that some banks are full of themselves, fraudulent in their practices, engaged in window dressing of financial information, involved in money laundering, scamming foreign exchange, and manipulating interest rates in their desperate attempt to declare bogus paper profits.

Cashing a check or transacting a business on a typical day in some commercial banks could take hours unless the customer concerned has friends across the counter. Banks are often crowded with long queues of people in a dirty, poorly ventilated, dully illuminated hall; the heat in such places is made worse by the large number of customers literally breathing down each other's neck. Such an environment constitutes a health hazard for people, especially with breathing problems because it could trigger a crisis. And airborne diseases could spread in banking halls, especially those with poor ventilation, where it is difficult or slow to get services.

Many banks introduced online services in an attempt to enable customers to have access to their accounts anywhere in Nigeria where a branch of the bank is located. Customers sometimes go to banks only to be told that the *system is down.* This is an euphemism for online failure and is often used as a cover up when banks do not have enough cash to pay their customers and want to keep them quiet until they get more cash from the Central Bank or when banks can no longer operate for the day because they are cash strapped. In fact, some banks or some of their branches keep little cash in their vaults because of the fear of armed robbers who at night raid banks with sophisticated guns and explosives. In fact, bank robberies are no longer news. The robbers often confront law enforcement agents and at times gain the upper hand, leaving behind blood, sweat, and sorrow, as they cart away millions of Nairas and even foreign currencies.

Another nagging issue is the problem being created by insurance companies. They are often seen as organizations that welcome you with open arms and smiling faces when you pay your insurance premiums but treat you with clenched fists and grinning faces when you demand compensation for losses incurred on insured goods. They may not point out your errors when you complete the insurance forms. They may be more concerned with the money you want to pay and quickly collect your cash or process your check. But, when you are about to make claims, you are likely to be confronted with excuses such as forms not properly completed, failure to dot the i's and cross the t's, and failure to cross one or two items and held responsible for falling into the traps they may have deliberately set for their customers to help them avoid paying insurance claims. This phenomenon has drastically affected insurance businesses in Nigeria. Therefore, it not surprising that some people may not patronize insurance businesses because they believe that God is the only genuine provider of insurance, and that man-made insurance often fails to provide cover.

Lack of Guarantee for Mechanical Goods

A traditional approach for manufacturers to secure trust and confidence of the users of their products is to ensure that the products reach consumers in a good condition and are able to provide satisfactory services. Normally, genuine manufacturers should be able to give a guarantee on their products. In Nigeria, it would appear that the retailer does not trust the customers to the extent of extending to him or her any guarantee because a customer could buy a product, open it, replace some of the new items in the product, and return it to the seller and lie that the product is bad. So, the culture does not give the seller the courage to guarantee a product. And when a guarantee is offered, it may be verbal, so that it could be denied. In some cases, it is the product that guarantees itself. For example, if one buys a television, it could be tested on the spot. If it works, that is guarantee! One cannot come back in the future and complain that the television is not working. After all, the seller of the television may not be able to give any guarantee in the face of fluctuating electricity current (common in Nigeria) that could damage the television transistors. So, there are so many constraints in the Nigerian business environment affecting the relationship between retailers and their customers.

Misleading Advertisements and
Deceptive Business Promotion

The issue of misleading advertisements is serious particularly in a predominantly illiterate society such as Nigeria. Misleading advertisements, wrong labeling, product adulteration and piracy, expired drugs, and other vices are a heavy social burden for the Nigerians, most of whom are living below poverty line. Packaging falsehood, half-truths, or facts slanted to give false impression are sources of social and health problems. For example, in 1991, the then health minister in Nigeria (Late Professor Olikoye Ransome-Kuti) observed that Nigerians, at a time, were being bombarded with misleading advertisements. It was noted that there might be ten or more varieties of chloroquine in the market under different brand names. The general public did not know that all those drugs were the same in reality but were advertised as if they were different, thus confusing the people watching the advertisements. When people contracted malaria, they often bought different brands, going from one brand to another and not seeing any improvement in their condition, all along not understanding that they were in fact buying the same pharmaceutical drug. This could lead to frustration or drug addition. This type of situation occurs with other drugs, especially expired drugs and food, resulting in lung cancer, kidney/liver infection or failure, and other related sicknesses. In 1974, a manufacturer of a brand of soft drinks came up with an advertisement that claimed that it could fight flu (influenza)! Also, targeting children or the general population to consume food and drinks with high sugar content has the potential for increasing the incidence of sugar-related diseases (e.g., diabetes).

Advance Fee Fraud and Money Laundering

Advance fee fraud (a.k.a. 419, named after the 419 criminal code in Nigeria) is the action of any person or group who by false pretense obtains from any person or group anything fraudulently. False inducement, misinformation, fraudulent advertisement, wrong labeling, product adulteration, and piracy would appear to fall under the ambit of 419. The issue of 419 is now global with the use of the Internet and more sophisticated techniques. Often, fraudsters pose as government officials capable of awarding significant contracts and lucrative employment and look for people who can lodge huge amounts of money into their bank accounts for attractive commission. These techniques have been used to fraud people. In Nigeria, many cases of 419 have been reported and the problem remains. Despite government efforts to crack down on the perpetrators of the crime, some gullible and greedy people still fall victim to fraudsters.

Apart from 419, other illegal methods being used to acquire wealth include money laundering, oil bunkering, cyber-crime, document racketeering, and other such devious activities. The victims, who are mostly foreigners, are often duped of large sums of money. In some cases, financial institutions serve as agents for money laundering between government officials (state governors, ministers, commissioners, etc.) and foreign banks. Since its inception in 2003, the Economic and Financial Crime Commission (EFCC) has been waging wars against illegal acquisition of wealth under any guise. For example, an inspector general of police (IGP) served a term in jail for corruption and a governor in Bayelsa State escaped from London while on trial for money laundering and other financial crimes in 2006. Also, some governors in Nigeria have been impeached as a result of the charges of corruption and other crimes that were brought against them.

Shortchanging Customers

According to Hornby (2001) in the *Oxford Advanced Learner's Dictionary*, the word "shortchange" is defined as giving back less than the correct amount of money to somebody who has paid for something with more than the exact price, or as treating somebody unfairly by not giving them what they have earned or deserve. So, when an individual or group is being given poor treatment they did not deserve, they are being shortchanged. Therefore, the business environment in Nigeria may be described as an environment where customers could be shortchanged.

Consider the following incident: As a visitor to Nigeria, you enter a supermarket to buy some items. At the end of the transaction, the salesperson tells you that because he or she does not have the right change, you could take some sweets to make up for the shortage. How would you react? There is another incident: You wanted to change some dollars into the local currency. You did not go to the bank for the transaction because you were told that you could change your money in the parallel market. You went to a foreign exchange dealer along the road and gave a dollar or some dollars for exchange. The person takes your dollar(s), looks at them, and returns them to you saying that he needs bills of higher denomination (e.g., $1,000 bills). You do not have such bills and so collect your dollar(s) and walk away. You go to another location to change the dollar(s) and you are shocked to be told that a dollar bill among the original dollars you wanted to exchange for the local currency was fake! Again, how would you react? Actually, the first person to whom you gave the dollar(s) to have it exchanged may have exchanged your original dollar for a fake one. The lesson here is that people should not hand over their original foreign currency to any dealer until it has been exchanged. The best place for exchange transaction is probably the bank, here too you are expected to be vigilant. Indeed, while the customer could be shortchanged, retailers could be shortchanged as well. For example, a customer could buy goods and pay for them with fake currency and the retailer could pay the change to the customer with fake currency. A comedian on Nigerian television captured this scenario: He joked about the story of a trader who complained that he was paid a substantial amount of money in fake currencies. When asked to tender the fake money as evidence, he said, "I have spent it!"

The Ethics Project 2006

Over a period of six months, during the course of teaching Human Resources Management at the 300 level (students complete first degrees at 400 level) and at the MBA level in the University of Benin in Nigeria, the roles of Human Resources in promoting business ethics were discussed. Students were given assignments on the relevant issues. At the 300 level, the students in the Department of Accounting, in groups, worked on the impact of corporate leadership on business ethics in Nigeria. At the MBA level each student in the Department of Business Administration worked on ethical behavior of Human Resources and its impact on development in Nigeria. Given the fact that the students were from different parts of Nigeria and were at the undergraduate and postgraduate levels, their reports were useful to the study of business ethics in the Nigerian context.

The project involved 852 respondents drawn from five major cities: Abuja (capital of Nigeria), Lagos, Benin City, Port Harcourt, and Asaba. All respondents were Nigerian, 62 percent being male and 38 percent being female. About 54 percent were engaged in full-time/part-time work or in self-employment, and the remaining 46 percent were unemployed. Specifically, the project was designed to find out personal opinions/views of the diverse Nigerian population on the following hypotheses: (1) firms that behave ethically perform better in the long-term than firms that compromise their code of conduct; (2) unethical behavior will be less prevalent in organizations that have a corporate code of ethics than organizations that do not; (3) employees will be more committed to organizations that have adopted a code of ethics than organizations that do not; (4) in a country where managers are ethical, the country would have more economic prosperity than a country where managers are unethical; and (5) Nigeria will not develop as long as financial crimes, advance fee fraud, product adulteration, and other vices in the economy are not targeted, reduced, or eliminated.

On the basis of the respondents' opinions, we concluded that the majority agreed that (1) firms with a code of business ethics perform better than those without a code of business ethics; (2) firms with a code of business ethics contribute more to the economic development of a country than firms without a code of business ethics; (3) a country that wants to develop creates and allows an environment for business ethics to thrive; (4) adherence to ethical behavior enhances the volume of local and foreign investment; (5) Nigeria may not develop to its full potential as long as financial crimes and product adulterations persist; (6) the government of Nigeria is addressing the country's various abuses and unethical business practices through policy formulation and establishment of watchdog agencies; (7) the government still needs to do more than what it is doing now to address unethical business practices; and (8) adulteration of products and services is the major problem faced by genuine manufacturers and service providers.

In addition, the majority agreed that (1) retailers misinform and give inadequate information to consumers; (2) the expiry dates of products (e.g., pharmaceutical drugs, medicines) are often manipulated by manufacturers, distributors, and retailers; (3) retailers often find it difficult to guarantee their products being sold to consumers; (4) expired goods are often sold to consumers by retailers; (5) the presence of NAFDAC has reduced availability of expired and counterfeit goods/drugs; (6) many lives have been lost through the use of expired and counterfeit drugs and goods; (7) advance fee fraud is still very much prevalent in Nigeria; and (8) there is no strict monitoring and enforcement of appropriate laws to deal with criminal activities.

However, the majority disagreed that (1) firms that behave ethically cannot really *make it*, unlike those firms that compromise; (2) almost all products, including drugs, are pirated; (3) operating instructions on manufactured and packaged goods are tampered with by manufacturers and retailers; (4) most banks render poor service to their customers; and (5) there is no consumer protection.

Some of our views in this chapter have been supported by these findings. According to the slogan of Boeing Company, between right and wrong is a troublesome gray area.

Government Policies and Watchdog Agencies

Turning to the findings of the ethics project and other issues raised in this chapter, it is not difficult to know the reasons why Nigeria in spite of her vast resources has difficulties in attracting major foreign investors. The government of Nigeria is aware of these problems and is making significant efforts to arrest the ugly trend. Unethical practices are corrupt practices that benefit only the perpetrators at the expense of the large society. Due to the negative impact of such practices on the common good of the society and the development of the Nigerian nation, the government, over the years, has drawn up policies and established watchdog agencies to check unwholesome practices among Nigerian businesses and their foreign collaborators. In 1975, Nigeria enacted a code of conduct, which was subsequently incorporated into the 1979 and 1989 constitutions. A variety of bodies have been established. These include the Economic and Financial Crimes Commission (EFCC), the Independent Corrupt Practices Commission (ICPC), National Drug Law Enforcement Agency (NDLEA), the Standard Organization of Nigeria (SON), the National Copyright Commission of Nigeria (NCC), and the National Agency for Food and Drug Administration Commission (NAFDAC), among others. The roles of these agencies and their limitations are discussed in the next section.

Economic and Financial Crimes Commission (EFCC)

The EFCC is a government agency with the responsibility to deal with unethical practices in the Nigerian economy. The commission is charged with the responsibility of investigating and enforcing all laws against economic and financial crimes. Also, the EFCC is expected to enforce all laws relating to banking, money laundering, and advance fee fraud. The commission has been widely acknowledged as a welcome development, given the corruption that has engulfed Nigeria like a poisonous gas. The critics of the commission, however, noted that it is selective in dealing with corrupt people, insisting that only the political opponents and those not in the good books of the government are usually the target of the commission. It may be put this way: the commission points its longest finger on political opponents but the remaining four fingers are pointed at itself—the commission—that is, those who established the commission are in key government positions and are corrupt and untouchable.

Independent Corrupt Practices and Other
Related Offences Commission (ICPC)

The ICPC was established by the ICPC Act passed into law on June 13, 2000. It is the apex body saddled with the responsibility of fighting corruption and other related offences; its mandate is to prohibit and prescribe punishment. It serves as a watchdog over illegal acquisition of wealth while the portfolio of the commission supports the aspiration of a society to make things work; however, the commission is often seen as a toothless bulldog. Its work has been seen to be similar to the activities of the EFCC. Critics argue that most of the activities being handled by the EFCC and the ICPC could be handled under the criminal laws already present in the constitution.

Nigerian Drug Law Enforcement Agency (NDLEA)

The NDLEA was established to fight hard drugs such as cocaine, heroine, and marijuana. The agency has the mandate to ensure that Nigeria is free from hard drugs and drug traffickers, who use Nigerian ports for smuggling hard drugs to Europe and other countries. In spite of the activities of this agency, so much remains to be done to clear the name of Nigeria as a transit point for hard drugs.

Standard Organization of Nigeria (SON) and
National Copyright Commission (NCC)

These agencies are set up to ensure that products are made to international standards and that creative works are protected from adulteration and pirates. The bodies are responsible for quality and the prevention of product adulteration and piracy.

National Agency for Food and Drug
Administration Commission (NAFDAC)

The NAFDAC has the responsibility to promote and protect public health by regulating imports, manufacturing, distributions, advertisements, sales of processed foods, drugs, cosmetics, medical devices, bottled or packaged water, drinks, and beverages. NAFDAC has created public awareness of the activities of product adulterators and pirates, regulated the activities of industries, promoted consumer awareness, and encouraged all the stakeholders to support government efforts to create a society that is free from poorly made injurious-to-life products.

These agencies and others have been designed to sanitize the system. They plug loopholes that individuals may take advantage of in business transactions and financial dealings. Indeed, Nigerians are aware of the need for positive change and are eager to enjoy its dividends. However, it should be stressed that positive changes are rather slow. People wonder about the factors making it difficult to use these agencies to transform the Nigerian society rapidly. The reasons are not far to seek: (1) the agencies' goals may look very good on paper, but very difficult to actualize; (2) we could be having good policies but are being actualized by the wrong people; and (3) the agencies are, perhaps unwisely, modeled after similar bodies in developed economies where the basic needs of the people have been met.

In Nigeria, the majority of the people are still poor, illiterate, underfed, and underclad. It puts forth the following questions: What do we gain by supporting government agencies? What do they see around them that makes them feel that the government is a time waster, hypocritical, lazy, and wasteful—no electricity, no good roads, no security, no water? And all that they now deserve is good government policies. If a government intends to add the burden to its people, the government should ensure that the people still have the strength to carry the load, otherwise, there could be consequences. First, the additional burden could make the people shed the entire burden suddenly at the doorstep of the government. Second, the additional burden breaks the back of the population and makes them snap. These are the genesis of the upheavals in societies that were once seen to be peaceful.

Efforts to deal with unethical practices using various agencies are in response to unethical behavior in Nigeria. The extent to which success could be achieved depends on the extent to which human behavior could be modified to suit government policies. Thus, like any other societies, the extent to which government policies could achieve their objectives rests squarely on the shoulders of the people. For example, Oludengun (2006) observed that when we examine government agencies in Nigeria, the initiatives were partially successful in achieving some of the immediate objectives of the agencies to deal with unethical practices but generally, substantial problems remain. The measures to sustain ethical behavior in Nigeria have failed because they were introduced in an overall political and policy environment that was not conducive to the success of the measures. In his opinion, when grand corruption is rampant at the top level of government and politics, the nature of governance is basically undemocratic, unaccountable, and patrimonial. And where patronage system has remained intact, one can hardly expect to enforce measures against unethical behavior with any degree of seriousness. By deduction, the state and governance and commitment at the highest political level are crucial to any successful drive to curb and punish ethical violations. Another problem with Nigeria is that the measures to curb unethical practices have focused more on sanctions than on the fundamental issues in the society responsible for unethical practices. Sadly, many of the institutions that were established to promote ethics and account-ability often lack the resources, public awareness, impartiality, and public support that are crucial for their success.

Based on these societal problems, we can see the difficulties in attracting foreign investment in Nigeria. A visitor to Nigeria who travels by road from Lagos to the northern or the eastern part of the country, an area spanning hundreds of kilometers, would probably marvel at the large expanses of uncultivated land, green vegetation, and bright sunshine. The visitor would also cross various bridges under which water is gushing through endlessly. Despite these resources, there is food scarcity. Something must be fundamentally wrong with Nigeria to import food that could be cultivated in the country. Equally, something should be fundamentally wrong for mak-ing Nigeria not attractive to foreign investors. After all, Nigeria is endowed with abundant natural resources for investors to take advan-tage of. All her natural resources notwithstanding, it is the oil and gas sector (petroleum) that is the mainstay of the economy and the driving force behind all investment opportunities from upstream to down-stream sectors. The proven Nigerian oil reserve is 23 billion barrels and the gas reserve is 160 trillion cubic meters.

The country has a petroleum and gas policy geared toward the vigorous exploration of the upstream and downstream sectors of the industry by local, foreign, or joint collaborative investors. In the upstream sector, investors are encouraged to participate in exploration and production of petroleum and gas. They are expected to apply for oil blocks for exploration through the Oil Prospecting License (OPL) and the Oil Mining Lease (OML). In the downstream sector, there are opportunities in oil refinery where an investor can set up and wholly own a refinery and where there is technological know-how that can help undertake turnaround maintenance of refineries. Also, opportunities exist in the manufacturing of special products such as spare parts, industrial and food grade solvents, insecticides, cosmetics, petroleum jelly, grease, bitumen-based materials (floor tiles, rubber products, and tarpaulin, etc.). Other investment opportunities include the export of refined products, asphalt storage, and packaging and blending plants. Apart from the petroleum industry, other investment opportunities include petrochemicals, gas development and conversion, and marketing of Nigerian crude oil. The non-oil sector includes coal and bitumen exploration, exploration of other solid minerals, and hotel and tourism, among others (NIPC, 2000).

The National Investment Promotion Commission, carved out from the Federal Ministry of Industry in 1995, provides services to encourage foreign investment. Despite the promulgation of investment decrees that the government claims are attractive or liberal, foreign investment in Nigeria is still problematic. These problems include but are not necessarily limited to political instability, porous security, weak infrastructure, and manpower problems. The other factors are nondemocratic government, international sanctions, advance fee fraud, and corruption.

Conclusion

Clearly, the enormity of the task to promote ethics and accountability should not be underestimated. A comprehensive agenda to promote ethics and accountability and to deal with corruption would benefit from the following ideas.

We need to foster and promote conditions of service to enhance professional and ethical standards. Poor pay, poor working conditions, job insecurity, and poor prospects after retirement create unethical practices. These should be avoided. Those who cannot survive with their salaries would have to survive by earning money illegally. Therefore, adequate salary that includes adequate retirement benefits and healthcare delivery at work for workers and their families are crucial. Sanctions against corrupt practices may not fully work if workers are not happy with their pay.

We need to set ethical standards by rewarding those who are ethical and projecting them as stars. It will not solve any problem if we believe that laws and the enforcement of laws could do the magic of dealing with unethical practices. Sanctions may only create people who will be more careful, play safe, and eventually become more sophisticated in unethical practices. Human beings anywhere, over time, could succeed in beating any sanction made by man.

Establishing coalitions of business associations, professional groups, and the civil society to explore and fight unethical practices is useful. Various business groups and professional bodies have ethical standards. Mass educational campaigns on the extent of corruption and the costs of unethical practices are needed. Systematic and impartial prosecutions of people using unethical practices are crucial. We get better results on this in developed countries where those indulging in corrupt and unethical practices are diligently prosecuted.

We need to look at work ethics vis-à-vis business ethics. Work ethics would appear before business ethics. Or do they complement each other? For example, in a society where people do not attach much value to honest work, quality work, or punctuality, and where people do not see work as the platform on which a country could launch itself to stardom, business ethics may not thrive.

Training in work and business ethics is paramount. Management, in reputable organizations should employ a full-time ethics officer who will give advice on ethical issues to top managements, disseminate information on ethical values, investigate ethic violations, advise the board of directors on ethics, and oversee an ethics training program.

We need to teach ethics in schools. We should begin to think about offering a degree course in Business Ethics and Corporate Culture. This should be a training ground for corporate leaders who should be able to make positive changes in their societies and in the international community.

Performance appraisal processes, promotion, salary increases, and other incentive schemes in organizations should be securely anchored on ethical values. These have the potential for promoting high ethical standards among employees who may wish to reciprocate the good intentions of management.

Attempts by top management to create an ethical atmosphere may have little effect on the ethical attitude and behavior of employees if management does not practice what it preaches. Therefore, top management should fully support an ethics program. The expectations of top management and its efforts related to ethical issues should be publicized in the organization handbook, newspapers, television, and radio commercials.

The international dimension to the ethical crisis ought not to be neglected. Businesspersons from the developed countries have often been accused of bribing public officials in developing countries as fair and legitimate methods for export promotion. In recent years, Transparency International has been blowing the whistle over this problem and demanding that action be taken to mend it. Any meaningful progress in this direction would require an agreement on strict enforcement of international conventions, punishing violators of ethical standards, and strengthening international integrity systems and strategies.

The fight against corruption in Nigeria is evident. It may be rough and slow, but in the long run, corruption will have to be defeated. There is no credible alternative. Corruption may not be totally eradicated; however, it could be reduced drastically to a level at which it becomes inconsequential and would not make development efforts difficult. Fighting corruption, unethical practices, and social vices is not the business of government alone. Everybody must be involved because corruption seems to be ubiquitous—government circles, marketplaces, streets, neighborhood, educational institutions, hospitals, religions, organizations, and among friends and family members.

Accordingly, corporate executives in Nigeria should provide honest leadership in business services and in their organizations, a leadership that would impact positively on the well-being of the larger society. For development, ethical behavior cannot be compromised. For Nigeria to attract foreign investments, the nation has to be ethical and this requires professionalism from the government, institutions, organizations, groups, and individuals. Further, negative factors such as corruption, poor infrastructure, insecurity, and political instability should be reduced. If the Nigerian economy is to get out of the vicious circle of underdevelopment, the government should provide the leadership to its agencies, institutions, corporate organizations, professional groups, and cognate others to create an environment for business ethics to thrive. Thus, government policies to deal with unethical behavior must be courageously implemented. We should respect the law that implements the policies relating to business ethics. Those who create disorder, harm, death, and destruction by flouting the relevant laws should be severely punished.

Finally, this chapter is not in any way designed to castigate Nigeria but to address some of the issues that prevent the country from attaining self-actualization. Self-actualization is a key issue for the individual, the group, the organization, and the society at large. Surely, Nigeria has good prospects for positive change but it requires diligent work. The direction of the change is clear—moving away from the unethical ways of doing things to a courageous strategy where integrity, honesty, and transparency would be the driving force behind the growth that would enable the Nigerian society to create wealth and share prosperity. Certainly, this is in accord with the view of Edmund Burke (Stewart, 1983) who quipped that a state without the means of some change was without the means of its conservation.

References

Adams, J.S., and Tashchian, A. "An Explanatory Study of Gender Difference in Experiences of Ethical Dilemmas at Work," paper presented at the Academy of Management Conference, Vancouver, Canada, 1995.

Agbonifoh, B.A. "Business Ethics." In *Introduction to Business: A Functional Approach*, ed. Ingbenebor, A.U., and Osaze, E.B., 174–90. Department of Business Administration, University of Benin, Benin City, Nigeria: Malthouse Press Ltd, 1999.

Akinmayowa, J.T. "A Psychological Approach to Human Resources Management in a Depressing Economic Environment." In *Environmental Challenges in the Third World*, ed. Folarin, B.A., and Orebamjo, T.O., Lagos: Environment and Behavior Association of Nigeria, University of Lagos, and Centre for Management Development, 1996.

Akinmayowa, J.T., and Bamgboye, E.D. "Product Adulteration and Piracy: A Major Economic Sabotage." *Benin Journal of Social Sciences* 8/9, no. 1/2 (2000): 42–45.

Chandan, J.S. *Management Theory and Practice*. New Delhi: Vikas Publishing House, 2001.

Clark, M.A., and Leonard, S.L. "Can Corporate Codes of Ethics influence Behavior?" *Journal of Business Ethics* 17, no. 6 (1998): 619–30.

Ethics Project 2006. *Contributions to the Ethics Project*. Benin City: Nigeria: Department of Business Administration, University of Benin, Nigeria, 2006.

Fry, F.L., Stoner C.R., and Hattwick R.E. *Business: An Integrative Approach*. New York: McGraw-Hill, 2000.

Hornby, A.S. *Oxford Advanced Learner's Dictionary*. Oxford: Oxford University Press, 2001.

Murphy, P.E., Smith, J.E., and Daley, J.M. "Executive Attitudes, Organizational Size and Ethical Issues: Perspectives on a Service Industry." *Journal of Business Ethics* 11, no. 1 (1992): 11–17.

NIPC. National Investment Promotion Commission. *Main Thrust of Nigeria's Trade Industrialization Policy*, no. 1–2 (2000).

Nickels, W.G., McHugh, J.M., and McHugh, S.M. *Understanding Business*. New York: McGraw-Hill, 2002.

Ojo, A.O. "The Social Impact of the Circulation of Fake Drugs in Edo State: A Case Study of Benin City." *MBA Thesis*, Department of Business Administration, University of Benin, Benin City, Nigeria, 1991.

Oludengun, Y.M. "Business Ethics." *Research Review*, Department of Business Administration, University of Benin, Benin City, Nigeria, 2006.

Onyenankeya, K. "Financial Crimes: The Nigerian Experience." *Nigerian Stock Market Annual*, 25–33, 2003.

Shea, G.F. *Practice Ethics*. New York: American Management Association, 1988.

Softkey Multimedia Inc. *Crompton's Interactive Encyclopedia*, Vision 1.0 (CD-ROM), 1997.

Somers, J.M. "Ethical Codes of Conduct and Organizational Context: A Study of the Relationship between Codes of Conduct, Employee Behavior and Organizational Values." *Journal of Business Ethics* 30, no. 2 (2001): 185–95.

Stewart, V. *Change: The Challenge for Management.* New York: McGraw-Hill Book Company, 1983.

Wotruba, T.R., Chonko, L.B., and Loe, T.W. "The Impact of Ethics Code Familiarity on Manager Behavior." *Journal of Business Ethics* 33, no. 1 (2001): 59–69.

Wulfson, M. "Rules of the Game: Do Corporate Codes of Ethics Work?" *Review of Business* 20 (1998): 1–9.

Yesufu, A.L. *Human Factors That Affect Foreign Investment in Nigeria*, MBA thesis, Department of Business Administration, University of Benin, Benin City, Nigeria, August 2001.

Part III

Emerging Lifestyle and Consumer Behavior

Chapter 6

Attitude of Indian Consumers toward Wine: Pleasure versus Prescription

Satyendra Singh

Wine is a sophisticated product and requires sophisticated marketing. Although wine purchasing is a behavioral process that involves choices and preferences based on attitude, it is also deeply rooted in traditions. The purpose of this chapter is to test the attitude model in a high-involvement situation to predict the consumer's choice—drinking wine for pleasure or prescription. The attitude is conceptualized as a three-component model—*affective (feelings)*, *behavioral (response tendencies)*, and *cognitive (beliefs)*. It is proposed that the *behavioral* component is the most significant predictor of consumers' *choices*, followed by *cognitive* and *affective* components. Results based on data provided by wine drinkers support this proposition. The chapter contributes to the literature by providing greater understanding of how consumers make choices about wine drinking, which is a recent phenomenon in Indian culture. The implication for managers is that they should be able to assess effectiveness of the components of attitude and market the product in the context of evolving culture and thus position the wine accordingly in the market.

Introduction

For a long time, wine has been mass marketed. This technique is often futile these days and has been criticized (Gluckman, 1990; Spawton, 1991; Jennings and Wood, 1994) for reasons such as the lack of marketing skills in the wine industry (Howley and Young, 1992; Lockshin, 1999), irrelevant marketing for smaller wineries (Sharp, 1991), and the wine market itself (Hall and Winchester, 1999), among others. Given the market of wine is changing, competition growing, and a new trend emerging, it can be suggested that consuming wine is considered as a lifestyle beverage—the more expensive the wine, the higher the status and, therefore, the more elegant the lifestyle, everything being equal. As a consequence, wine has become more acceptable and desirable to the consumers, creating a need for marketing managers to understand wine consumers' consumption pattern and thus their choice process.

To understand these patterns and choices, a great deal of attention is paid to mainly two types of segmentations: demographics and psychographics. Although demographic details provide a great deal of personal information about the consumer, it gives no pointers to the underlying motivations that drive that consumer's behavior; demography, therefore, is less useful in predicting consumer behavior (Grunert et al., 1997; Wedel and Kamakura, 2000). True, although wine consumers may be similar in demographics, they are different in psychographics (i.e., activities, interests, and opinions) and, therefore, in their attitude. For the purpose of the research, attitude is defined as comprising three components—affective, behavioral, and cognitive. These components are explained in detail later in this chapter.

Recently, scientists concluded that a low to moderate intake of wine is associated with lower mortality from cardiovascular and cerebrovascular diseases (Gronbaek et al., 1995; Auger et al., 2002). This finding seems to indicate that consumers appear to adjust their attitude toward drinking wine in moderation.

This leads us to believe that consumers who did not drink wine previously due to economic or religious reasons are now persuaded to drink wine for a healthy lifestyle. For this segment, wine is indeed more a prescription than pleasure.

Pleasure and *prescription*—two related but distinct lifestyle-based choices—are yet to be addressed in extant theoretical or empirical research. There are several reasons for the gap in the literature: first, due to the arrival of the Internet technology and the rise in educational qualification, today's consumers are more informative, discerning, and health conscious than in the past, so their decision-making process is more logical and rational; second, as these segments are related to behavior, it presents a useful starting point for research (Kotler and Armstrong, 1996); third, such an examination could identify differences between segments based on purchase and usages (Morris, 1996); and finally, segmenting based on lifestyle is more contemporary than personality and more comprehensive than personal values (Blackwell et al., 2001).

This chapter contributes to the body of knowledge by (1) proposing two lifestyle-based segments and choices—for pleasure (lifestyle), and for prescription (healthy lifestyle); (2) testing the impact of these choices on attitude formation; and (3) suggesting implications for managers. Further, the chapter enriches our knowledge of wine marketing in the emerging market of India, a market that has been a focal point for scholars and managers alike. In the next section, the chapter provides the rationale for focusing on these segmentations and choices, tests a central hypothesis, reports the results, and discusses the implications for managers.

The Context

Market segmentation is classified in terms of geographic, demographic, and psychographic properties to understand consumers' patterns for their choices (table 6.1). Motivated by the desire to understand these patterns and choices even further, researchers have segmented the market on the basis of wine-related lifestyle (Bruwer et al., 2002), demographics (Wedel and Kamakura, 2000), behavior (Johnson et al., 1991), benefit (Dubow, 1992), cultural background (Hall et al., 1997), volume purchased (Thomas, 2000), retail outlet (Sanchez and Gil, 1998), and involvement level (Lockshin et al., 2001), among others.

Table 6.1   Wine consumer segmentation

Spawton (1991)				
General:	Connoisseurs	Aspirations	Beverage	New wine drinkers
Dubow (1992)				
User-based:	Wine itself	Introspective	Semitemperate	Social image
Dubow (1992)				
Occasion-based:	Social introspective	Semitemperate	Food	Oenophilic
Hall and Winchester (2000a, b)				
General:	Connoisseurs	Image aspirations	Risk-averse	Enjoyment
Bruwer et al. (2001)				
General:	Conspicuous	Inconspicuous	Image-oriented enjoyment	Basic
This study (2007)				
Lifestyle-based:	Pleasure	Prescription		

The Choices: Pleasure versus Prescription
Prescription-Based Choice

Marketers have realized that wine can also be a part of a healthy diet and, thus, a healthy lifestyle. In 1993, the World Health Organization and the Harvard Medical School of Public Health developed a Mediterranean dietary pyramid that includes drinking wine in moderation (one to two glasses a day) as part of a recommended diet. One glass of wine is equivalent to 5oz containing 12 percent alcohol per volume. Recently, there has been a steady rise in wine consumption in India. The upward consumption trend is a reflection of changing consumer attitude toward wine, particularly because recent studies have shown the benefits of red wine (Wollin and Jones, 2001; Auger et al., 2002). Further, Whitten and Lipp (1994) prescribe, "If every adult in North American drank 2 glasses of wine a day . . . heart disease . . . would be cut by 40 percent and $40 billion be saved annually." Therefore, we label this kind of moderate drinking *prescription-based segment/lifestyle* and define such drinkers as a group of consumers who have adjusted their attitude by drinking wine in moderation in pursuit of a healthy lifestyle.

Pleasure-Based Choice

Admittedly, there are consumers who drink wine for the purpose of socializing and deriving a sense of pleasure. In fact, in some cultures, drinking wine is a norm, or a form of celebration at the end of grape harvest. Unlike many highly technologically driven or services industries, the wine industry is deeply rooted in traditions and is primarily agricultural-based. For countries such as France and Italy, wine drinking is a traditional part of everyday life and culture. Of course, the pleasure is mixed with blessing in that wine contributes to lower death rates from heart disease, as seen in countries such as France (Renaud and De Longeril, 1992). We label this segment as pleasure-based segment/lifestyle and define it as a group of consumers who drink wine to maintain a certain lifestyle and to get pleasure through various mode of expression; drinking wine for pleasure is one of them.

The Wine Consumer

India has increasingly become a key player in the world economy, as it is one of the most important emerging markets in the world with a significant potential for sustainable high rate of economic growth.

The impact of reform on industries, international trade, and financial areas is noticeable. Following economic liberalization in India, businesses saw an increase in spending by consumers.

Drinking wine is a newly developed trend in India. The consumers no longer perceive drinking wine as a taboo. As a result, several foreign and local firms are producing and selling wine in India by changing the attitude of Indian consumers toward wine, and by changing the local culture. The premise is that the behavioral pattern characteristics of a particular culture express the shared values and beliefs of that culture. Cultural values are also expressed through material objects (e.g., dress, food, housing, etc.) or characteristics of a particular culture (Royce, 1982). The values are prescriptive of attitudes and behavior. The measurement of values is an important tool for understanding and explaining consumer behavior (Larsen et al., 1999; Hall and Winchester, 2000b).

The Theoretical Framework

Researchers have always been interested in studying how consumers make decisions because understanding the process underlying consumer behavior is critical to explaining and predicting consumer choice. Consumer decision-making and choice models are researched based on several paradigms such as information processing (Johnson and Puto, 1987), theory of reasoned action (Ajzen and Fishbein, 1999), and multiattribute attitude research linking affective, behavioral, and cognitive components, among others. Although these models are useful, each of them has room for improvement; for example, the information process model does not include a motivational or emotional aspect of consumer decision (Bettman and Sujan, 1987) and the multiattribute attitude does not incorporate choice in the model for predicting behavior (Jaccard, 1981). On the other hand, some researchers have suggested that attitudinal research and information processing should be separate (Sheppard et al., 1988; Bagozzi and Van Loo, 1991), whereas relatively few have attempted to integrate the two (Fishbein, 1980).

For the purpose of this chapter, and for being consistent with the research by Dabholkar (1994), we incorporate choice into the attitudinal framework. Figure 6.1 illustrates this critical aspect of attitude—that is, all three components should be consistent. This means that a change in one attitude component tends to produce related changes in the other components. This is the basis for a substantial amount of marketing strategies (Dabholkar, 1994). The chapter tests specifically the predictive power of the components of the model in determining

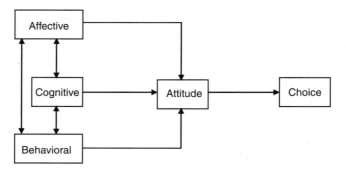

Figure 6.1   The attitude model

choices in a high-involvement situation such as purchasing wine. The general negative attitude of consumers about wine due to cultural reasons makes it appropriate for the study to test the attitude model to predict choice. The next section explains the interrelated components of attitude relating to wine purchasing and formulates a central hypothesis.

The *affective* component is defined as our feelings or emotional reactions to an object. Because wine is associated with negative feelings (because of alcohol content in it), modification of the component is required to change the attitude; for example, pairing an unconditioned stimulus (wine) with a conditioned stimulus (planning a joyous event such as a wedding or a family reunion) would evoke the same response as the conditioned stimulus (Baker, 1999). This type of conditioning is not only limited to low-involvement product but has shown to also directly influence a consumer's choice, especially in the area of brand selection. Therefore, highlighting the perceived positives of wine while detailing the negatives of not choosing wine may produce changes in the other components of attitude, resulting in wine being purchased as the best choice available in the avoidance-avoidance motivational conflict surrounding wine. Indeed, our initial affect to a product may be one of like or dislike without any cognitive basis for the feeling. This initial affect can then influence how we react to the product itself (Zajonc, 1980).

However, an alternative common and effective approach to change attitude is to focus on the *cognitive* component (Smith and Swinyard, 1988). The theory suggests that by influencing beliefs, cognitive interpretation will change. Also, the lower the general knowledge of the product amongst the consumers, the more likely it is that the consumers will follow opinion leaders within their reference group when making product decisions (Venkatraman, 1990). Thus, modifying the cognitive component by providing pertinent facts may be an effective strategy to shift the importance of and beliefs about wine.

The *behavioral* component of attitude is one's tendency to respond in a certain manner toward an object or activity. Therefore, a change in the affective or the cognitive component may not be sufficient to produce a change in the behavioral component unless consumers are willing or have an intention to respond to reflect the changes in their behavior. Purchasing a bottle of wine can be a difficult and daunting task for consumers to respond to and make choices. One of the reasons may be the doubt and anxiety about the fear of making *improper* choice, leading to stress. Therefore, formulating a strategy to reduce cognitive dissonance, after a consumer has responded, could increase the consumers' intention to make an informed choice. Further, reinforcing the belief that wine drinking in moderation is safe will save the consumers from the undue stress caused by societal perception. Drawing from the above discussion, the proposed central hypothesis to be tested is:

H1: Behavioral component is the most significant predictor of consumers' choice, followed by cognitive and affective components.

Methodology

The Attitude Scale and Data Collection

Over a period of one week, data were collected by administering the questionnaire (Appendix) in person to 500 randomly selected wine consumers in a luxury hotel in New Delhi, India. Given the sensitive nature of the study, personal administration of the survey was required. To increase response rate, we kept the questionnaire short and adapted items from Dabholkar's (1994) study to ensure that respondents understood the nature of the components of attitude. The majority of the respondents (96 percent) had no difficulty understanding it. Respondents were asked to distribute 100 points among the three components of the attitude scale and to indicate why they made the choice to purchase a bottle of wine. As mentioned before, respondents had two choices—pleasure or prescription. Respondents who did not purchase wine were not included in the survey. A total of 187 useable questionnaires was obtained, response rate being 38 percent. All respondents were assured of their anonymity.

Selection of the Product (Wine), Respondents, and Sample Characteristics

We approached respondents in a luxury restaurant for the following reasons: first, wine is still an expensive item, so those who could afford to dine in luxury restaurants could presumably also afford to buy wine; secondly, these consumers were thought of as being above the social stigma associated with drinking wine. The sample consisted of approximately 59 percent men and 37 percent women, which is representative of the population. Four percent of the respondents did not mention their age. The average age of respondents in the sample was about 34 years.

Analysis

A t-test indicated no significant differences between men and women, or between various age groups, or on any of the components of attitude. So no distinctions were made between men and women, and between age groups. We used discriminant analysis for the study. This technique is appropriate when the dependent variable is categorical (choice: *pleasure* versus *prescription*) and the independent variables (the three components of the attitude) are metric (Norusis, 1993). The analysis involves deriving the linear combination of the three independent variables (each of the three components of *attitude* was taken as an independent variable) that will discriminate best between the *pleasure* and *prescription* choices. Table 6.2 reports the mean scores and pooled correlation coefficients, whereas table 6.3 reports predictive power of the model. Further, the fact that

Table 6.2   Mean scores and pooled correlation coefficients

Attitude[a]	Means[b]				Structured matrix correlations[c]	F-ratio[d]	p-value[e]
	All	Pleasure group	Prescription group	S.D.			
Behavioral	40.34	37.14	43.52	13.12	.34	8.17	.01
Cognitive	38.40	35.39	41.39	12.81	.29	7.43	.03
Affective	35.31	31.43	39.17	11.71	.25	6.31	.04

Notes:
[a] Attitude components are rank ordered according to size of correlation with function.
[b] Numbers are mean of the three individual components of the Attitude variable.
[c] Pooled within-group correlations of discriminant function and independent variable.
[d] Significant Univariate difference between *pleasure* and *prescription* groups (with d.f. 1 and 179).
[e] p-value for Univariate F-ratio.

Table 6.3   Predictive validity

Actual group total	Predicted group		
	Pleasure group	Prescription group	Actual
Pleasure group	47 (60.25%)	31 (39.74%)	78
Prescription group	25 (22.93%)	84 (77.06%)	109
Predicted total	72	115	187

Note: $(C_{model}(64.57\%) \geq C_{maximum}(61.49\%) \geq C_{proportional}(60.75\%))$.

$Criterion_{model}$ (64.57 percent) $\geq$ $Criterion_{maximum}$ (61.49 percent) $\geq$ $Criterion_{proportional}$ (60.75 percent) suggests that the discriminant model is valid.

Results and Discussion

The results suggest that *behavioral (response tendencies)* $(.34, p < .05)$ is the most significant predictor of choices, followed by, in sequence, *cognitive (beliefs)* $(.29, p < .05)$ and *affective (feelings)* $(.25, p < .05)$. H1 is supported.

It is not surprising that intention to change behavior (response tendencies) is more important than the cognitive and affective components of attitude. However, other factors such as income, alcohol level in wine, and the like may increase the difficulty of changing behavior. It is important that managers highlight benefits associated with wine because the consumers may not be particularly knowledgeable about the positive aspects of wine. Because now Indian consumers have more disposable income, they may ignore the stigma associated with drinking wine and may begin consuming it. Further, the baby boomers' children have left the house and their financial resources that were once needed to pay for their children are now free for spending on expensive items such as wine. However, the ultimate outcome depends on the semantics and tactics of the advertisements that circumvents the social taboo and sensitive nature of the industry. Focusing on lifestyle appeals in advertisements could be effective.

The strategy to modify the *cognitive* component of attitude can be effective if managers try subtly to change consumer beliefs without compromising the strategy by diluting the message advertised. Curiosity generated by advertisements can be effective enough to change consumer beliefs. Generally, to a certain extent, cognitive choices can be mediated by opinion leaders within a reference group of a given consumer group (Venkatraman, 1990). Managers wishing to alter through attitude change the traditional view that discourages wine drinking may find the transformation a slow process, as the attitude is reinforced by several thousand years of social convention and culture prevalent in India.

It was found that the *affective* component was the least predictor of choices. Indeed, an excitement may arise from the thought of drinking wine, as it is a high-involvement product that when purchased requires both financial and emotional decision. Therefore, consumption of wine can involve decisions that could be regretted afterward (economically and emotionally), causing cognitive dissonance. However, the idea of drinking wine can be a good decision too. For example, drinking wine to celebrate success or to socialize can be seen as a celebration of life. Therefore, changing attitudes by changing feelings can be an effective strategy as well.

Like any other study, this study suffers from methodological limitations. Common method bias could not be eliminated because we needed to ask the same respondents their attitude and choices. It may be possible that some of the respondents gave socially desirable answers to the questions asked in the survey. Further, we assumed that the product is viewed as expensive and unwanted by the consumers, and that there is considerable amount of the baby boomer population that may like to drink wine. Finally, findings of the study are based on New Delhi's sample, so the generalization may be restricted to big cities only.

Future research should consider dyadic data to remove the problem of common method bias by capturing judgment from *sales people* and *respondents*. To avoid the problem of intellectually or socially desirable responses, future study should design a questionnaire based on scenarios (for more details, see Eroglu, 1987). Also, it would be interesting to test if self-image moderates or mediates the attitude-choice relationship. By attaching the concept of self-image to wine and by implying that wine enhances social standing, wine will possibly be viewed as more enticing to consumers. Finally, the study should be replicated in some other culture to validate the findings, as different cultures may have different viewpoints toward wine.

Implications for Managers and Conclusion

The objective of the chapter was to ascertain predictive power of the components of attitude in determining choices. Selecting a high-involvement socially taboo product, the findings indicate that the *behavioral* component contributes most to determining consumers' choice, followed by *cognitive* and *affective* components. Intuitively, managers may feel that all the attitude components are equally important, but in practice, it may not be the case. The implication of the study for the managers is that the emphasis should be on assessing intention of consumers to change their behavior (i.e., tendency to respond) rather than on merely trying to change behavior that may have only transitory effects on consumers. Therefore, the study contributes to the literature by providing greater understanding of how consumers make choices about purchasing wine in the Indian context.

The premise of the chapter is based on the fact that consumers are beginning to drink wine. The world is changing, so are lifestyles of consumers. Today's consumers are more informed and, therefore, more knowledgeable about wine. Changes are evident in distribution (retail consolidation), technology (grape harvesting), marketing (market orientation), and lifestyle (Rabobank International, 1999). In fact, informed consumers are able to trade up between price-points to brands and labels that offer superior value. Through these additional segments, managers can design and implement marketing strategies effectively (Smith, 1956). Further, understanding the pattern of the consumer choice process for each segment can contribute to positioning a wine brand and to maximizing profit (Hall and Winchester, 2000a) by achieving efficiencies and effectiveness in advertising and promotion (Dodd and Bigotte, 1997). Although appropriate segmentation can be purposeful and economical, in certain cases, other costs such as manufacturing, research, and promotions can increase as a result of the additional efforts needed to target such segments. Therefore, it is logical for firms to think in terms of the costs and the benefits of increasing the number of segments. Future research should examine the tradeoff between segmentations and revenues. Nonetheless, our findings on the consequences of segmentations on wine consumption do shed some light on Indian consumers' attitude toward wine.

Appendix

1. If you were to make decision to purchase wine, your decision would be based on (please distribute 100 points):
    a. my feelings/emotions/liking/disliking ———
    b. my beliefs/values/religion/tradition ———
    c. my intention to act on the information provided about the service ———
    Total   <u>100</u>

2. If you were to make a choice between a *pleasure* and a *prescription*, you would choose:

      [ ] *pleasure*   [ ] *prescription*

3. My age is about ———years.

4. I am   [ ] male   [ ] female

References

Ajzen, I., and Fishbein, M. *Understanding Attitudes and Predicting Social Behavior*. Englewood-Cliffs, NJ: Prentice-Hall, 1999.

Auger, C., Caporiccio, B., Landrault, N., Teissedre, P.L., Laurent, C., Cros, G., Besançon, P., and Rouanet, J. "Red Wine Phenolic Compounds Reduce Plasma Lipids and Apolipoprotein B and Prevent Early Aortic Atherosclerosis in Hypercholesterolemic Golden Syrian Hamsters (*Mesocricetus auratus*)." *Journal of Nutrition*, 132 (2002): 1207–13.

Bagozzi, R.P., and Van Loo, M.F. "Motivational and Reasoned Processes in the Theory of Consumer Choice." In *Handbook of Behavioral Economics*, ed. Frantz, R., 401–38, Greenwich: JAI Press, 1991.

Baker, W.E. "When Can Affective Conditioning and Mere Exposure Directly Influence Brand Choice?" *Journal of Advertising* 28, no. 4 (1999): 31–46.

Bettman, J.R., and Sujan, M. *Research in Consumer Information Processing*, paper presented at the American Marketing Association, 197–235. Chicago: 1987.

Blackwell, R.D., Miniard, P.W., and Engel, J.F. *Consumer Behavior*. Orlando, FL: Harcourt Brace College Publishers, 2001.

Bruwer, J., Li, E., and Reid, M.J. "Wine-Related Lifestyle Segmentation of the Australian Domestic Wine Market." *Australia New Zealand Wine Industry Journal* 16 (2001): 104–08.

———. "Segmentation of the Australian Wine Market Using a Wine-Related Lifestyle Approach." *Journal of Wine Research* 13, no. 3 (2002): 217–42.

Dabholkar, P. "Incorporating Choice into an Attitudinal Framework: Analyzing Models of Mental Comparison Processes." *Journal of Consumer Research* 21, no. 1 (1994): 100–18.

Dodd, T., and Bigotte, V. "Perceptual Differences among Visitor Groups to Wineries." *Journal of Travel Research* 35, no. 3 (1997): 46–51.

Dubow, J.S. "Occasion-Based vs. User-Based Benefit Segmentation: A Case Study," *Journal of Advertising Research* 32 (March/April 1992): 11–18.

Eroglu, S.A. "The Scenario Method: A Theoretical, Not Theatrical, Approach." In *AMA Summer Educators' Proceedings*, ed. Douglas, S.P., 236, Chicago: American Marketing Association, 1987.

Fishbein, M. "A Theory of Reasoned Action: Some Applications and Implications." In *Nebraska Symposium on Motivation*, ed. Howe, H., Jr., Monte, M., and Lincoln, P. 65–116, Nebraska: University Press, 1980.

Gluckman, R.L. "A Consumer Approach to Branded Wines." *International Journal of Wine Marketing* 2, no. 1 (1990): 27–46.

Gronbaek, M., Deis, A., Sorensen, T., Becker, U., Schnohr, P., and Jensen, G., "Mortality Associated with Moderate Intake of Wine, Beer and Spirit." *British Medical Journal*, 310 (1995): 1165–69.

Grunert, K.G., Brunso, K., and Bisp, S. "Food-Related Lifestyle: Development of a Cross-culturally Valid Instrument for Market Intelligence." In *Values, Lifestyles, and Psychographics*, ed. Kahle, L.R., and Chiagouris, L., 231–46. Mahwah, NJ: Lawrence Erlbaum Associates, 1997.

Hall, J., and Winchester, M. "An Empirical Confirmation of Segments in the Australian Wine Market." *International Journal of Wine Marketing* 11, no. 1 (1999): 19–35.

———. "Focus on Your Customer through Segmentation." *Australia New Zealand Wine Industry Journal* 15 (2000a): 93–96.

———. "What Is Really Driving Wine Consumers?" *Australia New Zealand Wine Industry Journal* 20, no. 5 (2000b): 68–72.

Hall, J., Shaw, M., and Doole, I. "Cross-cultural Analysis of Wine Consumption Motivations." *International Journal of Wine Marketing* 9, no. 2/3 (1997): 83–92.

Howley, M., and Young, N. "Low Alcohol Wines: The Consumers' Choice?" *International Journal of Wine Marketing* 4, no. 3 (1992): 45–56.

Jaccard, J. "Attitudes and Behavior: Implications of Attitudes towards Behavioral Alternatives." *Journal of Experimental Social Psychology* 17 (May 1981): 286–307.

Jennings, D., and Wood, C. "Wine: Achieving Competitive Advantage through Design." *International Journal of Wine Marketing* 6, no. 1 (1994): 49–61.

Johnson, L.W., Ringham, L., and Jurd, K. "Behavioral Segmentation in the Australian Wine Market Using Conjoint Choice Analysis." *International Journal of Wine Marketing* 3, no. 1 (1991): 26–31.

Johnson, M.D., and Puto, C.P. "A Review of Consumer Judgment and Choice." In *Review of Marketing*, ed. Houston, M.J., 236–92. Chicago: American Marketing Association, 1987.

Kotler, P., and Armstrong, G. *Principles of Marketing*. London: Prentice-Hall, 1996.

Larsen, T.B., Poulsen, J.B., and Grunert, K.G., "Acceptance of Functional Foods in Denmark, Finland and the US—a Cross-cultural Study of Consumers' Values and Preferences," proceedings of the Cross-cultural Consumer and Business Studies Research Conference, Mexico, 1999.

Lockshin, L., "Wine Marketing: Science or Fiction?" *Australian & New Zealand Wine Industry Journal* 14, no. 1 (1999): 65–67.

Lockshin, L., Quester, P., and Spawton, T., "Segmentation by Involvement or Nationality for Global Retailing: A Cross-national Comparative Study of Wine Shopping Behaviors." *Journal of Wine Research* 12, no. 3 (2001): 223–36.

Morris, J. "Segment Your Market to Survive." *Communications International* 23 (1996): 131.

Norusis, M.J. *SPSS for Windows Base System Users Guide*. Chicago: SPSS Inc., 1993.

Rabobank International. *The World Wine Business Report. Food and Agribusiness Research*. Utrecht, The Netherlands: Rabobank International, 1999.

Renaud, S., and De Longeril, M. "Heart Disease Mortality and Dairy Fat Consumption." *Lancet* 339 (1992): 1523–26.

Royce, A.P. *Ethnic Identity: Strategies of Diversity*. Bloomington, IN: Indiana University Press, 1982.

Sanchez, M., and Gil, J.M. "Consumer Preferences for Wine Attributes in Different Retail Stores: A Conjoint Approach." *International Journal of Wine Marketing* 10, no. 1 (1998): 25–38.

Sharp, B. "Marketing Orientation: More than Just a Customer Focus." *International Journal of Wine Marketing* 3, no. 1 (1991): 20–25.

Sheppard, B.H., Hartwick, J., and Warshaw, P. "The Theory of Reasoned Action Applied to Coupon Usage." *Journal of Consumer Research* 11 (December 1988): 795–809.

Smith, W.R. "Product Differentiation and Market Segmentation as Alternative Marketing Strategies." *Journal of Marketing* 21 (July 1956): 3–8.

Smith, R.E., and Swinyard, W.R. "Cognitive Response to Advertising and Trial: Beliefs, Confidence and Product Curiosity." *Journal of Advertising* 17, no. 3 (1988): 3–14.

Spawton, A.W., "Grapes and Wine Seminar-Prospering in the 1990s Changing Your View of the Consumer." *International Journal of Wine Marketing* 3, no. 1 (1991): 32–41.

Thomas, A. "Elements Influencing Wine Purchasing: A New Zealand View." *International Journal of Wine Marketing* 12, no. 3 (2000): 47–62.

Venkatraman, M.P. "Opinion Leadership, Enduring Involvement and Characteristics of Opinion Leaders: A Moderating or Mediating Relationship." In *Advances in Consumer Research*, ed. Goldberg, M.E., Gorn, G., and Pollay, R.B., 60–67. Provo, UT: Association for Community Research, 1990.

Wedel, M., and Kamakura, W. *Market Segmentation: Conceptual and Methodological Foundations*. Dordrecht: Kluwer Academic Publisher, 2000.

Whitten, D., and Lipp, M.R. *To Your Health*. New York: Harper Collins West, 1994.

Wollin, S.D., and Jones, P.J.H. "Alcohol, Red Wine and Cardiovascular Disease." *Journal of Nutrition* 131 (2001): 1401–04.

Zajonc, R.B., "Feeling and Thinking: Preferences Need No Inferences." *American Psychologist* (February 1980): 151–75.

Chapter 7

Culture, Creativity, and Advertising

Satyendra Singh
and Kwaku Appiah-Adu

This chapter proposes a comparison of Western and non-Western creative aspects of perfume advertisements. Based on a sample of the Western and the non-Western advertisements, findings suggest that national culture influences creativity of advertisements, and that Western advertisers are creative by using female allure, whereas non-Western advertisers are creative by using graphical designs. One major implication of the study is that managers can no longer rely on female allure when conveying creativity in advertisements in the non-Western culture. Instead, focus of the advertisement should be on the product and its utility only.

Introduction

In today's global environment, the development of advertising campaigns can be a difficult task for marketing products worldwide. The impact of advertising is no longer limited only to creating awareness of products or services, it also communicates—directly or indirectly—norms, judgments, and values that may have a relationship with the product advertised (Andrén et al., 1978). This leads us to an understanding of the cultural differences that is often considered necessary for successful international advertising (Keegan, 1996). The premise is that consumers grow up in a particular culture and become accustomed to that culture's value systems, beliefs, and perception processes. Consequently, consumers respond to advertising messages that are congruent with their culture, rewarding advertisers who understand the culture and tailor advertisements to reflect their values (Boodewyn et al., 1986).

A cross-cultural study of newspapers by Beniger and Westney (1981) found substantial cultural differences in the use of illustrations. Shapes, sizes, and symbols have different meanings and implications in different countries (Cutler and Javalgi, 1992). For example, in South America, advertisers should respect religious symbols and avoid national symbols such as flag colors. In the Middle East, sexual suggestiveness and some forms of physical contact such as kissing are considered offensive and are, therefore, not seen on television, in films, or in public places. Further, there are significant differences in meanings attached to body motions, greetings, colors, and the numbers. What is considered acceptable in one culture may be viewed as antagonistic in another. Even eating some types of foods may be regarded as a taboo in certain countries. For instance, in Arab countries, devout Muslims avoid not only pork products but also any foods that have not been prepared in accordance with the strict rules of Islam; whereas in the Western countries, one might find religious groups (e.g., Mormon Church) that do not consume products containing stimulants such as caffeine. These beliefs may conflict with advertising practices and images portrayed in media (El-Badry, 1994). Because cultural values and religious beliefs may differ from one part of the world to another, different issues and sensitivities need to be taken into consideration while designing advertising strategies for various international markets. For the purpose of this chapter, we follow McCracken's (1988) definition of advertising creative process as the transfer of cultural meaning from expressions to a product.

The foregoing discussion suggests that advertising may have to be adapted to the unique characteristics of local culture. True, while attempts may be made to standardize advertising messages, their execution may not be, as culture invariably dominates communications (Kanso, 1992). For most international advertisers, the tendency is to think globally but act locally. Although global advertising strategies generate efficiency and consistency in their international advertising efforts, copywriters and art directors are responsible for dreaming up creative concepts and crafting the executions that are in line with the local culture and values. The concept may come to mind as a visual, a phrase, or a thought that uses both visual and verbal expression. According to the philosophy of DDB Needham Worldwide, there are three characteristics—relevance, original, and impact—of advertisement that describe creativity in advertising. For the purpose of this study, we have followed the definition of creativity as original and imaginative work designed to produce goal-directed and problem-solving advertisements and commercials (Reid et al., 1998).

The key issues addressed in this study are: how creative directors translate creative themes of advertisements from one culture to another? What happens to the creativity of advertisements during transformation? Does it remain intact? Therefore, an understanding of the cultural differences is needed while communicating to people of diverse cultural backgrounds (Biswas et al., 1992). Creativity is one topic that has received insufficient attention in advertising research (Zinkhan, 1993). Except the analysis of advertising contents and tests of effectiveness of execution (Stewart and Koslow, 1989; Abernethy and Franke, 1996), very few studies relate to advertising creativity or the creativity process (Taylor et al., 1996; Reid et al., 1998). This chapter is designed to examine the effects of culture on the creativity of perfume advertising and to measure the extent to which creative directors are successful in retaining creativity while transforming advertisements from a Western culture to a non-Western culture.

We contribute to the literature by responding to the recommendations of Taylor et al. (1996) for academic researchers to investigate and identify peculiarities in advertising creative process in different cultures. Our knowledge of how advertising operates in other cultures is based on the content analysis of the end product (advertisements) rather than studies of the process itself. Further, Rotzoll and Haefner (1990) observe that advertising (as an institution) must be considered in the light of cultural expectations. Advertising plays different roles in different societies and thus influences how it is created in various cultures. In this chapter, we review cross-culture advertising-related literature, delineate the domain of culture and creativity, develop a methodology, and present analysis. Next, we offer a discussion that alerts managers to important issues involved in modifying creativity of advertisements in a culture. Finally, we construct a typology as a framework for directing future research.

The Culture-Creativity Framework

Literature Review and the Field Perspective

One of the difficulties faced by several firms is whether or not to standardize their advertising campaigns across countries. If a standardized approach is decided, the extent of standardization has to be determined. The proponents of the standardization approach emphasize that people around the world share the same basic needs and motivations, so standardization will yield benefits such as consistency in image and improved advertising quality (Levitt, 1983; Hammonds, 1990). However, the opponents of standardization contend that the universal approach to advertising is difficult because cultural and national differences exist among nations (Miracle, 1996; Goldman, 1992). Further, Lantos (1987) suggests that national cultural differences influence advertising practices and, therefore, it is reasonable to presume that influences should be observed at the component level of individual advertisements. For example, advertisements designed in the Western culture where nudity is a norm and widely accepted by the society may not be acceptable in the Islamic culture where due to cultural influences and religious norms, women must be fully clothed at all times in public. Hence, international print advertisements may have to be modified by superimposing long dresses on models or by shading their legs. Advertisers of cosmetics in Saudi Arabia refrain from picturing sensuous females; instead, they use drawings of women's faces in advertisements (Katz, 1986). In a typical advertisement, a pleasant-looking woman may appear in a robe with only her face showing (Luqmani et al., 1987). In some conservative Islamic countries, many religious authorities are opposed to advertising on the grounds that it promotes Western icons and non-Islamic consumerism (Al-Makaty et al., 1996).

The practicality and use of global advertising standardization has been quite controversial (Jain, 1989; Hammonds, 1990). Supporters of standardized advertising propose that the globe is becoming increasingly homogeneous in terms of needs and wants. Examples of standardization of advertising and the assumption of consumer homogeneity are common in the advertising industry and have sometimes led to disappointing results (Winski and Wentz, 1986). Some researchers have debated the issue of standardized advertising and consumer homogeneity. In fact, the standardized school questions the traditional belief in the heterogeneity of the market and the importance of localized approach. This school of thought assumes that better and faster communication has forged a convergence of art, literature, media availability, tastes, thoughts, religious beliefs, culture, living conditions, language and, therefore, advertising. Even when people are different, their physiological and psychological needs are still presumed to be the same (Onkvisit and Shaw, 1989).

Although standardization of advertisements may be applicable to certain product categories such as high-tech products or services (Hassan and Katsansis, 1991), it may not be applicable to other categories such as perfume advertising in the Middle East countries where public display of female allure is culturally almost unacceptable. A Western creative director of a multinational advertising agency in the United Kingdom said, "Islam is a part of everyday life and you have to be aware of that. You have to take it into consideration because there are certain sensitivities. There are things you cannot show. There are things you cannot say." Another Western director based in Dubai echoed the same sentiments,

> Perfume advertisements that are run in UAE are mostly just a pack of shots; that is, pictures of bottle of perfume. They [advertisers who create the advertisements for different parts of the world] do not run that kind of dry stuff in the West. What they do is just show us the pack. The advertisement is a pack-shot with a name, and that is very dull. There is no creativity.

On the contrary, an art director of a leading advertising agency in Dubai, who was critical of his Western directors' statements, commented,

> I agree that culture has its limitations in terms of what you can show and what you cannot. But the Western creative directors are not doing their jobs because they cannot come up with anything. What is sent from the principals [other companies that create the advertisements for them] is just being strapped up. Is this being creative? This is like totally giving up. Everybody has limitations, but you have to work within those limitations. Do you think that you can only communicate fragrances if you put sex in the middle? I guess that you are dead wrong.

Therefore, creative directors have to come up with different creative themes that are consistent with local social values and culture. Then, the question is as to what extent Arabic directors adapt Western-style advertisements to their culture without losing the original creativity. Based on the literature reviews and field perspectives, we advance the following proposition:

Adaptation of advertisements from one culture to another alters creativity of advertisements

Methodology

Using triangulation methodology, we examined four pairs of print advertisements of perfumes from the UK and UAE magazines. This method requires the use of multiple sources of data (Miles and Huberman, 1984), aids in the elimination of bias, and allows for plausible explanations (Denzin, 1978). The chapter focuses on illustrating pictorially creativity from across these cultures by studying equivalent advertisements. We used a combination of survey and interview techniques to explore the fundamental message of the advertisements being compared, because both the knowledge of the intention of the advertiser and research into the consumers' understanding of each advertisement were required before any valid comparison could be drawn.

Selection of Countries

We selected UAE, an Islamic country with a population of 2.8 million people. Dubai is one of the largest cities in the UAE and is considered to be the advertising capital of the Middle East. We assume that UAE is a fair representative of the Middle East culture (non-Western culture). Further, international advertising agencies such as Saatchi and Saatchi, and Lintas have independent offices in Dubai, whereas DDB Needham Worldwide, Bozell, BBDO, Dentsu, DMB&B, and Leo Burnett operate as partners in franchise tie-ups with local agencies TD&A, Prime, Impact, Publi-graphics, Tamra, and Radius, respectively. Dubai is also a cosmopolitan emirate with liberal values and a high tolerance for different lifestyles, even though its culture is still firmly rooted in the Islamic Arabic tradition. Oil revenues have given UAE one of the highest per capita GNPs in the world, which places the country at par with Western countries in terms of liberal lifestyles. UAE has been selected by some of the researchers for similar studies in the Middle East (Al-Olayan and Karande, 2000). On the other hand, our choice of the United Kingdom was based on the following two reasons: (1) it may be considered as a fair representative of Western culture; and (2) most of the franchisees in the UAE have their principals in the United Kingdom. Therefore, respondents were aware of the difficulties associated with the transformation of British advertisements to suit the Arabic culture.

Selection of the Product—Perfume Advertisements

To test whether creativity is altered across cultures, we used perfume advertisements for two reasons: first, creative themes of perfume advertisements may not be well accepted in Arabic culture; and second, unlike other advertisements that could demonstrate product benefits, the creative style of perfume advertising is basically image-oriented, and images cannot show fragrances—they can only attempt to suggest what happens if one does smell good. Advertisers cannot make an intellectual appeal about perfumes, so they have to generate different kinds of creativity to entice customers.

Selection of Magazines, Advertisements, and Respondents

For our analysis, we selected advertisements from women's magazines in the United Kingdom and UAE that appeared to be equivalent in both countries. An initial point of comparison was whether the advertisements in both countries shared a common picture. Keeping this criterion in mind, four matched-pairs of advertisements (two containing models and the rest otherwise) were randomly selected from the following magazines: Marie Claire (UK), Vogue (UK), Zeina (Arabic), and Osrati (Arabic). These magazines were recommended by respondents for their high circulation and their suitability to carry perfume advertisements to target young readers. No attempts were made to match the subject topics or the circulation numbers between the two sets of the magazines. A recent study found that readership in Arabic countries was relatively high due to large family sizes (Al-Olayan and Karande, 2000). During the pretesting of the picture-based questionnaire, four pairs of advertisements were considered adequate by a pool of nine creative directors (five from the United Kingdom and four from the UAE). For the purpose of cross-cultural examination of advertisements, Middle East Association of London and International Advertising Association (UAE chapter) were contacted for the list of advertising agencies (SIC Code 7311) that operated in both countries. Further, the advertising agencies listed in the *Advertisers' Guide to the Middle East* were also consulted to contact agencies in the UAE. Forty agencies in the United Kingdom and UAE were contacted over the telephone soliciting them to grant a short interview, so the interviewers could approach them with the picture-based questionnaire for a brief interview. Each participant was promised confidentiality. Respondents in both countries were asked to circle a number on a seven-point scale to indicate the extent to which they agreed that there was a loss of creativity during transformation of advertisements. On the Likert-type scale one represented no loss in creativity, whereas seven meant a significant loss. A total of sixty-five usable questionnaires (thirty-two from British respondents and thirty-three from Arabic respondents) were obtained. Eight agencies in the United Kingdom and seven in the UAE declined to participate in the study. The major reason for declining the interview was the lack of time to participate in the study. A total response rate of almost 81 percent was achieved. The characteristics of the sample are presented in table 7.1.

Results

A paired t-test was conducted to ascertain differences between the two sets of responses on the four pairs of pictures. Table 7.2 reveals significant differences between the perceptions of British and Arabic managers about loss of creativity during transformation of advertisements. The British respondents scored significantly higher (score of over five versus below 4.5) than their counterparts on pictures 1, 2, and 3. The results of the analysis indicated that the British respondents believed that creativity was lost during the adaptation process of the advertisements, whereas their counterparts disagreed. Both British and Arabic managers agreed that picture 4 had a little distortion of creativity.

Table 7.1 Characteristics of the sample

Position	No. (United Kingdom)	Turnover (UK)	No. (UAE)	Turnover (UAE)
Creative directors	11	>£10m	12	>£10m (equivalent)
Research managers	14	£4.9m–£9.9m	11	£4.9m–£9.9m
Copywriters/ artists	7	<£5m	10	<£5m
Total	32		33	

Table 7.2 Means, standard deviations, and t-values

Matched-pictures	Mean (S.D) United Kingdom	Mean (S.D) UAE	t-values
Picture 1	5.82 (.78)	4.35 (.67)	3.82*
Picture 2	5.65 (.65)	4.23 (.58)	3.75*
Picture 3	5.11 (.54)	4.27 (.63)	3.63*
Picture 4	4.25 (.67)	4.17 (.74)	n/s

Note: *p < .05.

Discussion

Picture 1 shows the advertisements for the Guy Laroche perfume Drakkar Noir in the United Kingdom and the UAE. The original advertisement (UK) depicted a woman's hand holding the wrist of a man's nude hand clenching a bottle of cologne. The UAE version of the advertisement showed the man's forearm covered by the jacket of a suit with only the cuff of the shirt showing, the woman's hand lightly touching his hand with one of her fingers. The creative theme of the advertisement was to communicate masculinity by the display of his wrist size, and to demonstrate the man's support for the woman by showing her clinging to the man's wrist, suggesting that she feels secure by holding his arm. According to the British respondents, the creative theme was altered in the UAE version of the original advertisement. However, Arabic managers believed that by covering the arm of the model in the advertisement and by letting a finger touch his hand, they were successful in conveying the same meaning symbolically. One Arabic respondent questioned, "Why do you need to hold his hand? I do not see any creativity in holding a hand as a result of application of the perfume. This is ridiculous; full stop."

Clearly, all efforts in the Arabic advertisement are geared toward reducing the exposure of the human flesh, be it male or female models. In addition, the contact between the male and the female is made less intimate. This is not surprising because it is inconsistent with the Arabic culture of minimizing contacts between men and women in public. This culture also prohibits depicting images that may be perceived as conveying sexual innuendos or promoting promiscuity.

While the UK advertisement is quite explicit in its appearance, the UAE advertisement is altered to suit the culture. Both advertisements are appropriate to the culture of their respective target audience and are attractive enough to market the product effectively. This approach

Picture 1 (United Kingdom)   Picture 1 (UAE)

Picture 2 (United Kingdom)   Picture 2 (UAE)

demonstrates the significance of culture in achieving advertising effectiveness through creativity and, thus, high levels of sales in the consumer marketing.

Pictures 2 and 3 reveal that the British advertisements had a feminine allure, whereas the translated version of these advertisements had almost no allure component, no facial expression, and no bare body. The creative theme developed in the original advertisements by injecting feminine allure as a persuasive element almost vanished in the translated version. A British respondent said, "As there is little creativity involved in the preparation of such advertisements, all advertising agencies have to do is: put the agent's name below the advertisements which they have received from their principals, translate the text into Arabic language, and run these advertisements in the local media." In fact, the lack of creativity is the reason why advertising agencies in the UAE receive only half the commission from advertisers compared to the commission they would receive for original advertisements.

However, an Arabic art director did not agree with the above statement, and said,

> Look, a feminine allure can be dressed up in any way you want; sex is not necessary. I will give you an example: The attention can be drawn toward a veil-clad woman because the veil draws the eyes of the

audience into the eyes of the model, and the skin around the eyes aids communication between the product and the model. Is it not being creative? Certainly, it is.

Indeed, exposure of the female body is severely restricted in the Arabian culture. On the contrary, in the Western world, nudity is not seriously frowned upon. As a result, advertisements show sensitive parts of models with a view to attract readers and sell products. Indeed, advertisements in the two cultures have been given different creative themes to achieve the desired effects.

Further, regulatory authorities in both cultures have their own standards regarding what is acceptable in advertisements and what is not. Therefore, an advertisement that may pass the screening test in the Western world is not likely to past the decency test in the UAE. Advertisers should take into account public reaction or response to images that are used in the creative themes. A public backlash is likely if an advertising agency exceeds "acceptable decency thresholds" in a particular culture. The end result may be twofold: first, complaints may be made to the authorities who are then likely to act under pressure; second, any negative sentiments could result in a mass boycott of the goods being promoted—both of which could be catastrophic for the advertiser and the agency. Thus, it is better to be safe than sorry.

Picture 3 (United Kingdom)   Picture 3 (UAE)

Picture 4 (United Kingdom)   Picture 4 (UAE)

The above considerations are possible reasons for the UK and UAE advertisements to have different creative themes.

Picture 4 convinced both sets of respondents that the UAE version of the advertisement was as good as the UK advertisement. The difference in creative themes between the two versions of for advertisement 1 (UK and UAE) is moderate, whereas the differences in advertisements 2 and 3 are quite considerable. However, in advertisement 4, the difference in creativity is marginal. It is therefore not surprising that respondents of this study indicated that the UK advertisement was as good as the UAE version.

The interesting issue about this particular advertisement is that female allure was utilized for both countries but the level of body exposure in the UAE advertisement was far less compared to that in the original UK advertisement. Hence, with a slight modification in the creative theme, an almost identical image was developed for the UAE market. This approach is closer to the standardization strategy. Despite what different schools of thought may dictate about the pros and cons of the standardization approach, a slight adaptation of the creative theme used in this instance (closer to standardization) appears to have had an effective impact in both the UK and UAE cultures. This said, it is a matter of choice for both advertisers and agencies as to which approach to adopt—standardization or differentiation—to select creative themes for different cultures. The final choice will depend on a number of factors—these include the audience or target market, type of product or service, prevailing influences on the nation's culture, cost considerations, and other pertinent factors that will be uncovered during the pretest stage of the advertising research process.

Recommendations

The appearance of women in advertising, designed for the Arab market, is difficult to recommend. Because Arabic culture emphasizes the shielding of women from men's eyes, even the placement of Arab-looking female models in advertisements shown in the UAE may be a risky strategy (picture 4). It would be a prudent policy to limit the portrayal of females in advertisements that are developed for the Arab market, because even the slightest oversight could backfire on the advertisers. For example, there once was a tremendous row over an advertisement showing Omar Sharif, a famous Egyptian actor, with a woman, because she wore a ring but he did not. The advertisement was not well received because it was considered improper for a married woman to be closely associated with an unmarried man.

Second, a women's role in an advertisement should be contemplated, only if there is a direct relation between the product and the women's use of it. Even then, there could be a number of restrictions, for example, lipstick manufacturers are not allowed to show their products on a lady's lips, a woman cannot be shown alone with a man in an advertisement—a child should be present and the woman's head has to be covered. Advertisers are also forbidden to show immodest exposure or to use women as sexual symbols. Also, some of these restrictions are applied on the basis of the subjective interpretation of authorities, so it is difficult to predict what would be acceptable when women are shown in advertisements. Most advertisers learn to comply with these strict rules regarding women in advertising or else turn to using male models in roles that would typically be played by female models in Western advertising.

It was also learnt during the interviews with the respondents that magazines imported to the UAE are censored on arrival for any material considered vulgar, obscene, or politically sensitive. For example, an advertisement for butter, in the German magazine *Archives*, showed cows lying around in fields, resting on their elbows; the creative theme was used to put across the message that "cows that are content make better butter." When the magazines arrived in the UAE, the censors had blackened the mammals. This indicates the extent to which messages conveyed through creative themes could be lost in the Arab market as a result of cultural differences.

Implications for Managers

This study has implications for managers. When a female model is being used to advertise perfumes in the UAE, the focus of the advertisement should be on the product and its utility. Use of female allure to attract readers should be avoided, even if machismo and feminine allure are relevant to almost every culture. It is important to acknowledge the cultural subtleties and allow those kinds of latitudes that accept cultural differences. Generally, it is of paramount importance that advertisers be sensitive to the cultural implications of their creative strategies. In this regard, advertising and marketing practitioners need to appreciate individual country differences; for example, historical values and religious practices may serve to form customer impressions and perceptions about advertising. In general, creative directors cannot apply universal standards of perfume advertisement to the UAE market.

Limitations

Although complexities in this cross-cultural research, including difficulties in comparing culture and language problems were, controlled, it may be possible that responses from the respondents of this study contained some bias. For example, respondents' responses on a Likert-type scale are subjective. Further, some respondents, in order to protect their cultural values and norms, might have scored low on the scale. Finally, the collection of advertisements was limited to print media. This choice was appropriate because these magazines were the dominant and most widespread media in UAE for perfume advertisements. In spite of these limitations, the results will be beneficial in assisting advertising agencies in the development of creativity in advertisements. Because this study examined only perfume products with limited pictures and utilized a relatively small sample size due to time and financial constraints, the results of the study should be interpreted in the light of these limitations.

Future Research Directions

During the interviews with the creative directors in both countries, it became apparent that Western creative directors held the view that

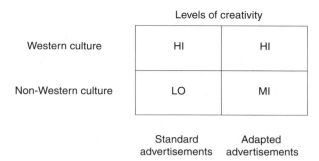

Figure 7.1   The Typology: Culture versus creativity

Note: LO, MI, and HI stand for low, medium, and high, respectively.

perfume advertising could be communicated well through creating glamour, whereas their Arabic counterparts believed that creativity in perfume advertising could also be communicated by using digital graphics. Therefore, it would be interesting to investigate whether creativity in perfume advertising can be effectively expressed by the use of graphics, as opposed to the show of female allure.

Although this study has provided additional insight into creativity and cultural issues in the Arab culture, replication of this study in other emerging markets would increase our understanding of creativity in advertising across a wider range of cultures and thus provide a broader perspective on the role of culture in moderating the creative effects of advertising.

Finally, combining the concept of culture and creativity, we propose a typology in figure 7.1 of four conditions that indicates levels of creativity under certain combinations. Future research should test the typology empirically by using the median split method and comparing them using analysis of variance.

Conclusion

This study examines creativity in advertisements in two international settings, demonstrates the creative process relevant to general societal values and beliefs and supports the proposition that the creative process of advertising is influenced by culture. Therefore, McCracken's (1988) cultural definition of the advertising creative process as the transfer of cultural meaning from expressions to a product is correct, at least in the Arab culture.

Further, the findings suggested that the British creative directors encountered cultural limitations as impediments to the creative process of perfume advertising in the UAE. Although there may be creative talents in the UAE, advertisements for most of the major brands of perfumes are brought from the Western countries. Only a few advertisements are made in the UAE. Creative directors based in the UAE should consider local cultural values when conceiving ideas for advertising, even if there is little room to maneuver in the area of creativity. The message of perfume advertising is like selling a sort of illusion of style and glamour, so it may be difficult to conceive an idea that sells glamour without showing glamour. These cultural limitations may hamper the creative process of advertising. Indeed, machismo, femininity, and feminine allure may not be always displayed in the advertisement. All these sensitivities, censors, and perceptions of the target audience may impede the creative process of advertising in the UAE.

Acknowledgments

The authors would like to thank Aziz Merchant and Abdul Khan for selecting the advertisements, collecting data, and interviewing the respondents.

References

Abernethy, A.M., and Franke, G.R. "The Information Content of Advertising: A Meta Analysis." *The Journal of Advertising* 25, no. 2 (1996): 1–17.

Al-Makaty, S.S., Norman van Tubergen, G., Whitlow, S.S., and Boyd, D.A. "Attitudes towards Advertising in Islam." *Journal of Advertising Research* 36, no. 3 (1996): 16–26.

Al-Olayan, F.S., and Karande, K. "A Content Analysis of Magazine Advertisements from the United States and the Arab World." *Journal of Advertising* 29, no. 3 (2000): 69–82.

Andrén, G., Ericsson, O., Ohlsson, R., and Tannsjo, T. *Rhetoric and Ideology.* New York: Advertising, 1978.

Beniger, J.R., and Westney, D.E. "Japanese and US Media: Graphics as a Reflection of Newspaper' Social Role." *Journal of Communication* 31, no. 4 (1981): 28–36.

Biswas, A., Olsen, J., and Carlet, V. "A Comparison of Print Advertising from the United States and France." *Journal of Advertising* 21, no. 4 (1992): 1–13.

Boodewyn, J., Soehl, R., and Picard, J. "Standardization in International Marketing: Is Ted Levitt in Fact Right?" *Business Horizon* 29 (November/December 1986): 69–75.

Cutler, B.D., and Javalgi, R.G. "A Cross-cultural Analysis of the Visual Components of Print Advertising: The US and the European Community." *Journal of Advertising Research* 32, no. 1 (1992): 71–80.

Denzin, N.K. *Sociological Methods: A Source Book*. New York: McGraw-Hill, 1978.

El-Badry, S. "Understanding Islam in America." *American Demographics* (January 1994): 10.

Goldman, K. "Professor Who Started Debate on Global Ads Still Backs Theory." *The Wall Street Journal* (October 1992), B8.

Hammonds, K.H. "Ted Levitt Is Back in the Trenches." *Business Week* 9 (April 1990), 82–84.

Hassan, S.S., and Katsansis, L.P. "Identification of Global Consumer Segments: A Behavioural Framework." *Journal of International Consumer Marketing* 3, no. 2 (1991): 11–28.

Jain, S.C. "Standardization of International Marketing Strategy: Some Research Hypotheses." *Journal of Marketing* 53, no. 1 (1989): 70–79.

Kanso, A. "International Advertising Strategies of Multinational Corporations: Global Commitment to Local Vision." *Journal of Advertising Research* 32, no. 1 (1992): 10–14.

Katz, M. "No Women, No Alcohol: Learn Saudi Taboos Before Placing Ads." *International Advertiser* (February 1986): 11–12.

Keegan, W.J. *Global Marketing Management*. New York: Prentice-Hall, 1996.

Lantos, G.P. "Advertising: Looking Glass or Moulder of the Masses?" *Journal of Public Policy and Marketing* 6, no. 1 (1987): 104–27.

Levitt, T. "The Globalisation of Markets." *Harvard Business Review* 61, no. 3 (1983): 92–102.

Luqmani, M., Yavas, Y., and Quraeshi, Z. "Advertising in Saudi Arabia: Content and Regulation." *International Marketing Review* 6, no. 1 (1987): 59–72.

McCracken, G. "Culture and Consumption: A Theoretical Account of the Structure and Movement of the Cultural Meaning of Consumer Goods." *Journal of Consumer Research* 13, no. 1 (1988): 71–84.

Miles, M.B., and Huberman, A.M. *Qualitative Data Analysis*. London: Sage Publications, 1984.

Miracle, G.E. *Communication with Foreign Consumers*. Miami: Bureau of Business Research, University of Michigan, 1996.

Onkvisit, S., and Shaw, J.J. *International Marketing: Analysis and Strategy*. New York: Merrill Publishing Company, 1989.

Reid, L., Karen, N., King, W., and Delong, D.E. "Top-Level Agency Creatives Look at Advertising Creativity Then and Now." *Journal of Advertising* 27, no. 2 (1998): 1–15.

Rotzoll, K., and Haefner, J. *Advertising in Contemporary Society*. New York: South-Western, 1990.

Stewart, D.W., and Koslow, S. "Executional Factors and Advertising Effectiveness: A Replication." *Journal of Advertising* 18, no. 3 (1989): 21–32.

Taylor, R., Hoy, M., and Haley, E. "How French Advertising Professionals Develop Creative Strategies?" *Journal of Advertising* 25, no. 1 (1996): 1–13.

Winski, J.M., and Wentz, L. "Parker Pen: What Went Wrong? Why Company Global Marketing Plan Founded." *Advertising Age* 2 (June 1986): 60–61.

Zinkhan, G.M. "Creativity in Advertising: Creativity in the Journal of Advertising." *Journal of Advertising* 22, no. 2 (1993): 1–3.

Part IV

Emerging Business Practices

Chapter 8

The Current Marketing Practices in Ghana

Kwaku Appiah-Adu and
Satyendra Singh

The purpose of this study is to conduct an empirical investigation into the differences between the marketing orientation of foreign and domestic manufacturing firms in Ghana. Specifically, an attempt was made to determine the marketing functions and to distinguish between the actual performance of marketing activities in the firms selected. Data was obtained from 79 companies representing local and foreign firms in eight foreign countries spread across Europe, North America, and Asia. Our analysis indicates that, on the whole, foreign firms perceive marketing functions as more important and tend to perform more marketing activities compared with domestic firms. Managerial implications of our findings and study limitations are discussed alongside future research directions.

Introduction

In the last decade, considerable scholarly attention has focused on marketing in developing countries (Dadzie et al., 1988; Okoraofo, 1996; Appiah-Adu, 1997). Although some of these studies have been based on the applicability of marketing concepts in developing markets (Samli and Kaynak, 1984; Maholtra, 1986; Akaah and Riordan, 1988), other scholars examine the general impact of economic reform on marketing practices of firms operating in developing economies (Steel and Webster, 1992; Okoroafo and Kotabe, 1993). Yet another strand of research has addressed the impact of marketing activities upon performance in these liberalized environments (Okoroafo and Russow, 1993; Okoroafo and Torkonoo, 1995).

The increased academic and practitioner interest in the marketing concept and its implementation stems from the important contribution of marketing to the survival and sustained growth of many organizations in today's fiercely competitive business environment. Moreover, scholars argue that marketing is becoming increasingly relevant to several developing nations as they liberalize their economies and move toward a free market system. Given the importance of and interest in the marketing practices of firms operating in developing nations, particularly in economic reform countries, the objective of this study is to conduct an investigation into the differences between the perceived importance and performance of marketing activities in foreign and domestic firms operating in Ghana. Ghana was selected for this study because it was among the first sub-Sahara African countries to subscribe to the international Monetary Fund's (IMF) structural adjustment program (SAP) and is considered by IMF and World Bank experts as a model of success in the Third World (*West Africa Magazine*, 1995). The rest of this paper is organized as follows. First, a background of the study is provided. Second, a literature review is conducted, followed by the hypothesis development and methodology sections. Then, the results are reported and discussed. Next, implications of the findings for foreign and domestic managers are addressed. Finally, limitations of the study are highlighted alongside suggestions for future research directions.

Background to the Study

Ghana has a population of 15.9 m, a GDP of $6970 (Ghana Budget, 1998). The country has been cited by economic analysts as a role model of success in Africa because of the growth rates that have been achieved by pursuing the IMF's SAP and the subsequent nurturing of a free market economy. Like many other transition developing markets, Ghana has sought to transform its economy through an Economic Recovery Program (ERP). This evolution began in 1983 and comprised reform policies aimed at expanding the private sector, particularly through export-oriented initiatives. These new policies, which are outlined in the next section, have transformed the business environments in which many firms operate.

Structural Adjustment Program

The major policies of the SAP include reforms in foreign exchange regulations to reflect the real value of the currency (Cedi) and the abolition of foreign exchange restrictions to make the availability of foreign currencies more widespread. In addition, reforms have been instituted to encourage investments with the introduction of a wide range of incentives introduced to attract foreign investors into the country. Further, business policies have been amended to foster trade liberalization and export promotion. Finally, other reforms include the relaxation of price controls, privatization of state-owned enterprises, and improvement in food and agricultural production. Of all the various reform mechanisms, those that have had the most significant impact on the marketing activities of firms are the financial, trade, and investment policy.

Literature Review

Marketing Orientation

In this chapter, marketing orientation reflects the perceived importance and performance of activities that focus on product, price, promotion, and distribution (McCarthy and Perrault, 1993). The main objective of marketing activities is to understand and satisfy customer needs and this is realized when all elements of the marketing system (i.e., suppliers and distributors) are working together effectively. In addition to the conventional 4Ps (product, price, promotion, and place), this research incorporates another dimension of marketing—customer orientation—into its definition of marketing orientation, since the customer is central to the definition of marketing orientation and all marketing efforts. A firm's level of marketing orientation is a measure of the perceived importance of the five dimensions of marketing mentioned above and its actual performance of these activities.

Pre-SAP Market Conditions and Practices

Like many other developing countries, Ghana was not attractive for direct investments due to environmental conditions characterized by rigid trade barriers, high inflation rates, poor growth, inadequate communications, substandard infrastructure, and high political risk. These sentiments are confirmed in a study of several *Fortune 500* firms that suggests that factors such as soaring inflation, government bureaucracy, poor communications, and changing business laws served as obstacles to investments in the developing world (Elsaid and El-Hennawi, 1982). Moreover, as in other Third World nations, performance of marketing activities in these conditions were limited and highly constrained at the firm level (Samli and Kaynak, 1984). This stemmed from the fact that products were manufactured and sold regardless of compatibility with customer needs. Market research and promotion were difficult to undertake because disclosure of information to the general public was rigorously vetted and pricing of goods was generally dependant upon government regulations. Thus, the marketing concept might have been accepted in theory but its practice was limited.

Emerging Marketing Practices in the Post-SAP Environment

The SAP, with its concomitant free market policies, has given rise to a steadily evolving buyers' economy in which sellers compete for the custom of purchasers. Hence, the portrayal of developing countries as oligopolistic sellers' markets may not be typical of transitional developing economies. It is expected that organizations will make marketing decisions in the context of their domestic and international environments. Empirical evidence (Dadzie et al., 1988) suggests that the new environment has led to increased performance of marketing activities. It has also been found that small firms in Ghana are becoming more innovative in order to survive, especially in conditions marked by weak demand, low-cost competing imports, and escalating operating costs (Steel and Webster, 1992).

With Ghana's gradual shift toward a buyers' economy, it is expected that firms will begin to conduct marketing activities that focus on customer satisfaction, hence, marketing decisions involving research and development, pricing policy, promotional budgets, media selection, personal selling, and the like, will place more emphasis on quality via better manufacturing processes, improvements to satisfy customer preferences, and new product development in response to customers' evolving requirements. To gain an edge over competitors, firms will seek to become price competitive, focus on sound logistical practices, and work closely with intermediaries. Distribution activities will be performed efficiently to provide the customer with the required goods at the right time and place, while promotional efforts will take into account customer attitudes and benefits.

Hypotheses Development

Marketing Orientation of Domestic and Foreign Firms

In discussing the similarities and differences between the marketing orientation of domestic and foreign companies and for the purpose of hypotheses testing, we draw upon evidence established in prior research. Studies conducted during the early 1980s suggest that marketing activities were not adequately practiced (Samli and Kaynak, 1984; Mitchell and Agenmonmen, 1984) in most developing countries.

However, by the latter part of the same decade, the picture had begun to change, with empirical findings reporting an increase in the incidence and regularity of marketing principles in a gradually evolving buyers' market instead of a sellers' economy (Akaah and Riordan, 1988; Dadzie et al., 1988). Research that specifically examined the marketing activities of domestic and foreign organizations identified differences in their practices (e.g., Chong, 1973; Akaah and Riordan, 1988), with foreign firms outperforming their domestic counterparts in most areas. Although a similar and more recent effort by Okoroafo (1996) revealed an improvement in the marketing activities of domestic firms in Nigeria's reformed economy, foreign companies were still found to be ahead. As noted earlier, foreign organizations tend to emphasize customer service and superior product and quality package delivery. Their products are characterized by distinguishable brand names and they follow practices that have been tried, tested, and refined in their home markets. In addition, foreign managers are well versed in competitive marketing strategies due to the experience gained in their home markets. Hence, it is expected that foreign executives will have a relatively greater perception of the importance of marketing and will generally perform more marketing activities than domestic managers. This leads to the main hypothesis for this study:

H1: Foreign manufacturing firms operating in Ghana will perceive marketing activities to be more important than their domestic counterparts.

H2: Foreign manufacturing firms are more likely to perform marketing activities than their domestic counterparts.

Research Design

Survey Administration

The sample for this study comprised 200 domestic and foreign manufacturing organizations operating in Ghana. Local firms represented approximately 62 percent of the sample and the remaining 38 percent were foreign businesses with parent companies headquartered in North America, Europe, and Asia. Foreign firms were defined as those with some proportion of ownership overseas. The organizations were compiled from the *Ghana Business Directory* (1996). Data for this research were generated using self-administering questionnaires, following pretests with a group of business executives in Ghana. After completing final revisions to the pilot instrument, a questionnaire, a covering letter, and a reply-paid envelope were posted to chief executive officers (CEOs) of the sample firms and follow-up mails were sent a month later to those who did not respond to the initial survey. The items employed in the questionnaire were based on a seven-point Likert-type scale. From the first and second waves of mailing, 62 and 20 responses respectively were received. A total response of 82 was obtained but three were rejected due to missing key items, providing 79 usable questionnaires, which represented a response rate of 39.5 percent. An analysis of the results of early and late respondents was conducted to test for nonresponse bias. A series of chi square tests indicated no significant differences between the two sets of respondents (Armstrong and Overton, 1977) on any of the measures analyzed (e.g., consumer products versus industrial products, $X^2 = 0.81$, $p > 0.05$; Ghanaian and non-Ghanaian firms, $X^2 = 0.075$, $p > 0.05$).

Characteristics of Respondent Firms

Approximately half of the respondents (51.90 percent) were domestic firms. The remainder comprised foreign firms with headquarters in the United States (12.66 percent), United Kingdom (18.99 percent), Germany (6.33 percent), France (3.80 percent), South Korea (2.53 percent), Switzerland (1.26 percent), Netherlands (1.26 percent) and Sweden (1.26 percent). Most firms (75.95 percent) had an annual sales turnover equivalent of at least $4 million. The combined respondent sample for both domestic and foreign companies represented a wide spectrum of businesses, including manufacturers of food, pharmaceuticals, beverages, chemicals, metals, and industrial equipment. Those offering durable and nondurable consumer products accounted for 69.62 percent of the respondent firms, while industrial product manufacturers were represented by 30.38 percent. The mean age of all organizations was 12.1 years and the average size, based on number of staff, was approximately 198. About 87 percent of the firms employed between 100 to 1000 employees, and thus the majority of firms could be classified as large businesses (c.f., Liedholm and Mead, 1987; Okoroafo and Russow, 1993).

Operationalization of Measures

The marketing orientation measure was designed to reflect the fundamentals of the marketing concept. Hence, the four marketing Ps (product, price, promotion, and place) proposed by McCarthy and Perrault (1993) were included. In addition, important activities associated with the marketing function in transition economies such as market research (Okoroafo, 1996), customer service, and customer satisfaction programs (Golden et al., 1995) were also employed. To assess the perceived importance and performance of marketing, executives were asked to provide responses pertaining to the perceived importance of product, pricing, promotion, distribution, and customer orientation activities as well as of the actual performance of these functions on a seven-point Likert-type scale (1 = not at all important or not performed at all to 7 = very important or performed extensively).

Results and Discussion

Perceived Importance of Marketing Activities

The mean values for perceived importance of marketing activities are exhibited in table 8.1. All mean scores are statistically at the 0.05 level. For the purposes of interpretation, items with means higher than the midpoint value of four represent perceived importance of an activity while items scoring less than four denote perceived nonimportance.

Standard deviations signify the level of consensus around the mean. The difference between perceived importance in foreign and domestic firms was found to be statistically significant at the 0.05 level. On product-related activities, foreign executives tend to have a higher perception of the importance of product quality while domestic managers view product improvement and new product development as important activities. This may be due to the renewed zest among domestic managers to catch up on modifications and new developments that are long overdue. Additionally, foreign managers perceive pricing as a very important activity compared with their domestic counterparts who do not appear to have a high perception of the importance of pricing activities other than the actual setting of prices. This finding may stem from foreign executives' greater appreciation of the advantages competitive pricing strategies can offer. Next, domestic managers perceive advertising as the only important promotional activity while foreign managers seem to understand the importance of activities such as personal selling and sales promotion in addition to advertising. Further, both domestic and foreign managers do appreciate the value of effective distribution and customer-oriented activities, though the latter group has a higher perception of the importance of these activities. Worthy of note is that domestic firms managed a score

Table 8.1 Mean and standard deviation scores for perceived importance of marketing activities

Marketing orientation variables	Mean (S.D)	
	Domestic firms	Foreign firms
Product activities		
Product quality	4.31 (1.52)	5.31 (1.03)
Product modification	4.52 (1.77)	4.35 (1.13)
New product development	4.36 (1.32)	4.25 (1.41)
Pricing activities		
Analyzing competitors prices	3.89 (1.11)	4.02 (1.08)
Actual setting of prices	4.21 (1.08)	4.89 (1.33)
Discounts for different buyers	3.78 (1.07)	4.40 (1.31)
Promotion activities		
Advertising	4.28 (1.14)	5.11 (1.02)
Personal selling	3.67 (1.19)	5.21 (1.31)
Sales promotion	3.81 (1.16)	4.47 (1.12)
Distribution activities		
Establishing distribution outlets	4.09 (1.21)	5.21 (1.10)
Efficient product service handling	4.58 (1.00)	5.71 (1.15)
Minimizing distribution cost	4.30 (0.89)	5.58 (1.04)
Customer-focused activities		
Customer satisfaction	4.43 (0.91)	6.01 (1.23)
Customer service	5.50 (1.31)	5.54 (1.16)
Market research	4.81 (1.14)	5.71 (1.12)

Note: All means are significant at the 0.05 level.

just above the critical value of four for market research, suggesting that its importance is not yet widely appreciated.

Performance of Marketing Activities

The mean values for performance of marketing activities are exhibited in table 8.2. Similar to the method used to interpret perceived importance, items with a mean score greater than four indicate performance of an activity whereas items scoring less than four suggest nonperformance. The results indicate that though domestic managers perceive product improvement and new product development to be important, they are still outperformed in these areas by their foreign counterparts. This may be due to lack of technology or funds to pursue these activities. Foreign firms tend to be most concerned with providing high quality products. Pricing activities are more widespread in foreign companies compared with their indigenous counterparts. Generally, analysis of competitors' prices and the utilization of discounts are not well performed in domestic firms. This may be attributed to the lack of expertise required to conduct these activities effectively. Although advertising seems to be prevalent among domestic firms, personal selling and sales promotion activities are not performed extensively. Foreign firms tend to be utilizing all promotional elements quite well.

Worthy of note, however, is the overall low scores for promotional elements, a factor that could be attributed to limited media availability. On the issue of distribution, both foreign and domestic firms score quite well, confirming the consensus regarding the importance of distribution as a marketing function in developing markets (Akaah and Riordan, 1988). It also appears that customer-focused activities are being taken seriously by both groups of firms. This supports the argument that the customer is gradually becoming the focus of

Table 8.2 Mean and standard deviation scores for performance of marketing activities

Marketing orientation variables	Mean (S.D)	
	Domestic firms	Foreign firms
Product activities		
Product quality	4.11 (1.31)	5.21 (1.02)
Product modification	4.32 (1.11)	4.88 (1.17)
New product development	4.12 (1.58)	5.01 (0.82)
Pricing activities		
Analyzing competitors prices	3.77 (1.42)	4.87 (1.22)
Actual setting of prices	4.01 (1.26)	4.77 (1.13)
Discounts for different buyers	3.51 (0.87)	4.69 (1.21)
Promotion activities		
Advertising	4.15 (1.32)	4.45 (1.32)
Personal selling	3.02 (1.15)	4.12 (1.19)
Sales promotion	3.11 (1.44)	4.25 (1.20)
Distribution activities		
Establishing distribution outlets	4.02 (1.12)	5.11 (1.02)
Efficient product service handling	4.52 (1.31)	5.32 (1.17)
Minimizing distribution cost	4.19 (1.21)	5.19 (1.23)
Customer-focused activities		
Customer satisfaction	4.39 (1.42)	5.41 (1.24)
Customer service	4.03 (1.19)	5.42 (1.33)
Market research	4.21 (1.23)	5.61 (1.43)

Note: All means are significant at the 0.05 level.

improved marketing activities among firms operating in economic reform developing countries.

This chapter seeks to contribute to existing knowledge through an examination of managerial perceptions of the importance and performance of marketing activities in foreign and domestic firms in a transition developing economy. In this context, the study facilitates the identification of differences between perceptions and practices of foreign and domestic firms. Moreover, for each group of firms, it is possible to determine whether perceived importance is matched by actual performance of the activity. From a methodological standpoint, this study recognizes the central role of customers in marketing activities and, therefore, adds a fifth dimension to the fundamental 4Ps in the conceptualization of the marketing orientation construct. Given the increasing scholarly attention devoted to marketing in developing countries in recent years, and the growing interest of Western multinational companies in emerging markets of the developing world, these findings are important to both academic researchers and business practitioners.

Earlier suggestion that marketing principles are perceived as important more among foreign executives than among indigenous managers is largely substantiated by our findings. Additionally, the contention that foreign firms are more likely to perform marketing activities than their domestic counterparts is supported. Consistent with our expectations, it seems that managers of both domestic and foreign organizations have reasonably high perceptions of the importance of marketing activities such as product quality improvements, price setting, advertising, efficient distribution planning, customer service and satisfaction programs, as well as market research.

Managerial Implications

Although marketing practice is on the increase, foreign companies tend to outperform domestic firms in all areas. This portends long-term anxieties for indigenous firms that need to maintain a competitive edge in order to survive. These results may stem from the fact that domestic managers still do not *fully* appreciate the benefits of certain marketing functions, as evidenced in the scores for analyzing competitors' prices, providing discounts for different categories of buyers, and utilizing personal selling and sales promotion tools. This problem could be resolved by providing training on the relevance of all marketing activities to the firm, with an emphasis on the customer as the focus of all marketing efforts. Given the highly competitive environment, this issue is quite crucial because effective marketing activities will become increasingly important for survival or for maintaining a competitive advantage.

In addition to in-company training efforts, there is a pressing need for transfer of marketing knowledge to transition developing economies. New forms of marketing could also be developed through the modification of Western techniques and adaptation of these tools to suit the country's culture. Both managers and employees can benefit from these transfers through more formal educational procedures that lead to the attainment of academic qualifications. In this context, tertiary institutions will serve as the primary agents of such transfers and seriously consider providing educational funding for these purposes.

Evidence from this study suggests that domestic and foreign executives who tend to adopt marketing principles wholeheartedly do so because of the perceived importance of these activities to the firms. The differences in perceived importance and actual performance scores indicate that managerial perceptions are not matched by actual performance. However, if from a conventional wisdom standpoint it is accepted that effective marketing practice results in higher performance (Buzzell and Gale, 1987; Jacobson and Aaker, 1987; Okoroafo and Russow, 1993; Kotler, 1997), it is important for managers to fully understand the benefits associated with marketing activities in order to perform them effectively. This calls for procedures to formalize marketing programs with an aim of redressing the apparently ad hoc approach that generally characterizes certain aspects of marketing practice, particularly among indigenous businesses.

With respect to investment prospects, the background provided on the economy indicates that numerous opportunities are available to entrepreneurs from both industrialized and developing countries. Establishing subsidiaries or branches can be cost effective, particularly in countries that have floated their currencies and experienced a sharp drop in value relative to currencies of developed nations. Although misplaced policies of the pre-SAP periods do plague the economy, a long-range view can yield tremendous gains. Quite clearly, Western firms that are skilled in performing all marketing activities effectively are likely to be viewed as attractive joint venture partners for Ghanaian firms that recognize the importance of marketing practice but are underperforming in certain areas.

Limitations and Future Research Avenues

The utilization of subjective measures could lead to bias and may not be consistent with actual data. Additionally, the use of a cross-sectional sample of firms is an inherent weakness. However, these methods were adopted due to time and financial constraints. From an academic viewpoint, a number of future research issues arise from this study. Clearly the dynamics of marketing orientation are adapting in response to the changing Ghanaian business environment, hence, it is recommended that scholars examine those specific marketing activity areas where formalization is vital and most profitable to both domestic and foreign companies. Moreover, future research may focus on internal corporate variables that influence the importance and performance of marketing activities in firms. A further area that warrants academic investigation is the consequence of effective marketing practice on organizational performance measures such as productivity, innovativeness, and adaptability. These issues would shed light on the antecedents and consequences of a marketing orientation in both foreign and domestic firms operating in transition developing economies and also provide guidelines on how marketing practice could be improved in these countries. Finally, an intriguing line of future research may be to use a case study approach to examine the similarities and differences between foreign firms' marketing activities in their home countries and abroad to determine the degree to which the environment influences perceptions and importance of marketing practice.

References

Akaah, I., and Riordan, E. "Applicability of Marketing Know-How in the Third World." *International Marketing Review* 5 (Spring 1988): 41–55.

Appiah-Adu, K. "Marketing in Emerging Countries: Evidence from a Liberalized Economy." *Marketing Intelligence and Planning* 15, no. 6 (1997): 291–98.

Armstrong, S., and Overton, T. "Estimating Non-response in Mailed Surveys." *Journal of Marketing* 14 (August 1977): 396–402.

Buzzell, R.D., and Gale, T.B. *The PIMS Principle: Linkage of Strategy to Performance.* New York: Free Press, 1987.

Chong, S. "Comparative Marketing Practices of Foreign and Domestic Firms in Developing Countries: A Case of Malaysia." *Management International Review* 13 (1973): 91–98.

Dadzie, K., Akkah, I., and Riordan, E. "Incidence of Market Typologies and Pattern of Marketing Activity Performance in Selected African Countries." *Journal of Global Marketing* 1, no. 3 (1988): 87–107.

Elsaid, H., and El-Hennawi, M. "Foreign Direct Investments in LDCs: Egypt." *California Management Review* 24, no. 4 (1982): 85–92.

Ghana Budget. Accra: Government of Ghana Office, 1988.

Ghana Business Directory. 5th edition, Accra: L'Indicateur Fit Ghana Limited, 1996.

Golden, P., Doney, P., Johnson, D., and Smith, J. "The Dynamics of a Marketing Orientation in Transition Economies: A Study of Russian Firms." *Journal of International Marketing* 3, no. 2 (1995): 29–49.

Jacobson, R., and Aaker, D. "The Role of Risk in Explaining Differences in Profitability." *Academy of Management Journal* 30, no. 2 (1987): 277–96.

Kotler, P. *Marketing Management, Analysis, Planning, Implementation and Control.* Englewood Cliffs, NJ: Prentice Hall, 1997.

Liedholm, C., and Mead, M. "Small-Scale Industries in Developing Countries: Empirical Evidence and Policy Implications." *International Development Paper* 9, Michigan State University, Department of Agricultural Economics, East Lansing, 1987, 973–74.

Maholtra, N. "Why Developing Countries Need Technology." *International Marketing Review* 3, no. 1 (1986): 61–73.

McCarthy, J., and Perrault, W. *Basic Marketing.* Homewood: Irwin Inc., 1993.

Mitchell, I., and Agenmonmen, A. "Marketers Attitudes toward the Marketing Concept in Nigerian Business and Non-business Operations." *Columbia Journal of World Business* 19, no. 3 (1984): 62–71.

Okoroafo, S. "Differences in Marketing Activities and Performance of Foreign and Domestic Manufacturing Firms in Nigeria." *Journal of Global Marketing* 9, no. 4 (1996): 109–18.

Okoroafo, S., and Kotabe, L. "The IMF's Structural Adjustment Program and Its Impact on Firm Performance: A Case of Foreign and Domestic Firms in Nigeria." *Management International Review* 33, no. 2 (1993): 139–56.

Okoroafo, S., and Russow, L. "Impact of Marketing Strategy on Performance: Empirical Evidence from a Liberalized Developing Country." *International Marketing Review* 10, no. 1 (1993): 4–18.

Okoroafo, S., and Torkonoo, H. "Marketing Decisions and Performance in Economic Reform African Countries." *Journal of Global Marketing* 8, no. 3 (1995): 85–102.

Samli, A., and Kaynak, E. "Marketing Practices in Less Developed Countries." *Journal of Business Research* 12, no. 1 (1984): 5–18.

Steel, W., and Webster L. "How Small Enterprises in Ghana Have Responded to Adjustment." *The World Bank Economic Review* 6, no. 3 (1992): 423–38.

West Africa Magazine. Britain and Ghana (May 22–29, 1995): 788–802.

Chapter 9

Performance Measurements of the International Joint Ventures in an Emerging Market

Gin Chong

This chapter identifies ten major internal and external factors that may affect the processes of measuring performance of international joint ventures (IJVs) by its parents. A parent is defined as the business unit that administers, including giving continuing resources and support, and formulates the strategies of the IJVs. The factors are generally divided into internal and external factors. The internal factors include agency, control, strategy, technology, and transaction costs whereas the external elements include culture and society, economy and market size, government and politics, industrial structure, and resources.

Based on a series of semistructured interviews with the CEOs and CFOs of five organizations (three manufacturing and two services) whose parents are based in Houston, Texas, and their IJVs in the People's Republic of China, this chapter concludes that all the factors have impact, one way or another, on performance of the IJVs. Thus, it is essential that the parents should consider these factors when evaluating and rewarding their IJVs. Further, the parents should assess the performance based on both the financial and nonfinancial returns of the IJVs. Results of this finding have implications for the parents, IJVs, and stakeholders of the organizations.

Introduction

This chapter intends to evaluate the factors that a business organization uses in measuring the performance of its international business unit. An organization consists of the parent and all its international business units. Discussions as to how performance should be measured arise due to the increasing importance and volume of trade through joint ventures as a result of international strategies. This strategy has led to substantial research on the antecedents and outcomes of IJVs, especially among strategy and international business researchers. However, there is a lack of consistency in the research findings on how performance of these IJVs is measured and the links between the internal and external factors that lead to a different set of measurements. In fact, strategy and international business research on large and well-internationalized firms (McDougall and Oviatt, 1996) do not necessarily reflect those of the smaller counterparts operating under a different environment and exposed to a different category of challenges, because the large and small IJVs are two different species (Shuman and Seeger, 1986).

Many studies have been conducted on IJVs in emerging markets, in particular China, on the benefits of IJVs as a mode of overseas investors' entry into the markets. These studies have obtained inconsistent findings on planting an IJV in China on two issues. First, while some authors believe that IJVs are a better mode of entry to the Chinese market (Luo, 1995), others show that IJVs are less beneficial for an organization's performance than wholly owned investment vehicles (Pan and Chi, 1999). By analyzing data drawn from U.S. firms in the computer and pharmaceutical sectors, Li (1995) finds that IJVs experience a higher rate of failure than wholly owned investment projects. This could be due to the extent of technology transfers and exchanges between the partners. Second, some authors (Luo and Peng, 1998) acknowledge the advantages of early entry into the Chinese market but others (Li et al., 1999) do not support the notion of added advantages. Lieberman and Montgomery (1998) show that the inconsistency in testing first mover advantage among the IJVs in China may be due to (1) a lack of control of important institutional or environmental factors; (2) the nature of industries in which IJVs compete; and (3) small sample size.

Nonetheless, even though much research has been conducted, some important issues concerning overseas investment in China remain unclear, in particular on how the performance of IJVs is being measured. This suggests that there is a need to consider more factors in exploring the behavior and performance of IJVs. One such factor is the societal culture of the IJVs' host country. Past research has suggested that there is a moderating effect of societal culture on an IJV's behavior or performance (Porter, 1990). The effect of a given business policy or management approach such as early market entry can vary depending on the societal culture of the IJVs (Hofstede, 1980). In studying international IJVs in China, some authors suggest that the cultural distance between home and host countries and other external and internal factors may have great influence on the parents' choices and selections of the IJVs' locations in China (Pan, 1997).

To fill the gap, this chapter, first, defines an emerging market, analyzes the benefits of IJVs, and discusses the elements that influence decisions on performance measurements based on a theoretical framework that systematically maps these internal and external factors. Based on grounded theory and cross-case analysis, a section is devoted to discussions on the methods and findings of semistructured interviews with representatives of the parent organizations, whose administrative office is located in Texas and their IJVs in China. The findings have useful references to many existing and potential parents on how to measure IJV performances. The findings are useful for business managers who are planning to have their IJVs in China.

Definition of Emerging Market

This section defines an emerging market and joint venture. Although Welsh et al. (2006) report that there is no consensus on what constitutes an emerging market, Czinkota and Ronkainen (1997) identify three characteristics associated with an emerging market. These are based on the level of economic development, economic growth, and market governance.

The level of economic development is measured by gross domestic product (GDP) per capita. GDP per capita is a useful measurement of economic development because it relates to the population's wealth, extent of middle class, and level of industrial and service sector development of a country or location (Alon and McKee, 1999). The usage of the level of economic development as a demarcation criterion for distinguishing emerging markets equates with the anachronisms of the World Bank and the United Nations that include terms such as less developed countries (LDCs), third world countries, and developing countries. The World Bank divides countries on the basis of GDP per capita into four classes. Three of the big emerging countries (India, China, and Vietnam) fall into the lowest-income class, but these territories have seen a surge of growth in recent years. According to the United Nations, only 15 percent of the world's population resides in developed market economy countries (Czinkota and Ronkainen, 1997).

Economic growth is usually measured in terms of a country's GDP growth rate. Most of the countries referred to as emerging markets have enjoyed GDP growth rates exceeding 5 percent from 1990 to 1997, with some exceptions in East Asia that have displayed double-digit growth rates (Czinkota and Ronkainen, 1997). From 1997 to 1999, East Asia, Brazil, and Russia encountered the financial crises that set back their economies' growth. Such crises demonstrate that the often-touted high growth rates of emerging markets may not be sustainable in the long run. Alon and McKee (1999) report that when tracing economic growth of an emerging market, growth in GDP must be studied vis-à-vis growth in population. This means that if the population growth rates exceed the GDP growth rates, then the standard of living in these countries drops over time. The most useful measure that captures both growth rates is GDP per capita growth rate.

The third criterion for judging emerging markets is the country's market governance. Market governance includes the level of free-market activities, government control of key resources, stability of the market system, and the regulatory environment. Countries that liberalize their economic institutions and democratize their political structures are often referred to as transitional economies/countries. These transitions have been welcomed by the Western economies and are regarded as opportunities for international retail and trade expansion. Among the most important transitional elements with respect to international investors are the political and economic risks introduced by the reorganization of economic and political units in emerging markets (Czinkota and Ronkainen, 1997). Economist Intelligence Unit, Institutional Investor, and International Country Risk Guide (ICRG) have evaluated such risks. The ICRG is a business venture risk rating system in which an independent collaborative group attaches a number to a foreign country after considering weights of relevant factors. Market governance influences a wide range of country risk elements such as government regulations and red tapes, political stability, briberies, ownership restrictions, controls over capital flows, restricted access to rare local resources, and import restrictions. These are important to a parent organization when evaluating a foreign market potential, and thus it is essential to determine the potential for trade expansions and economic exchanges in the given arena (Alon and McKee, 1999). In summary, Millar et al. (2005) conclude that an emerging market business system includes a broad range of countries that are rapidly entering the world business system. These include some of the East European countries, Asian countries such as some provinces of China (e.g., Shanghai, Guangzhou, and Shenzen), Malaysia, Thailand, Indonesia, The Philippines, and some of the Latin

American countries such as Mexico, Chile, and Brazil. This suggests that as long as a country is at its developing and expanding stage of its economic empowerment, it will be classified as an emerging market.

Joint ventures are defined as legally and economically distinct organizational entities created by two or more parent organizations that collectively invest capital and other resources to pursue certain strategic objectives (Pfeffer and Nowak, 1976). Barringer and Harrison (2000) emphasize that a joint venture includes an entity that is created when two or more firms pool a portion of their resources to create a separate jointly owned organization. Both these definitions emphasize on pursuing specific objectives, in particular building resources and fostering for closer relationships. In fact, the relationships of an IJV sustain and flourish based on the concepts of compatibility, trust, understanding, and mutual respect between the IJVs and their parents and among the IJVs, and their willingness to share the resources within the team. IJVs have long been a preferred mode for entering into the foreign markets (Beamish and Banks, 1987) because they have the advantage of local knowledge, cultures, needs, and expectations. However, they need to balance the price of survival. This depends on the closeness in relationships among the team players while sharing common goals and objectives. Relationships can be molded only through time, mutual trust, respect, and understanding. This has a significant impact upon the performance of an IJV and the organization as a whole. In the next section, we explore the perceived benefits of having IJVs, the underlying reasons for having trades through the IJVs, and the performance of the IJVs.

Potential Benefits of IJVs

Sullivan (1994) identifies three key benefits of an IJV partnership. First, foreign market penetration, that is, the extent of dependence on the foreign markets; second, foreign production presence or the degree to which the enterprise is engaged in production-based activities across borders (Annavarjula and Beldona, 2000); and third, country scope, which is the geographic range or breadth of the firm's international presence (Goerzen and Beamish, 2003). The first two components answer the depth of participation of the IJVs' overseas businesses whereas the third component captures the breadth of IJVs. Sullivan (1994) observes that each component seems to rely on a particular set of ratios for measurements. For example, most parents use the foreign sales–total sales ratio to evaluate the IJVs' depth of market penetration, and foreign assets–total assets ratio and foreign employment–total employment ratios for evaluating the extent of IJVs' production presence. For the third component, that is, country scope, the commonly used variables are the numbers of foreign countries and numbers of foreign affiliates that an organization associates with (Mishra and Gobeli, 1998). Depending upon the scenarios, an organization may score high on one component but relatively lower on the others.

Rather than merely measuring the breadth and depth of the IJVs' involvement, Allen and Pantzalis (1996) feel that it is essential for the IJVs to optimize their operations and results by projecting social responsibilities with positive images as the ambassadors for their home countries, and by providing products and services to local partners and protecting the local environment. Thus, the parents should not focus solely on financial returns but also on the nonfinancial elements and factors. Even if a parent intends to rely upon financial elements, these elements and bases of allocating a higher or lower weighting for each element should be clearly explained and consistently applied. A regular review of the weighting should be conducted and dialogues with the local IJVs promoted. This ensures a sense of transparency and assurance to the IJVs on rewarding and allocating scarce resources. Goerzen and Beamish (2003) find that the IJVs' depth is negatively related to an organization's performance, but breadth has a positive relation with its performance. However, Allen and Pantzalis (1996) find a tradeoff between breadth and depth; that is, performance levels are highest if an organization has a broad but not deep IJV network. This suggests that negative returns from IJVs can be attributed to overinvestments in a particular country or territory as opposed to across a number of countries as part of the international expansion plans. It is thus essential for a parent to review every stage of international expansion and use appropriate bases to measure performance of these overseas investment plans. The returns from these foreign territories should take into account unexpected factors and challenges that affect return on investments (ROI).

The additional benefits that IJVs may enjoy include the ability to exploit sources of competitive advantage that are not readily available to the locals and thus help improve the sense of interdependence on each other's supports (Subramaniam and Watson, 2006). These potential benefits are not necessarily available to all the organizations due to inaccessibility or the costs associated with exploitation. An IJV could take advantage of opportunities to leverage the differences between the parent and its IJVs, because as the level of international diversification increases, the potential opportunities and risk for the IJVs may increase proportionately. These include the following:

Differences in Tastes, Demands, and Income Levels

IJVs can shift sales from low-income to high-income markets, generating higher profits on the IJVs' resources. Foreign direct investment (FDI) is designed to exploit profitable opportunities in higher-income markets. As products become obsolete in high-income markets, FDI can be used to shift sales to low-income markets, thereby reviving and extending the lifecycle of declining product lines to help gain from the exchanges. This benefits not only the IJVs but also the local economy, whereby unemployment is minimized and social problems are avoided. Certainly, boosting the local economy projects a good image to the locals and gains faith as the savior for the people living in the surroundings.

Differences in Factor Endowments

Through FDI, an IJV can reap gains from specialization by shifting production to lower cost locations when updating their production techniques and approaches to take advantage of the differences in factors between the countries and territories. This process of specialization improves either the horizontal integrated FDI (i.e., producing the same product lines in two or more countries) or vertically integrated FDI (i.e., segmenting the stages along the value chain across countries). The diversification process evens out any sudden unexpected drops in sales, changes in government regulations, or fluctuations in economic conditions. These factors cannot be controlled by IJVs but significantly affect performance and returns.

Differences in Knowledge-Based Assets

Acquisition of knowledge-based assets motivates FDI (Dunning, 1993). Researchers have argued (Kostova and Roth, 2002) and shown that a parent with IJVs in more than one country can draw upon the knowledge base in their foreign affiliates to improve their own products, services, and processes while generating worldwide organizational learning processes within the IJV network. This check-and-balance process encourages brainstorming sessions among the team players within the organization on new products and services, determines how well the players approach and serve the customers, and prepares for unexpected scenarios. The end results motivate team players to strive for a higher level of targeted achievements and expectations. The internal forces of continuing interactions and encouragements add value to the processes and better serve the communities.

Differences in Government Regulations

Investments can be used to shift production to locations where the host governments offer lower taxes, higher subsidies, protected trade zones and facilities, and easier exit regulations. These conditions are conducive to the survival of IJVs.

Cross-border Flexibility

Managing IJVs' risk has long been considered a motivation for FDI (Rugman, 1976) to deal with sudden changes and shocks in the external environments (Kogut, 1984). For example, during the Asian Financial Crisis in 1997, many domestic Asian firms, without access to the U.S. marketing and distribution networks, were unable to expand their exports as quickly as IJVs in the United States. Availability of an overseas IJV mitigates unexpected economic and political downturns.

Bargaining Power

Larger IJVs, due to their ability to move and access assets and resources relatively quickly between the countries, have more bargaining power than those location-bound actors such as governments, trade unions, and domestic firms. To have investments in IJVs, however, is not a one-sided proposition. The parents should be aware of the levels of costs and risks involved due to cross-border exercises, exposure, and opportunities. As an organization increases its number of IJVs, the level of exposure to rising costs and other risks increase exponentially. These include the following:

Costs and Risks of Multiple Sources of Value
One of the key characteristics of IJVs is that they operate with multiple sources of value (Sundaram and Black, 1992) due to different exchange rates between the countries that create foreign exchange risks. The sales, market value of the IJVs, and ability to raise capital are negatively affected by translation exposure. Indeed, the greater

the number of countries in which the IJVs operate, the more the IJVs face foreign exchange risks. On the other hand, international diversification of markets and production locations may cushion the IJVs from exchange rate shocks that are regional or country specific (e.g., the Asian currency crisis and revaluation of Renminbi).

Costs and Risks of Multiple Levels of Authority

As the IJVs expand into several countries, it is faced with higher cross-border transactions costs and higher interaction costs with different regulatory requirements. Political risks may increase (Chase, et al., 1988) with increasing difficulties to establish legitimacy (Kostova and Zaheer, 1999). On the other hand, as IJVs become established actors in the host countries, the liability of foreignness should decrease at the individual affiliate level.

Presence of the After-Sales Services

It is essential that IJVs have an efficient mechanism to follow up on the after-sales services to ensure that customers are well served by the products and services. Without such services, customers will opt for alternative supplies that are easily accessible. Once the no-turning-back option has been adopted, the chances for the customers remaining loyal to the organization's products and services become slim and, in many cases, the possibility of referrals to new customers is reduced. Reputations and the brand name of the IJVs will greatly be affected and it will take a significant period of time to recoup lost confidence and market shares. Indeed, it affects the measurement of performance of the IJVs.

The Theoretical Framework

This section assesses how the various theories have impacted on the performance and strategies of IJVs. The framework is divided into the internal and external factors that influence a parent in the course of measuring performance. These factors are classified according to the sources of pressure and forces faced by an IJV. The internal factors are those that normally arise within the IJV, whereas external factors are those beyond the control of the IJV and external sources. The internal factors include (1) agency; (2) control; (3) strategy; (4) technology; and (5) transaction costs. The external factors are (1) culture and social; (2) economy and market size; (3) government and politics; (4) industrial structure; and (5) resources.

Agency

Agency theory sheds light on the relationship between control and performance. A relationship exists when one economic entity (the principal) authorizes the other (the agent) to act on behalf of the principal (Eisenhardt, 1989). However, due to inherent conflicts between self-interests of the principal and the agent; agency costs and conflicts occur when an agent does not act in the best interest of the principal (Jensen and Meckling, 1976). Alchian and Demsetz (1972) observe that metering problems may occur when two economic entities, acting as a team, jointly produce output or provide for relatively similar services to a small group of customers. Unless monitoring and mediation occur, each team member may not necessarily pursue the best interests of the other or the team as a whole but may act opportunistically pursuing its own strategic interests, reaping the resources and retaining the profits. As such, IJVs should resemble a team. Fama (1980) argues that a team exists if all the team members behave with a selfless attitude and realize that their destinies depend on the survival of the other team members. The agency problem exists due to divergent self-interests and goals between parents and their IJVs, in particular where the IJVs were not created from the same political and cultural background. For example, if the parents are from a developed country while their IJVs are mainly situated in the less-developed countries (Subramaniam and Watson, 2006), imbalances will occur. Even though each partner has its strategic interests and objectives, these goals may not necessarily be salient for the others. It is important to note that each of them needs the others for survival in order to achieve the intended overall goals (Fox, 1984). Both the transaction costs theory and agency theory predict that the team with the greatest control of the IJVs, as a group, normally uses the common pool of resources to pursue its own interests and to achieve its own objectives rather than sharing them among all the partners or using them for the best interest of the organization as a whole. Killing (1983) reports that, in effect, the management control structure becomes a critical vehicle through which decisions about whose objectives to pursue are made and performance evaluated. As a result, an IJV with a dominant control structure is expected to satisfy more of its dominant parent's objectives than those with dominant parents. By the same token, Killing (1983) concludes that when sharing the controls of the IJVs, the extent to which the objectives of both the parent and IJVs have been achieved should be relatively equal. Thus, positive relationships between the degree of a parent's control and the extent of achieving its objectives have a great impact on the performance of its IJVs.

Apart from structure, other factors have also been posited to have an effect on the IJVs' performance. For example, some researchers report that the quality of the working relationships among the IJVs affects the overall performance (Zajac and Olsen, 1993; Child et al., 1997). Other factors include parent-IJV trust, consensus, and conflict about goals. We discuss these factors below.

Trust

Multiple conceptions of trust have a positive impact on the performance of IJVs (Nooteboom et al., 1997). However, there are various degrees of trust. Ring and Van de Ven (1992) distinguish calculative forms of trust from confidence in another's goodwill, whereas Lewis and Weigert (1985) differentiate leaps of faith from trust based on reasons and experiences. Lewicki and Bunker (1995) conclude that trust consist of three components—calculus-based, knowledge-based, and identification-based trust. Calculative trust occurs when far-sighted parties recognize the potential benefits of their continuing interactions and expect that other parties will behave predictably (Williamson, 1993). For the knowledge-based trust, one person relies on another because of direct knowledge about their behavior. The IJVs with identification-based trust develop a social bond with their parents and between the IJVs based on mutual appreciation of each other's needs. These three components are interrelated and will affect the performance of the individual IJVs, and in turn that of the parents. The presence/absence of any of these three components could erode the relationships and cooperation within the partnerships, thereby causing long-term damage to the organization's survival (Subramaniam and Watson, 2006).

The development of trust among IJVs can have a direct positive effect on performance. For example, Barney and Hansen (1994) conclude that a strong form of trust can reduce the costs of governance mechanisms that would otherwise be required for lesser forms of trusts and could eventually exploit exchange opportunities, in turn, gaining competitive advantages. A strong form of trust is exogenous to the IJVs' governance structure and is derived from values, beliefs, integrity, principles, and standards that are shared among the IJVs. This is akin to Lewicki and Bunker's (1995) identity-based trust where the presence of such trust enables the parties to trash ambiguities in the contracts, correct errors, cope with uncertainties, solve problems in better manners (Lee and Cavusgil, 2006), and achieve integrative outcomes that allow all the parties to achieve their objectives and improve performance (Lax and Sebenius, 1986). Mohr and

Spekman (1994) report that a strong correlation between the trust satisfaction level and profit exists; for example, a strong alliance relationship exists between automobile manufacturers and dealers. Saxton (1997) reports a positive relationship between shared decision-making processes and the level of trust, coexistence, and performance.

A higher level of trust within IJVs cuts costs and unnecessary red tapes and bureaucracy. If trust exists, transaction costs are reduced as formal contracts are done away with (Lee and Cavusgil, 2006). Apart from costs savings and smooth flows of information and goods, trust becomes an alternative mechanism to safeguard against opportunism (Zaheer and Venkatraman, 1995). Both trust and control contribute to the IJVs' confidence that their counterparts will pursue mutually beneficial goals in the alliance, rather than act opportunistically (Das and Teng, 1998), whereas Nooteboom et al. (1997) find that trust greatly reduces the probability of perceived loss for IJVs and improves the overall performance and financial results of an organization. This notion is supported by Newman (1992) who analyzes how trust plays an important part in strengthening U.S. parents' willingness to accept a minority equity ownership and to transfer responsibilities, technologies, and knowledge to its Chinese IJVs (Harzing and Noorderhaven, 2006). Apart from the Chinese perspective, Hennart (1988) finds a similar phenomenon among Canadian manufacturing IJVs in that trust is positively related to performance, whereas Inkpen and Beamish (1997) report a symbiosis between trust and performance on the North American–Japanese IJVs arrangements.

Nonetheless, trust and control may influence performance. Lee and Cavusgil (2006) find that for shared control IJVs where trust level is higher, control may be sufficient to predict performance. However, in a dominant controlled IJV scenario, trust becomes a necessary companion of control if high levels of performance are desired. This relationship shows that the level of trust and control will influence the performance of IJVs.

Consensus or Conflicts about Goals

A superior working relationship between the parent and the IJVs could make improvements to the organization's performance (Yan and Gray, 1994). Ring and Van de Ven (1994) note that parent-IJV and inter-IJV relationships are pivotal for the organization to create a consensus on key cultural expectations, purposes, beliefs, and values. These relationships contribute to performance and the IJVs' formal commitments to the organization. As the level of consensus among the IJVs improves, the amount of contributions to the organization's overall missions, goals, and operating procedures increases while conflicts and misunderstandings are significantly reduced. Opportunism and monitoring costs decrease while the overall performance of the organization improves (Das and Teng, 1998).

Decision-making serves the purpose of controlling. This is due to an increase in the frequency and amount of interactions among the IJVs and between parents and their IJVs. This shares a better understanding of each other's strengths and weaknesses and develops the organization's collective norms and values. As the goal-setting process allows all parties to form a consensus, the individual IJV will have a greater incentive to drive forward and strive for a better level of return. If major problems occur, the IJVs lend their hands to one another for support in order to avoid future disasters. Mutual supports improve performance once the waves of threats have disappeared.

Mohr (2006) observes that those IJVs that experience considerable conflicts in working together are less likely to reach decisions that they both can support and will affect the services and, in turn, performance. Conflict between the team members may arise due to disagreements over goals or operational and managerial expectations. These conflicts will send confusing signals to the IJV managers, employees, and stakeholders (Lyles and Salk, 1997) and will have negative impact on performance (Anderson and Narus, 1990). While Geringer and Hebert (1989) find that the level of conflict was negatively related to performance, the relationships held for dominant IJVs but not for shared-control IJVs. On the other hand, Mohr and Spekman (1994) find a positive relationship between conflict resolution and IJVs' satisfaction. In the short-term, conflict can jeopardize performance, except for some IJVs that are capable of finding integrative resolutions to such conflict and improving the performance; but in the long-term, all conflict will be ironed out among parties and repercussions, if any, to the performance, is minimized. Trust and goal consensus are thus interrelated; a combination of these two elements will improve performance of IJVs and the organization as a whole.

Context-Based Bargaining Power

Mohr (2006) postulates that the power-dependence theory emphasizes on context-dependent relationships between bargainers. The relative bargaining power of a player depends on the extent of mutual dependence among the team members that eventually affect performance of the individual player (Thompson, 1967). Thus, the bargaining power and performance of an IJV are determined by the availability of alternatives, significance of the parent's stakes in the current relationships, and potential outcomes of the bargains (Bacharach and Lawler, 1984). The IJVs with the most potential supports, alternative modal choices to enter a market, and bargaining power and the least dependence on the other existing IJVs perform better. This is due to its ability to threaten and leave the team and terminate the current negotiation while exercising its best alternatives to pursue its own interests and resources. Thus, IJVs with strong bargaining power and little or no reason to compromise during the negotiations processes emerge as a winner and are, in turn, in a better position to improve its performance (Fisher and Ury, 1981).

Nonetheless, very few IJV partnerships are important to their over-all strategic portfolio and performance. Bartlett and Ghoshal (1986) conclude that parents justify preferential treatment being given to a particular IJV if the IJV invests a greater stake in the venture and negotiates for a stronger control. In fact, this process negatively affects IJVs because the IJVs themselves become the victims and dependent on their partners and lose their incentives to strive hard and improve performance. The increase in reliance means a significant reduction in the bargaining power of IJVs. The increasing dependence deteriorates the IJVs' performance unless the parent takes strategic actions to offset this dependence; for example, by making specific resource allocations or by deciding to turn around the bargain and negotiate for more autonomy and resources. Excessive dependence on the parent and other team players cause serious repercussions on the IJVs' performance (Mjoen and Tallman, 1997).

Partners' Host Country Knowledge

Adequate knowledge about the host countries is a critical resource for success and survival of an IJV (Harzing and Noorderhaven, 2006). It is possible to acquire local knowledge and develop new organizational capabilities internally through incremental experience accumulation in new markets (Johanson and Vahlne, 1977), but this process takes time and resources and sometimes results in mistakes (Dierickx and Cool, 1989). As a result of size and lack of knowledge, any mistake can endanger the survival and relationships between IJVs and parents (Beamish, 1999). A local or host-country partner represents an alter-native choice of primary sources of local knowledge and this process reaps financial returns in a relatively short period of time (Yan and Gray, 1994). A local IJV will have an in-depth, updated, and detailed knowledge about various aspects of the host country, particularly when identifying needs, customs, legal and regulatory requirements, competitions, and tastes of the locals. The local networks can provide

IJVs with timely information and feedback on the changes in the local environment and thus overcome the parent's concerns on foreignness (Hymer, 1976) and improve performance and profitability (Beamish and Banks, 1987). As the parents accumulate experience and skills in the local environment, they tend to reduce their dependence on the IJVs for knowledge and may even find that the role of these IJVs will eventually become redundant (Makino and Delios, 1996). As the dependence level decreases, the parent's bargaining power over the IJVs increases. This leads to a change in the balance of bargaining power between the parent and the IJVs and causes instability or dissolution of the organization (Inkpen and Beamish, 1997).

Until this learning goal is not completed, the relationships between the parents and IJVs continue to survive while each attempts to strive for better financial and performance results (Parkhe, 1991). From this perspective, the longer a parent takes to acquire the knowledge from its IJVs, the slower the chance of change in the bargaining power. This prolongs their relationships and thus maintains performance levels and results. The time taken to develop a relationship between a parent and its IJVs should be taken into consideration when measuring performance. A longer relationship promotes a better understanding and thus improved financial and performance results.

Control

Positive and reliable management control over the IJVs' daily operations exerts a strong effect on the IJVs' performance (Mjoen and Tallman, 1997). Management control refers to the process by which a parent influences its IJVs to achieve the expected goals and objectives (Flamholtz et al., 1985). Geringer and Hebert (1989) define control as a multidimensional construct comprising of scope, extent, and mechanisms of influence that the IJVs' parents exercise and as a process by which behavior and output of an IJV are influenced by its surrounding IJVs. Control depends on the extent of decision power the parent exercises and exerts upon the IJVs' daily operations, processes of making strategic decisions and designing the IJVs' corporate structure, and operating procedures (Killing, 1983). Control is the extent of influence exercised by each team player over the strategic, operational, and structural issues of the others (Galaskiewicz, 1985). The control structure could be in the form of shareholdings or human resource practices such as nomination of the parents' key personnel to the committees of the IJVs where the decision-making processes take place (Wahlstrom, 2006). Yan and Gray (1994) conclude that by nominating a parent's representatives to the IJVs' committees equates to a critical mean of control at the strategic and operational level. This reflects the level of trust a parent has on IJVs. The finding shows that control, either in the form of shareholdings, human resource practices, or a combination of both, has a positive impact on the performance of IJVs.

It is critically important to understand and identify how control is being acquired and maintained IJVs and whether by exercising such control produces the desired outcomes (Tomlinson, 1970). A parent gains and maintains control over its IJVs by creating, maintaining, and ensuring that the strategies of the parents fit into those of the IJVs and eventually yield improved and positive returns on investment (Franko, 1971). We support the notion that a parent should either tighten its control over the IJVs or decrease the IJVs' autonomy whenever the parent needs to standardize or centralize its international strategic goals, policies, and plans to consolidate the production facilities. Blodgett (1991) argues that increasing control would mean the need for a parent to transfer more critical strategic resources such as proprietary technologies and intellectual properties to curb opportunism by its IJVs and to prevent unauthorized technology leakage (Wahlstrom, 2006). Although the view of intention to control (Tomlinson, 1970) suggests that the IJVs' corporate strategies could influence each other's desire for control over other team players, it offers an insufficient explanation in situations where an IJV seeks influence and control over the remaining players. In that situation, the parent needs to negotiate and mediate between the IJVs and avoid conflict among the players. The mediation process may need space, time, and resources to bear fruit. Clearly, it affects performance and results of the organization as a whole.

It is thus essential for the parent to exert its management control at the time of the IJV's founding, and subsequently the level of control should be reviewed and revised in light of the parents' relative bargaining power, strategic fit, negotiations, and mutual alignments. Once the control structure is established and stabilized, changes in the relative bargaining power are subsequently forgotten among the players. In view of this, the level of control and length of time needed to establish the relationships between the parent and its IJVs have a direct influence on the extent of control, negotiations, and alignments. This causes stress and uncertainties, and subsequently affects the IJVs' performance and results (Inkpen and Beamish, 1997).

In fact, the notion of bargaining power is rooted in the power-dependence theory (Emerson, 1962), which posits that one player's power is derived from another's dependency. The theory conceptualizes bargaining power as a relative phenomenon that is assessed through interplayer comparisons (Galaskiewicz, 1985). The parent's control in IJVs is relational and assessed by the extent of division and controls among the players. The degree of diversity in terms of control over a particular IJV will have a direct impact on its financial performance. For example, if an IJV is being monitored and controlled closely compared to the others, the IJV will normally yield stronger and better financial results and returns than the other team players (Yan and Gray, 1994). This is due to the pressure, expectations, and trust that a parent has asserted on a particular IJV. To gain its own independence and control, the IJV needs to outperform all the others, obtain its parent's trust, and emerge as the champion. In the course of striving for independence, the IJV will make attempts to capture the required level of self-control, self-confidence, and autonomy. Once the independence status has been granted, compliance with the expectations of the parent will reduce gradually and the IJV may or may not continue to receive resource supports to enhance its own performance.

Size of the IJVs

Size and number of players in a team affect performance of both the individual IJVs and its parent. For small- and medium-sized enterprises (SMEs), the IJVs do not have as much resources as their larger counterparts who can withstand mistakes, challenges, or losses. They are constantly exposed to environmental pressures (Aldrich and Auster, 1986). The challenge of being small is found to be closely and positively related to organizational mortality rates and performance results (Singh et al., 1986). Stinchcombe (1965) reports that when comparing the level of public awareness between an IJV that belongs to an SME and a larger corporation, the former tends to receive a lower level of awareness and thus makes it difficult to gain access to local resources, develop local business networks, and capture local market shares. This is because large corporations have the needed resources and established reputations to gain more confidence and easier penetration to local markets. These resource-rich large corporations have better facilities to hire skilled professionals and are in a better position to gain access to information due to its networks, political, and social ties with the local governments and communities. Through this process, IJVs achieve their full potential for growth in a relatively short time frame.

In addition, partnering with large corporations accelerates the pace of leverage and the reputations of IJVs. The institutional theory emphasizes the importance of institutional environments that include cognitive and sociological elements such as shared norms, standards, and expectations (DiMaggio and Powell, 1991). This institutional environment is an underlying driving force behind the organizational activities because of organizations' desire for legitimacy (Martinez and Dacin, 1999). Large size tends to legitimate an IJV easily because a larger corporation is being interpreted by the external stakeholders as being successful with better wealth-generating capabilities, knowledge, skills, returns, and a caring attitude toward the local communities and environments (Baum and Oliver, 1991). Barringer and Harrison (2000) support this notion and conclude that those IJVs that belong or work closely with a resource-rich parent can shorten their time to establish legitimacy because the parent has a strong presence and commitment to the local needs. This means that a parent may take a relatively short time to recoup its initial investments (Stuart et al., 1999) and reduce mortality rate of IJVs (Baum and Oliver, 1991). Alvarez and Barney (2001) view that unless the stocks of parents are listed, profitability is not a major factor because stakeholders are keen to know about the extent of contributions that IJVs can offer to the local communities and infrastructure rather than financial returns. Financial returns and wealth creation may not be the main criteria for local firms. The size of the parent and its IJV play an important part in the success and survival stories because the IJV is under pressure of social responsibilities, social citizenships, and governance. However, Osborn and Baughn (1990) report that many large parents tend to make unreasonable demands, introduce unreasonable expectations, impose unfair contractual and noncontractual terms in the business transactions, and put undue pressure on IJVs to maximize profit margins and investment returns. Even though evidence supports this perception, in particular regarding IJV potentialities and resources due to their size and position, the extent of exploitation depends on the level of equity ownership of the parents in the IJVs. The higher the level of equity ownership, the higher the level of exploitation and the greater the expectations a parent has from its IJVs in terms of returns on profitability and wealth (Anderson and Gatignon, 1986). These expectations of exceptional returns and profitability become mandatory for hostages and collaterals (Mjoen and Tallman, 1997). Gray and Yan (1997) support this view and conclude that those IJVs that are in this situation are expected to meet their key goals and missions not only for their own interest but also for the sake of the other team players including the parent. IJVs that are branded as high performers are subject to regular reviews and inspections on their abilities and contributions. Failure to meet these targets may mean that the IJV may be sidelined from being one of the team players. To return to the team, the player may have to perform better. The parent may now raise the bar for returns and resource supports. These added challenges make IJVs work harder to gain lost ground and trust in exchange for continuing support from the team members. At this stage, the IJV needs to convince all the other players for a second chance or otherwise will eventually be phased out, expelled, or left alone to fight its own battles for survival. Performance measurement has become an important tool for the parents to evaluate the continuing relationships and trust. Loyalty of the individual IJV will be judged based on their promised returns and the size of their investments (Yan and Luo, 2001).

Strategy

Parents play important roles that may affect their IJVs' performance. These include setting strategic directions, designing governance mechanisms, agreeing on incentives, monitoring performance, allocating scarce resources, designing coordination mechanisms to facilitate sharing, and transferring resources between the IJVs (Hoskisson et al., 1993; Collis and Montgomery, 1998). Apart from creating value and wealth, the IJVs face a constant flow of challenges due to external environment pressure such as compliance with legislative requirements on how profits and tax should be reported, and how the value chain should be improved (Porter, 1985). Day and Wensley (1988) conclude that the value chain strategy lies in deciding whether an IJV has its own local production sites or needs to import raw materials for further processing for local sales. Local production processes allow the IJV to capture a larger share of the market, add value to the products and after-sales services, and improve the IJV's performance. This is because the IJV has an autonomy and a sense of responsibility in its production and services chain. To achieve this, the IJV needs to formulate appropriate strategies to fit into the local environment and the parents' missions and goals. The extent of reliance on the chains of supplies and services will have implications on the IJV's performance. For example, an R&D strategy tends to be important and relevant for high-technology industries, whereas a branded industry needs to pay attention to its marketing strategies. The market position of an IJV is a reflection of a proxy for the organization's preparedness for the local competitive advantage, presence, interests, and contributions to meet the local needs. This impacts the IJV's and the organization's profitability (Prescott et al., 1986). In some cases, disputes over the directions of causality may arise due to difficulties in focusing and predicting the local expectations and needs (Jacobson, 1988). Thus, if an IJV intends to modify its market position, this process needs to be considered seriously as it may jeopardize the IJV's performance, at least in the short-term (Rumelt and Wensley, 1981). In the long-term, the situation will be adjusted and performance will return to a normal or expected level.

Technology

The extent of technological skills of a parent influences the IJVs' performance, profitability, and financial returns. If a parent invests significantly in R&D and technological knowledge, the parent may pressurize the IJVs to do the same even more. This process encourages transfers of intellectual properties and skills among the team players. Sohn, Kim, and Moon (2007) stipulate that a close relationship exists between the level of technology transfers and performance. As the volume of investments in R&D on products and services by the parent increases, the returns for the IJVs increase exponentially. Anderson and Sedatole (2003) conclude that technology, among others factors, ensures the IJVs to be in a cutting edge position on their products and services and improve its efficiency and effective usage of resources. The transfer and sharing of technical knowledge and skills between team players enhances the level of performance. Using the Croatian experiences, Cui et al., (2006) conclude that the large volume of technology transfers and sharing among the players builds a team spirit of faith and confidence. Once all the team members have the same level of mindset, habits of sharing technology flow freely within the organization. This forces the organization to seek more challenging tasks and higher goals. This becomes a synergic force for returns and performance. Thus, the culture of free technological transfers and the willingness to share knowledge among players fosters relationships and eventually improves performance.

Transaction Costs

The transaction costs theory can be divided into incomplete contracts and opportunism. For an incomplete contract scenario, the parents form IJVs to overcome uncertainties associated with the incompleteness of market contracts (Crocker and Masten, 1988) and to improve their financial performance. An incomplete contract situation arises when the IJVs have to live with a substantial extent of uncertainties (Crocker and Masten, 1988), that is, the outcomes of their cooperation will not be apparent until a few years later. In view of this, when a parent evaluates the performance of its IJVs, it is essential to ascertain the extent of uncertainties in the relationships and incompleteness of the contracts. To minimize these uncertainties, IJVs seek management control, trusts, confidence, and opportunism (Williamson, 1975). Each party attempts to maximize financial results through available opportunities. Eventually, the opportunistic IJVs will gain a large share of negotiated contracts and opportunities and get the upper hand in management control. These reap good financial returns. Each team player will continue to strive for a larger economic share. Then, a champion emerges to dominate while the others hope for a continuing supply of resources (Hill and Hoskisson, 1987). The parent needs to take the appropriate management control of their IJVs to attenuate uncertainties and to attain the overall strategic interests the organization. Depending on how the structure of the IJVs is being designed, a complete elimination of selfish behavior is deemed impossible (Chi and McGuire, 1996), particularly in situations where IJVs' commitments are monitored or verified. For example, an IJV exists due to its parent's attempts to establish presence in the local market, or to gain access to resources or technology. As long as an opportunity arises, an IJV pursues its own interests at the expense of the other team players. This is because many IJVs are under pressure from their parents to attain the expected returns. The unnecessary pressure affects performance and financial results of the IJVs (O'Clock and Devine, 2003).

From the transaction costs theory perspective, exercising management control by a team player enables alleviation of potential opportunism. This prevents the other team players from using a common pool of resources and gaining their own strategic interests. As a result, each player guards its own position while pushing the unwanted uncertainties to the others. Thus, when measuring performance, it is essential that parents assess the extent its IJVs are exposed to the transaction costs. Different levels and stages of opportunism and uncertainties cause different levels of financial returns to the IJVs.

Culture and Society

Local culture and environments influence organization's culture (Teece, 1986). According to the institutional theory, institutional environments generate two sets of constraints that influence an organization's behavior and performance. One set consists of formal constraints that include factors such as economic, political, and judicial rules (O'Connor et al., 2006), whereas the other consists of informal constraints that include the culture and ideology of a society (North, 1981). Hofstede (1999) concludes that in China, the formal institutional environments exist where a parent is expected to observe factors such as economy, political, and regulatory requirements. These factors greatly affect performance of its Chinese IJVs. However, the Chinese informal institutional constraints that include societal culture do not seem to create much impact on the IJVs' performance (O'Connor et al., 2006). Both sets of constraints affect an organization's behavior and performance. For example, Porter (1990) concludes that institutional elements of a given country have a great impact on the international competitiveness whereas Hill (1995) reports that institutional framework adds value to organizations. For example, in the United States, the institutional environment could stimulate not only the individual organizational prowess but also the country's economic development; whereas in Japan, institutional environment creates organizational competitiveness. Buckley et al. (2006) conclude that both *guanxi* (close relationships) and *mianzi* (giving opportunities) to others play an important role to secure contracts and the IJVs' relationships. These cultural institutional elements have great impact on the relationships and level of performance among the players.

Adler (1986) finds that a national culture has an impact on a wide range of organizational situations such as the employee performance, the organizational culture, managerial decision-making processes, leadership style, and human resource management practices. The national culture could thus influence the organization's ability to acquire and deploy resources (Puffer, 1993). Societal culture has become part of an organization's resources that leads to competitive advantage due to the accumulation of specialized assets, skills, greater commitments and desire for better performance results (Porter, 1991). National cultures can be divided into individualistic and collective cultures. Dunning and Bansal (1997) report that in a individualistic culture environment such as the United States, the society enjoys a better and higher level of technological assets, whilst in a collectivistic culture society, such as Japan and China, an organization may benefit from how the society organizes its workforce and establishes the relationships between contractors, suppliers, and IJVs. In view of differences in cultural impetus, it is essential for a parent to evaluate the national cultures and ensure its IJV strategies fit into the system to capture the needed resources and maximize returns.

Different cultures dictate different forms of investments. For example, in a collective culture such as China, IJVs prefer more labor-intensive operations and activities, with little investment in equipment and technological intensiveness (Li et al., 1999), whereas in the individualistic culture environment where more emphasis is on technological intensity, it is essential that the parent and IJVs invest significantly in the latest production facilities, equipment, and technologies (Boulton, 1997). An organization needs to adjust its strategies to align with the local and national cultures, needs, values, beliefs, and expectations to maximize its financial returns. Failure to adapt and adopt the host country's cultures would mean a disaster to the IJVs' survival and performance.

Long-term Orientation

Hofstede (1999) points out that Asian cultures are characterized by a long-term orientation. The parents should be aware that Asian IJVs seek long-term continuing relationships, investments in education and training, mutual respect, persistence, thriftiness, and delayed gratification. Long-term orientation tests the relationships between the parents and IJVs to pursue the common goals and financial targets of the organization. Time is an essential factor when measuring performance and returns. Cheng (1997) observes that in many cases, setting up a Chinese IJV involves establishing long-term trust and confidence, and thus evaluations of performance within a short space of time may not yield desired results. Similarly, Tung (1982) reports that Asians, in particular the Chinese, have a different concept of interpreting time compared to the Westerners as they are interested in building long-term relationships. This means that once an IJV has gained their trust and the parent has demonstrated its goodwill and willingness to lend assistance to the host country, the Chinese try to reciprocate in kind when it is possible. Time frame should be taken into consideration when measuring the performance of a Chinese IJV.

Economy and Market Size

Stability of the economy and market size affect business performance. A large market usually has a strong demand for products and services. The size of the Indian and Chinese markets means easy marketability of products and services, this bolsters the confidence of parents investing in these countries. Apart from these growing Asian giants, countries in South America and Africa are potential marketplaces for investments. However, political stability is needed to attract a continuing flow of investments and resources from the parents. Based on a range of factors that could influence the measurement of performance, Mainela (2007) concludes that both market size and economic stability lead to investor trust and confidence and thus have a positive impact on the performance of the IJVs. The parents need assurance of continuing growth and stability. This helps parents take decisions on allocating resources to areas where there are justifications for enduring economic stability and growing purchasing power. These factors influence the performance of IJVs.

Government and Politics

Stability of governments and policies create a reliable marketplace for investors and IJVs. Under a democratic government, its policies and processes build a strong and stable market compared to those of governments that constantly pose challenges to the economies and purchasing powers of consumers. Different government policies and structures have different degrees of impact on the performance of the IJVs (O'Connor et al., 2006). A country's characteristics also affect a parent's decisions on foreign direct investment (FDI) and competitive performance (O'Connor et al., 2006). Other factors including the market size and growth (Terpstra and Yu, 1988), labor costs (Veugelers, 1991), political stability (Fatehi-Sedeh and Saflzadeh, 1989), and government policies (Loree and Guisinger, 1995) positively influence IJV performance. For example, Kogut and Singh (1988) find that industry, firm, and country-specific factors influence a parent's selection decision, financial results, and entry modes. Kim and Hwang (1992) support this notion that different international geographical regions have different influence on the international performance of an organization. The strategic choice theory asserts that even though performance of an organization is greatly influenced by external factors, these factors are beyond the control of the organization, and thus the parent should evaluate the performance of IJVs based on what is controllable (Hannan and Freeman, 1989). The theory advises parents to avoid countries that offer little or no guarantee for organizational returns. The parent should rank a country based on factors such as government policies, political climate, infrastructure, regulatory requirements, and location. Based on these rankings, firms should assess the levels of risks and opportunities provided by the controllable and uncontrollable factors.

Caves (1989) finds that government policies and political climate affect IJV performance in two ways. First, the policies affect the industrial structure and competitive rivalries of either one particular sector or all the sectors within a country. This then affects individual corporate identity and performance. Second, different economic and political conditions affect the industrial structure, corporate characteristics, and IJV strategies, thus affecting returns from the IJVs. Loree and Guisinger (1995) find that the effects of government policies on foreign direct investment differ between countries with different levels of economic development (i.e., emerging markets). This is because governments are the gatekeepers to many critical resources and regulatory requirements such as foreign exchange or import licenses, and thus IJV performance in these countries is, to a certain extent, restricted and determined by the administrative preferences and processes of governments rather than by the industrial, corporate, and IJV characteristics. These factors eventually affect the IJVs' performance.

The economic development of a country has a direct impact on per capita income, and in turn on its buying power. This impact has repercussions on IJV performance because the standard and cost of living determines the amount of surplus money consumers can spend on products and services. When economic development is at its peak, other developments such as infrastructure building, urbanization, and specialization of physical and mental labor may also take place. A large country provides significant potential market and business opportunities, and thus economies of scale and IJV performance (Armstrong, 1970). A country with a stable rate of inflation gives confidence to the investors, as countries with relatively high inflation are associated with unwarranted costs. This affects the profitability of the IJVs due to escalating costs (Austin, 1990). Instability in exchange rates complicates the planning process and performance measurement of an IJV. Lessard (1986) observes that economic and political situations of a country affect an IJV's performance because political risk, unpredictable government interventions, regulatory constraints, and unwarranted tax rates have adverse effects on the IJVs' performance.

Industrial Structure

The industrial structure of a country affects the performance of the business units (Montgomery and Porter, 1991). The industrial organizational theory stipulates a close relationship between structure, conduct, and performance (Bain, 1956). This triangular paradigm suggests that structural conditions of an industry impact the conduct of the organizations within the industry, which, in turn, affects the performance of the organization. Conduct arises as an implicit result of the industrial structure such as the degree of rivalry between the organizations and within an industry. Porter's five-force framework analyzes the impact of industry structure on an organization's performance (Porter, 1985). These are the bargaining powers of buyers, the bargaining powers of suppliers, pressure from substitute products, the threat of new entrants, and the rivalry among existing competitors. The extent of impact on performance by these forces varies from one country and industry to another. Birkinshaw and Morrison (1995) find that the choice of industry may have a critical influence on the ability of an IJV to identify the factors of individual country and industry. The more an IJV is being managed on a globally integrated basis—that is, with differentiation of strategic roles (Birkinshaw and Morrison, 1995) and financial cross-subsidization across IJVs (Hamel and Prahalad, 1985)—the less meaningful are the intercountry differences in term of profitability and returns. The impact of choice and structure of industries remains vague due to the range of external forces affecting IJVs.

Resources

A resource-based concept focuses on the availability of resources and the extent of capabilities that enables an organization to exploit an imperfect and incomplete market while generating above-normal rate of returns and sustaining competitive advantages (Peteraf, 1993). Conner (1991) observes that an organization's decisions about selecting and accumulating resources should be economically rational within the constraints of limited information, cognitive biasness, and causal ambiguity. Success and measurement of performance of an IJV depend on the extent of accessibility and the identification and use of valuable, difficult-to-copy, and irreplaceable resources (Teece, 1986). The concept suggests that factors such as market position (Buzzell and Gale, 1987) and resources and capabilities (Barney, 1991) of the IJVs are the main determinants of performance due to intraindustry differences. The strategies of a parent and their IJV must be aligned by the extent of secured resources (Hoskisson et al., 1993). Performance of an organization should be based on the extent of providing economies associated with the sharing and transferring of rent-created resources among the IJVs (Collis and Montgomery, 1998). The IJVs' financial returns stem from their market positions in relation to their competitors and resources specific to the IJVs.

The size of firms has an impact on the extent of accessibility and volume of resources, and on their performance. Wernerfelt and

Montgomery (1988) observe that for small IJVs, the affect of accessibility to resources on performance is less than 1 percent of the variance in a firm's overall performance; however, Rumelt (1991) finds that for large firms, the correlation between accessibility to resources and performance is as much as 32 and 83 percent of variance. This shows a positive correlation between accessibility to resources, size of the IJVs, and overall performance of the firm.

For the IJVs, Grant (1987) concludes that most empirical studies focused on manufacturing firms that showed a strong relationship between a firm's degree of internationalization, size, accessibility to resources, and performance. However, geographic diversifications and resource availability may lead to an enhanced corporate performance up to a certain point, beyond which the organizational costs and complexity associated with managing the scattered operations outweigh the advantages. Apart from considering financial returns, a parent needs to assess its IJVs' position in diversifying into international markets to reduce the risk of bankruptcy and to increase sales and, in turn, to accrue for higher values to the organization (Gomes and Ramaswarny, 1999). These factors contribute to measuring business performance.

Performance Measurement

The commonly used measure to examine the degree of internationalization is the ratio of foreign to total sales (Geringer et al., 1989). Other measures include the ratio of foreign assets to total assets (Ramaswamy, 1993), and the ratio of employees in foreign locations to total employees (Kim et al., 1989). These measures aim at capturing neither the depth nor the scope or breadth of internationalization. For scope or breadth of internationalization, performance is based on geographical dispersion of operations across countries. IJVs tend to leverage location-based advantages to enhance their performance (Kogut, 1985). Ramaswamy (1993) concludes that a positive relationship exists between number of IJVs and a firm's performance due to diversity of risk, accessibility of resources, and opportunities.

For revenue-based measurements, IJVs tend to use either or both gross margin and pretax as a percentage of revenues due to the following reasons. First, these ratios avoid the noncontrollable factors— currency conversions between parents and cross-border IJVs. Second, the investment-based measures, which are based on the nature of the industry and the cross-country nature of the firm's operational activities, may not reflect returns on their achievements (Yip, 1984).

For example, return on sales is an important criterion for evaluating an IJV's performance (Choi and Czechowicz, 1983) but cross-country assets are subject to parent's allocations, valuation differences, and depreciation rules. Also, it is difficult to determine whether a particular class of assets ought to be included in the calculations. For example, within the fixed asset category, some parents do not include plant and machinery in the calculations because these are meant for a particular IJV, not for others. To streamline comparisons, this category of fixed assets may be excluded in all the calculations even though they generate revenues for the IJV being evaluated. To avoid complications and confusions, revenue-based measures are considered suitable for an international comparison. Third, a pretax measure is more relevant than other variables because this reflects the performance of the management of the IJV being evaluated. The pretax figure is being used because the IJV managers may have little or no control over the local tax rates. And as for tax concessions, if any, these tend to be negotiated by the parent at the first instance when the IJVs are being considered for a particular geographical location or country. Fourth, profits are measured before deducting the corporate overhead charges, because allocations of the latter tend to be largely discretionary on the part of the parent's management, not controllable by the IJV managers. Nonetheless, Atrill and McLaney (2002) argue that ROI is a popular method of evaluating the profitability of divisions because the IJV managers have control over the allocated investments. They suggest that ROI should be expressed as a divisional profit to divisional investment (or assets employed) ratio because ROI is a measure of profitability as it relates profits to the size of investment. Broadbent and Cullen (2003) support this mathematical formula but suggest that ROI is an appropriate financial measure of performance only when the IJV is designated as an investment center. ROI is in fact a popular measure of divisional performance in the United Kingdom for the following reasons: (1) it is widely used and understood by managers; (2) it can be used for comparison because it is expressed in ratios; (3) it focuses on assets and profits; and (4) it is a comprehensive measure because all divisions are reflected in it.

However, a parent may need to pay particular attention to how an individual IJV reports its profits because profits can be distorted in many ways. First, the parent needs to establish the extent of cross-subsidization between IJVs (Hamel and Prahalad, 1985). Second, the parent and IJVs may manipulate the transfer prices and enable the firm as a whole to benefit from the differential tax rates, local subsidies, free trade benefits and supports, and exchange differences

(Yunker, 1983). The magnitude of profit manipulation is a closely guarded secret (Lecraw, 1983). Thus in some cases, a parent may use both revenue and investment approaches.

If a parent decides to use the investment-based measurements, which are based on returns on assets, it needs to define *asset* with justification because assets are subject to revaluation and depreciation, and the amount can be based on pre-tax, gross, or after-tax profits. These judgmental measurements add distortions to the computations when comparing and measuring the performance of IJVs and the organization as a whole. The parent should thus consider adopting both the revenue-based and the investment-based measurements. This hybrid approach complements each other's shortcomings and evens out possible distortions. The methods and bases of measurements need to be clearly stated and consistently applied from one period to another. Consistency avoids misunderstanding and misinterpretation of results. Any change to the methods or basis of measurements should be properly recorded and justified with reasons. The effects, if any, due to the changes should be shared among the IJVs. Transparency and accountability improve trust, confidence, responsibilities, and achievements among IJVs. To identify the winners, the IJVs should be put on a level playing field in the evaluation process. The achievers should be recognized and rewarded, and low performers need to find ways to improve their activities and results.

Apart from financial returns, the parent and IJVs should also consider nonfinancial results. These include market and political risk, employment creation rate, employee turnover ratios, corporate social responsibilities and contributions, customer satisfaction, rate of referrals, and market share. These are a useful guide to both parents and IJVs to formulate plans and strategies for catering the markets when securing the needed resources and opportunities. In many cases, the parent tends to use both financial and nonfinancial returns to even out any shortcomings of the measurements. An integrated paradigm is the appropriate approach for almost all firms.

Methodology

Data Collection

This is an exploratory study reflecting the lack of prior research on how parents would measure performance of their IJVs. This study is based on interviews with the highest officers (three of them are CEOs and the remaining two are CFOs) of five firms in Houston, Texas. Grounded theory was used to discover a specific phenomenon.

Strauss and Corbin (1998) state that grounded theory is driven by data systematically gathered and analyzed through a research process. In this method, data collection, analysis, and eventual theory stand in close relationship to one another.

To gain understanding of accounting practices in their natural setting, the qualitative approach is effective (Tomkins and Groves, 1983). Five cases were selected for obtaining an in-depth understanding of how the parents measure performance of their IJVs through semistructured interviews with representatives of parent organizations. Out of the five cases, three cases are from service industries whose activities include banking, financial, and real estate investment, whereas the remaining two cases are from manufacturing industries that manufacture automobiles and computer components. For the purpose of this study, a parent organization is defined as the office or business unit that is responsible for monitoring and administrating IJVs. The business unit may not be the head office of the organization but is responsible for all the decisions and activities of those Chinese IJVs. All the interviewees were assured of confidentiality of their identity and data. On average, the interviewees had eight years of experience working with the organization and were aware of how performance was being measured and monitored. Each interview lasted for about an hour. The interviewees preferred to be interviewed within their office premises. The interviews were conducted in a friendly manner and in many cases, the interviewees were asked to illustrate and substantiate the discussion with examples and evidence. Notes were taken during the interviews as the interviewees refused to be taped. The interviewing notes were then transcribed in proper format and discussed with the respective interviewees to ensure their accuracy and completion. This process was repeated for the next interview held after a period of over three weeks.

Data Analysis

The grounded theory requires data to have three coding—open, axial, and selective. First, data from the interviews are analyzed sentence by sentence using open coding (Strauss and Corbin, 1998). Because many questions were raised and discussed during the open coding, each interview was analyzed based on the main points made by the interviewees. Relationships between these points were noted, as they were useful in facilitating and developing coding procedures. Second, the axial coding aims at identifying the relationships between these open codes to form independent categories. An axial coding refers to the coding that revolves around categories and their properties. Further, Strauss and Corbin (1990) explain that axial coding is a set of procedures whereby data are put back together in new ways after open coding by making connections between categories. Third, selective coding is a process of integrating categories and refining the theory. This approach redefines the categories to various focal categories under investigation. Further, Strauss and Corbin (1990) suggest that this could be in terms of causal conditions, environmental conditions, organizational conditions, management strategies, and consequences. These categories should be expanded to subcategories to reflect the aim of the investigations. There is no fixed rule on the number and types of categories for a particular research as long as these classifications achieve the aims and refine the theory. The selective process should be expanded to include identified issues even though they are eventually neglected. These should be regrouped, evaluated, and analyzed to confirm with the original sources before being ignored. These neglected categories could eventually be found relevant or useful to the current or future investigation processes. The following section gives the background of each participating firm in the study. The focus is to determine how a parent measures the performance of its IJVs.

Case Studies

Table 9.1 reports a brief description of the five participating firms. Interviewees in the firms were from the parent organizations who analyzed, interpreted and monitored the measurement of performance. They also ensured that the purpose and reasons for adopting certain elements of performance measurement were identified and justified.

Service Firm A

Firm A was established in the early 1950s as a retail bank. It now has over 15 percent of the U.S. market share. It has branches in the United States and other countries. New York is its head office but the Houston office is in charge of the Asian IJVs including those in China. The management team in the parent office has an average of 13 years of work experience in the banking sector, during eight years of which it operated from its Houston branch. Due to competition in the local market, Firm A opened an IJV in Shanghai two years ago. Firm A uses both financial (gross profit and turnover ratios) and nonfinancial measurements (employee turnover) for measuring performance.

Table 9.1   Profile of the firms participated in the case study

Interviewee	Nature of IJV	Years of relationship	% holding	Key financial measures	Key nonfinancial measures
A (CFO)	Services	2	80	Gross profit; turnover ratio; returns on investment	employee turnover; customer satisfaction; referrals by customers
B (CEO)	Manufacturing	4	50	Net profit before tax; returns on investment	Customer satisfaction; employee turnover; production/delivery time lag; number of new customers
C (CEO)	Services	3.5	75	Net profit before tax; returns on investment; market shares	Customer satisfaction; customer waiting time; employee turnover
D (CEO)	Manufacturing	2	70	Net profit before tax; returns on investment; customer satisfaction	Market size, customer referrals, number of new products; employee turnover
E (CFO)	Services	1	60	Gross profit; returns on investment; turnover ratio	Customer satisfaction; referral rate; employee turnover

Manufacturing Firm B

Firm B manufactures and supplies computer components to the U.S. market and has factories in central and southern United States. Due to increasing competitions and manufacturing costs, Firm B has two factories in China—one is outside Shanghai and another in Shenzhen (South East China). Both plants were established four years ago. The manufactured components are either for the Asian market including the local Chinese market or for the United States. This is an equal partnership with the local Chinese organization. The intention for having the Chinese IJV is to diversify risk, expand the market, and explore low-cost structures. The main performance measurement indicators are net profit before tax, and returns on investments. The parent office in Houston uses both financial and nonfinancial measurements. In the next few years, the parent intends to implement the balanced scorecard model for performance measurement for the entire organization. A hybrid approach was adopted in order to have a balanced form of measuring performance and to ensure long-term results rather than short-term returns, avoiding any bias on either the financial or the nonfinancial measurements.

Service Firm C

The main activity of Firm C is to provide insurance, unit trust, and financial services to its customers. It has two IJVs in China—Beijing and Shanghai. These two IJVs were established four years ago and each provides a broad range of financial services to the individuals, small- and medium-sized enterprises, and public sector organizations. The management has an average of 11 years of work experience at the parent office, out of which six years were at the Houston office. Currently the parent uses both financial (net profit before tax, and returns on investments), and nonfinancial (customer satisfaction and employee turnover) measurements. The limitations of the financial approach are one of the reasons why this firm adopted the nonfinancial measures to supplement the measurement processes. The parent weights both the financial and nonfinancial measurement equally.

Manufacturing Firm D

Firm D assembles automobiles for sales within the United States. It was established in the mid-1960s. Most parts of its plant in Texas are automated. It has an IJV in Shenzhen (South East China) that assembles automobiles for the local Chinese and U.S. markets. Due to local competition, the parent set up the Chinese IJV two years ago in search of a low-cost structure and a large market. Since its inception, the parent has been using both the financial and the nonfinancial approaches in particular the customer-focused strategy that intends to increase its market share. Customer satisfaction and employee turnover are the key nonfinancial measurements. The IJV instills the *fear of customer* attitude and behavior to make the parent use nonfinancial measures.

Service Firm E

The main activities of E include purchasing of properties for leasing and management. The vibrant pace of development in Shenzhen (South East China) has prompted the parent to have its IJV invest in properties for leasing. The firm needs significant funding for constructing and leasing a wide range of houses to the locals. The houses are for rentals either to the individuals or the visitors of nearby factories and organizations. Rental incomes are meant for paying staff salaries, maintaining the properties, and meeting the cost of operating the IJV. The parent organization uses both financial and nonfinancial (including customer satisfaction, and employee turnover) elements for measuring performance. According to the firm, the combined approach of using both financial and nonfinancial elements is useful for the board of directors and shareholders, but the nonfinancial elements of measures are useful for evaluating operational activities and the management competency of the IJV. The nonfinancial elements focus on long-term returns, relationships, motivations of the IJV's management and employees because sometimes the financial returns do not present the full picture of an IJV: its overall challenges, situations, and achievements. Both the parent and the IJV use the balanced scorecard approach for evaluating performance.

Cross-case Analysis

A cross-case analysis involves comparisons of the five cases to understand how the parents measure performance of their IJVs and justify adoption of a particular measure (Strauss and Corbin, 1998). Yin (1994) regards the development of consistent findings over multiple cases as a strong finding to challenge the hypotheses. The following section presents the analysis and findings.

Findings

This section discusses the major findings of the interviews and links them to each of the elements of the framework identified earlier. These elements are (1) Agency; (2) Control; (3) Strategy; (4) Technology; (5) Transaction costs; (6) Culture and society; (7) Economy and market size; (8) Government and politics; (9) Industrial structure; and (10) Resources.

Agency

The framework conceptualizes that an agent exists to pursue its own interests and goals rather than those of its parent or the organization as a whole. Interviewee C agrees with this notion to a certain extent and said,

> in the short-term, an IJV tends to exist or gets alliance with us [as the parent] to build its own aims and strategies. In the long-term, both of us [IJV and the parent] have an aligned mission and visions. This relationship builds an increased level of trust and performance. As the level of trust increases, especially with our Chinese IJVs, we feel that there is a reduction on cost of governance, and uncertainties, and [that we] have relatively similar beliefs, values, expectations and mutual supports.

"As the level of trust and confidence increases over time, the level of risk that the IJV prepares to undertake increases, and thus the rate of returns on investments," says Interviewee D. In the short-term, Firm D uses net profit before tax and returns on investments to evaluate the contributions of its IJV; whereas in the long-term, the market size, numbers, percentage of customer referrals, and numbers of new products are the main measuring elements.

Interviewees A and B emphasize the importance of ensuring that both the parent and the IJVs have common goals and visions to avoid conflicts and improve performance. "These can be achieved over time with the level of trust we have. It is not unusual to have different sets of goals and aims at the beginning, but take time to adjust," comments Interviewee A. However, Interviewee E takes into account the level of interactions that the IJV has with the local environment, networks, and connections and comments, "the Chinese IJVs emphasize on local networking and connections to gain access to resources, and all these need time and space." These interviewees agree that when measuring performance, agency relationships should be taken into consideration.

Control

The framework postulates that strong management control over an IJV's daily operations exerts a positive effect on performance due to IJVs' commitments and strategic importance. However, the framework does not stipulate the control through shareholdings. Firm E said, "it becomes impractical to have daily control and supervision on the operation of an IJV due to its physical distance and the constant changing local environment." Thus, the control should be based on the extent of control, trust, and parents' control on its IJVs. Interviewees B and D both hold weekly conferencing with the general managers of the IJVs. Regular communication has built confidence, respect, and mutual trust between the parties. Performance of Firm D has improved as its local managers feel that their views are being appreciated and that they are being considered as team players. The interviewees agree that a higher proportion of shareholdings will mean a stronger influence on the operations of the IJVs, and thus on performance and returns.

Strategy

Both parents and IJVs are jointly responsible for formulating the IJVs' strategies. The agreed strategies should be reviewed and updated regularly to reflect changes in the local environment. However, the overall mission and vision of the organization should be the same. Interviewee A comments, "it is essential for our IJV's to have their own strategies, but these must be comparable to ours—the organization as a whole." "As long as," Interviewee B said, "both sets of strategies are not far apart, we should leave the IJVs alone sorting out their own strategies since they have a better and clearer knowledge of the local environment than us." When measuring performance, the parent should consider the stage of an IJV, as different stages of the IJVs' lifecycle will yield different results. If an IJV is in the process of changing its strategy, performance may be affected due to the changeover, but if it is at the maturity stage, the returns and results should be relatively consistent with the past performance. The interviewees agreed that the parents needed to know exactly the lifecycle stage of their IJVs because a different stage of completing a particular plan and mission yielded a different level of risks and uncertainties, and thus of financial returns. For example, Firm B was to launch a major advertising campaign for its new products and after-sale services. Indeed, performance is greatly dependent on the success of the initiative.

Value chain strategy synchronizes the production and marketing processes. Accessibility to local resources throughout the process adds value, cuts costs, and improves efficiency on deliveries. Interviewees B and D from the manufacturing sectors agreed that the value chain strategies built healthier financial results and returns due to their IJVs' better control over the situations. This is practical for the Chinese IJVs due to the availability of resources, infrastructure, and close networks for business-to-business and business-to-consumers environments. Clearly, parents need to consider the facilities and resources available to the individual IJV.

Technology

The extent of technology transfer from a parent to its IJVs and among IJVs affects the levels of returns and profitability of the IJVs. A higher level of technology transfer from the parent improves operations and efficiency and provides more efficient and up-to-date products and services to their customers. Interviewees B and D support the view that their IJVs' request for the latest technologies and ideas enable them to compete with the others in an increasingly sophisticated market. However, this is not applicable in the services sectors. Interviewees A, C, and E do not feel that there is any significant correlation between the level of technology transfers and profitability. The only link between technology transfers in the services sector is the extent of new ideas that the parent is prepared to share with its IJVs and its flexibility in providing services. Indeed, firms like to have flexibility in their approach to meet local demands. For the manufacturing sector, interviewees B and D agreed that continuous improvements through R&D provided a significant support to advance their products, services, and procedures. Therefore, the level of R&D transfer is an important indicators of performance and results.

Transaction Costs

All the interviewees agreed that transaction costs existed in the early stages of their relationship with their IJVs. It was due to uncertainties (e.g., incomplete contracts) and opportunism (opportunities in transactions). Each party tends to maximize its profits and returns due to selfishness and opportunism (agreed by all the interviewees). However, as the level of relationships and trust improves, the level of transaction costs reduces to a minimum. This process significantly reduces the costs of governance and the level of bureaucracy, while improving transparency, accountability, and caring among the team players. Interviewee E commented, "even though we have a relatively short period of relationship (one year) with our Chinese IJV, we feel that we have a long way to go. We have the confidence that once we have established the appropriate level of trust and confidence with the Chinese IJV (e.g., over the next few years), this will greatly reduce the transaction costs." Transaction costs hinder profitability and performance of IJVs. However, Interviewee A observed, "it was difficult to ascertain the exact amount of transaction costs—both uncertainties and opportunities—as this depends on the relationship between us and our IJVs. Nonetheless, we feel that these costs will gradually be reduced to a minimum level as time progresses."

Culture and Society

Culture and social background of a country affects the survival rate and performance of an IJV. "The internal culture of an IJV will change over time, but not the external culture," Interviewee B said. "It is thus important to understand both the organizational and societal cultures, as both of these are, to a certain extent, interrelated and influence the strategies, market size, and performance of the IJVs," Interviewee C added. The Chinese emphasize long-term relationships. Thus, when measuring performance of Chinese IJVs, as Interviewee A suggested, "evaluators should look into the length of time that the relationships have cultivated. Longevity is the key that the Chinese consider." The longer the relationships, the more stable the financial and nonfinancial returns, trust, confidence, employees' loyalty, rates of retentions, and referrals by customers. Further, because China is a collectivistic society, the environment emphasizes a close relationship between contractors and suppliers. Also, a parent needs to ensure that the societal emphasis is on success.

Economy and Market Size

An IJV located in a large market performs better than those situated in small local markets. This is particularly true in the Chinese context. A stable macroeconomy creates a large market size and strengthens consumers' purchasing power. When measuring performance and comparing the returns among IJVs, Interviewee A recommended, "to express the results in relative terms using percentages to differentiate between those IJVs that are situated in a relatively large market and those in a smaller and sparsely populated place. This makes the comparisons meaningful." However, Interviewee E pointed out that "it is difficult for us to ascertain the size of a market due to lack of information and difficulties to draw an exact boundary on our markets. Also there are many competitive products, so we need to review the bases of measurements—gross profit and turnover ratios—on a regular basis." "The measurements should be based on sustainability in the growth rather than solely on a particular period of time," Interviewee B clarified.

The economic situation of a particular location and country should be considered when measuring performance. In a location where a high inflation rate exists, adverse impact on the purchasing power of the locals may be felt. Interviewee A adds, "within China, certain locations in large cities may have a higher rate of inflation than a rural area, and thus may cause imbalances on the performance of two IJVs located in two different towns and cities even though they are situated within the same country." In some cases, it is difficult to arrive at the updated official inflation rates, making comparisons and evaluations challenging. The parents need to ensure that updated information is being used while measuring performance to project fairness across the board and among the team players. Interviewee A suggested, "the official guidance is the best bet, but if we could not get it, we will have to rely upon our IJVs to provide the needed information. We normally compare the information with the local chamber of commerce and [the United States] Department of Commerce." The whole process of measurements should be properly discussed and agreed upon among the team players before they are implemented. This avoids misunderstandings, confusions, and disincentives to the players.

Government and Politics

Stability of a government attracts FDI. As the confidence level increases, so does the level of FDI. However, parents are equally concerned with the level of bureaucracy, red tapes, and legislative requirements. All the interviewees were concerned with the increasing level of bureaucracy in dealing with their Chinese IJVs, but stability in the government's system compensates with a continuing trend of returns on the investments. Interviewee D supported the view and said, "a stable government and no unexpected changes in government regulatory requirements make the measuring process easier and budgets much reliable." Further, interviewee B takes into consideration the different stages of investments in China because the learning curve during the initial stages of investment is relatively high (c.f., four years ago) with a large volume of paperwork; but now the level of bureaucracy has greatly reduced. These factors have given confidence to the parents in selecting IJVs.

Interviewee C commented, "We have a number of IJVs and we regularly monitor the political climate of the host governments and adjust our measuring yardsticks." Indeed, the yardsticks change as the political climate of the host country becomes relatively unstable. Interviewee C continued, "to be fair, the parents—including us— should inform their IJVs if they decide to change the measuring processes." Political and economic situations of a country work in tandem to attract FDI. Interviewee C used the trend analysis to measure the performance of its IJVs and adjusted for political instability in the host countries. This adjustment was shared among the team players whenever such situations arose.

Industrial Structure

Competition in China is fierce due to the high expectations and demands of the parents and the power of the consumers. In urban areas, where the level of competition is high, parents tend to use the market share, percentages of referrals, and new customers as the yardsticks; whereas in rural areas, where the competition and infrastructure is relatively less challenging, the parents tend to use profitability and returns on investments for evaluation purposes. Interviewee E emphasized the need for different sets of measuring rules for different industrial structures as competition, industrial structure and infrastructure, and uneven spread of government investments vary from region to region. There appears to be no fixed basis for selecting the measurements among the interviewees but all seem to suggest that GDP of the region will be taken into consideration. The maturity and duration of investments that the parents have made in the IJVs need to be taken into consideration. For example, Interviewee B, who has been running an IJV in China for the last four years, tends to focus on *net profit before tax* and *profitability returns*, in comparison to *market share* in the initial stages of investment. Firm B used both financial and nonfinancial elements for measuring performance.

The above discussion shows that parents change the measuring standards during their relationships and investments. "As long as the IJVs are fully informed and understand the measuring process, these will not upset the relationships and strategies of the organization as a whole," Interviewee C confirmed.

Resources

Availability of resources from the parents or other team players affects performance and strategies of an IJV. IJVs are situated in locations where the resources (i.e., human skills, technology, raw materials, and infrastructures) are relatively abundant; the IJVs have the added advantage of implementing their strategies and plans compared with those in relatively remote areas where resources are scare and expensive. Interviewee B supports the calls for setting up an IJV where accessibility to resources is not a major problem. Resources, in particular those that are rare, are needed for success stories. Apart from looking at resources, the parents should consider the availability of having a good and reliable infrastructure, both road and railway systems, and multimedia connections. All the interviewees revealed that they constantly reviewed the current status of resource supports and were prepared to shift the investments to places where these could be obtained relatively cheaply and easily.

Contribution of the Chapter

This chapter discusses the theoretical framework that determines and identifies factors that may improve or hinder performance of IJVs. The framework maps internal and external factors that a parent and its team players need to consider for performance measurement. These factors should be reviewed and updated regularly due to the changing environment of IJVs. The framework consists of factors relating to agency, control, strategy, technology, transaction costs, control and society, economy and market size, government and policies, industrial structure, and resources. It is essential that both parents and their IJVs be sensitive to the constantly changing business environment, in particular the rules and regulations passed by the host governments, the level of competition, and demands from the customers, employees, and other stakeholders. The continuing wave of demands and requests by the customers for cheaper and better services and products may sometimes cause misunderstandings by other groups of stakeholders due to an uneven spread of returns. This arises because of a conflict of interest—customers want a better quality product with a lower price while the shareholders expect the organization to maximize their wealth and returns. Reconciling these differences in interests and expectations is challenging and may suggest that IJVs may have to forego some or all of their intended plans to balance the needs and expectations of these different groups of stakeholders. Parent need to negotiate and declare their intentions and reach agreements with their IJVs as to how and who will exercise control and make decisions. True, the extent of direct control and daily supervision of the IJVs reduces as time progresses. Time builds the needed trust, relationships, and friendships between the parent and its IJVs, and more importantly between the IJVs and the local stakeholders. Performance of the IJVs improves over time. Apart from the external threat (e.g., competitions, host government's actions on policies and regulations, and economic stability), the parent should consider other factors such as the availability of resources, maturity, and dependence on resources by the IJVs. Resources include human resources, technological know-how, and natural supplies of materials from within and outside the location. Human resources include the level of skills and knowledge, willingness to strive for common goals, mission of the organization as a whole, and flexibility of labor relationships with the unions. Technological level and infrastructure of the host countries should also be taken into consideration. For the natural supplies of resources, the parent needs to consider the costs, relevance, accessibility, and resources. Transfer costs may be included when measuring the performance and returns. Although there is no fixed rule as to how these nonfinancial factors could be translated into financial data for the calculations, it is essential for the parent to communicate and agree with the IJVs as to how these factors should be incorporated in the calculating processes.

Maturity of the relationships depends on the length of time that a parent has with their IJVs and the level of mutual trust and respect that one enjoys with another. In the case of Chinese IJVs, it is obvious that time frame is inversely related to the level of trust and confidence that the parent has invested over time. Sometimes, length of time should not be the sole measurement of maturity, the degree of trust, accountability, care, and transparency too are good indicators. The yardstick should be based on quality and selfless dealings rather than merely on the quantitative time. As long as both parties are willing to work in tandem and for the benefit of the organization as a whole, performance should improve. Thus, when measuring performance, the parent needs to consider the extent of the journey—time and space that both have traveled. The longer the journey they have accomplished together, the better the level of relationships and trust between them. These factors contribute to business performance, results, and returns.

However, in effect, trust may be a necessary supplement to formal control to ensure high levels of performance under certain circumstances. Trust not only serves as a safeguard against opportunism but also, coupled with productive resolutions, enables the partners to capitalize on synergies and create competitive advantages. This boosts performance of the organization (Barney and Hansen, 1994).

For measuring performance of firms, parents use a range of financial ratios such as foreign assets versus total assets of the organization ratio, IJVs' turnover versus total turnover of the organization ratio, gross profit, net profit before tax and interests, and returns on capital employed. Each of these financial ratios has its own merits and limitations but it is essential to note that financial returns should be used as a form of guidance, not as firm indicators of the IJV's performance. Nonfinancial elements such as causes of underperformance, organizational and environmental conditions, management strategies, and consequences should also be considered. The organizational and environmental conditions include customer satisfaction (e.g., the number of new, referral, and lost customers; customer evaluation), service quality (e.g., employee attitude, customer waiting time, friendliness, and appearance of employees), and human resources (e.g., employee turnover, and employee training and development programs). However, Chong (2003) concludes that financial yardsticks ensure that what gets measured gets done. Indeed, both financial and nonfinancial measurements are equally important and the two should complement and not replace one another.

Like any other study, this study has limitations too. A conscious or unconscious bias in the interactions between the interviewer and interviewees can exist; however, by using multiple data collection methods such as interviews, document inspections, and further inquiries, we enhanced the reliability and validity of the study. This study used the multiple case study approach that ensured a degree of representative proportional in the quantity of cases studied (Yin, 1994).

Future Research Directions

Due to the high degree of exposure of IJVs to external factors, surroundings and parents' dynamic nature of control, the bases of measuring performance of IJVs should be reviewed on a regular basis. Although the theoretical framework remains static, it captures only a snapshot situation of the IJV. Measurement of performance should be stretched over a period of time. Trend analysis enables parents to gauge the real performance of their IJVs. The IJVs are situated in extremely dynamic, harsh, and notoriously unstable locations. It would be interesting to compare these performance measurements with those of IJVs situated in a relatively stable environment (Doz, 1996). This can be accomplished by using the dynamic theory (Yan and Gray, 1994).

More empirical tests should be conducted on the factors included in the framework—specifically the methodological issues concerning data collection, and range and size of the samples—using different geographical and political arenas. Further research should compare IJVs' perspectives with the parents' perspective for performance measurement. More research should contribute to the body of knowledge as to how the measuring process will have ramifications on the perceived challenges to meet the needs and expectations of the external stakeholders as well as those of the parents.

Performance measurement is linked to the extent of control, direct and indirect, by the parents. However, measuring management control is a challenging task because it deals with control at different levels, for example, strategic, operational, and structural controls (Yan and Gray, 1994), and on different dimensions, for example, scope, extent, mechanisms, and overall control (Geringer and Hebert, 1989).

With respect to performance measurements, both Yan and Gray (1994) and Osland and Cavusgil (1996) observe that different IJVs may have different goals and objectives, and each may consider some measurements extremely relevant and critical, and some as unimportant or irrelevant. Another line of inquiry will be to match performance measurement of a particular parent with that of the IJV based on external factors by using the framework discussed in the chapter. Indeed, the framework needs to be reviewed and updated with the passage of time.

References

Adler, N.J. *International Dimensions of Organizational Behavior.* Boston: Kent Publishing, 1986.

Alchian, A.A., and Demsetz, H. "Production, Information Costs, and Economic Organization." *American Economic Review* 62, no. 5 (1972): 777–95.

Aldrich, H.E., and Auster, E.R. "Even Dwarfs Started Small: Liabilities of Age and Size and Their Strategic Implications." In *Research in Organizational Behavior*, ed. Cummings, L.L., and Staw B.M., Vol. 8, 165–98. Greenwich, CT: SAT Press, 1986.

Allen, L., and Pantzalis, C. "Valuation of the Operating Flexibility of Multinational Corporations." *Journal of International Business Studies* 27, no. 4 (1996): 633–53.

Alon, I., and McKee, D.I. "Toward a Macro-environmental Model of International Franchising." *Multinational Business Review* 7, no. 1 (1999): 76–82.

Alvarez, S.A., and Barney, J.B. "How Entrepreneurial Firms Can Benefit from Alliances with Large Partners." *Academy of Management Executive* 15, no. 1 (2001): 139–48.

Anderson, E., and Gatignon, H. "Modes of Entry: A Transaction Cost Analysis and Propositions." *Journal of International Business Studies* 17, no. 3 (1986): 1–26.

Anderson, J.C., and Narus, J.A. "A Model of Distributor Firm and Manufacturer Firm Working Partnerships." *Journal of Marketing* 54 (January 1990): 42–58.

Anderson, S.W., and Sedatole, K.L. "Management Accounting for the Extended Enterprise: Performance Management for Strategic Alliances and Networked Partners." In *Management Accounting in the Digital Economy*, ed. Bhimani, A. Oxford, UK: Oxford University Press, 2003.

Annavarjula, M., and Beldona, S. "Multinationality-Performance Relationship: A Review and Re-conceptualization." *International Journal of Organizational Analysis* 8, no. 1 (2000): 48–67.

Armstrong, S. "An Application of Econometric Models to International Marketing." *Journal of Marketing Research* 7, no. 2 (1970): 190–98.

Atrill, P., and McLaney, E. *Management Accounting for Non-specialists*. London: Prentice Hall-Financial Times, 2002.

Austin, J.E. *Managing in Developing Countries*. New York: Free Press, 1990.

Bacharach, S.B., and Lawler, E.J. *Bargaining: Power, Tactics, and Outcomes*. San Francisco, CA: Jossey-Bass, 1984.

Bain, J.S. *Barriers to New Competition*. Cambridge, MA: Harvard University Press, 1956.

Barney, J. "Firm Resources and Sustained Competitive Advantage." *Journal of Management* 91, no. 17 (1991): 99–120.

Barney, J.B., Hansen, M.H. "Trustworthiness as a Source of Competitive Advantage." *Strategic Management Journal* 15, no. 8 (1994): 175–90.

Barringer, B.R., and Harrison, J.S. "Walking a Tightrope: Creating Value through Inter-organizational Relationships." *Journal of Management* 26, no. 3 (2000): 367–403.

Bartlett, C.A., and Ghoshal, S. "Tap Your Subsidiaries for Global Reach." *Harvard Business Review* 6 (1986): 87–94.

Baum, J.A.C., and Oliver, C. "Institutional Linkages and Organizational Morality." *Administrative Science Quarterly* 36, no. 2 (1991): 187–218.

Beamish, P.W. "The Role of Alliances in International Entrepreneurship." *Research in Global Strategic Management* 7 (1999): 43–61.

Beamish, P.W., and Banks, J.C. "Equity Joint Ventures and the Theory of the Multinational Enterprises." *Journal of International Business Studies* 18, no. 2 (1987): 1–16.

Birkinshaw, J.M., and Morrison, A.J. "Configurations of Strategy and Structure in Subsidiaries of Multinational Corporations." *Journal of International Business Studies* 26, no. 4 (1995): 729–53.

Blodgett, L.L. "Partner Contributions as Predictors of Equity Share in International Joint Ventures." *Journal of Marketing Business Studies* (First Quarter 1991): 63–78.

Boulton, W.B. *Electronics Manufacturing in Korea and China*. Baltimore, MD: Loyola College. USA. NTIS Report #PB95–188116 (1997).

Broadbent, M., and Cullen, J. *Managing Financial Resources*. London: Butterworth Heinemann, 2003.

Buckley, P., Clegg, J., and Tan, H. "Cultural Awareness in Knowledge Transfer to Chine—The Role of Guanxi and Mianzi." *Journal of World Business* 41, no. 3 (2006): 275–88.

Buzzell, R.D., Gale, B.T. *The PIMS Principles: Linking Strategy to Performance*. New York: Free Press, 1987.

Caves, R.E. "International Differences in Industrial Organization." In *Handbook of Industrial Organization*, ed. Schmalensee, R., Willig, D. Vol. 2, 1225–50. Amsterdam, The Netherlands: Elsevier Science Publishers B.V., 1989.

Chase, C.D., Kuhle, J.L., and Walther, C.H. "The Relevance of Political Risk in Direct Foreign Investment." *Management International Review* 28, no. 3 (1988): 31–38.

Cheng, A.T. "Gambling on Guanxi." *Asia Inc.* (July 1997): 30–35.

Chi, T., and McGuire, D.J. "Collaborative Ventures and Value of Learning: Integrating the Transaction Cost and Strategic Option Perspectives on the Choice of Market." *Journal of International Business Studies* 27, no. 2 (1996): 285–307.

Child, J., Yan, Y., and Lu, Y. "Ownership and Control in Sino-Foreign Joint Ventures." In *Cooperative Strategies: Asian Pacific Perspectives*, ed. Beamish, P.W., and Killing, J.P., 403–27. San Francisco, CA: New Lexington Press, 1997.

Choi, F.D.S., and Czechowicz, I.J. "Assessing Foreign Subsidiary Performance: A Multinational Comparison." *Management International Review* 23, no. 4 (1983): 14–28.

Chong, H.G. "Performance Measurements for SMEs." *The International Journal of Condition Monitoring* & *Diagnostic Engineering Management* 6, no. 3 (2003): 11–15.

Collis, D.J., and Montgomery, C.A. "Creating Corporate Advantage." *Harvard Business Review* 76, no. 3 (1998): 70–83.

Conner, K. "A Historical Comparison of Resource-Based Theory and Five Schools of Thought within Industrial Economics: Do We Have a New Theory of the Firm?" *Journal of Management* 17, no. 1 (1991): 121–54.

Crocker, K.J., and Masten, S.E. "Mitigating Contractual Hazards: Unilateral Options and Contract Length." *Rand Journal of Economics* 19, no. 3 (1988): 327–43.

Cui, A.S., Griffith, D.A., Cavusgil, S.T., and Dabic, M. "The Influence of Market and Cultural Environmental Factors on Technology Transfer between Foreign MNCs and Local Subsidiaries: A Croatian Illustration." *Journal of World Business* 41, no. 2 (2006): 100–11.

Czinkota, M.R., and Ronkainen, I.A. "International Business and Trade in the Next Decade: Report from a Delphi Study." *Journal of International Business Studies* 28, no. 4 (1997): 827–44.

Das, T.K., and Teng, B.S. "Between Trust and Control: Developing Confidence in Partner Cooperation in Alliances." *Academy of Management Review* 23, no. 3 (1998): 491–512.

Day, G.S., and Wensley, R. "Assessing Advantage: A Framework for Diagnosing Competitive Superiority." *Journal of Marketing* 52, no. 2 (1988): 1–20.

Dierickx, L., and Cool, K. "Asset Stock Accumulation and Sustainability of Competitive Advantage." *Management Science* 35, no. 12 (1989): 1504–10.

DiMaggio, P., and Powell, W. *The New Institutionalism in Organizational Analysis*. Chicago: University of Chicago Press, 1991.

Doz, Y.L. "The Evolution of Cooperation in Strategic Alliances: Initial Conditions or Learning Processes?" *Strategic Management Journal* 17 (Summer 1996): 55–85.

Dunning, J., and Bansal, S. "The Cultural Sensitivity of the Eclectic Paradigm." *Multinational Business Review* 5, no. 1 (1997): 1–16.

Eisenhardt, K.M. "Agency Theory: An Assessment and Review." *Academy of Management Review* 14, no. 1 (1989): 57–74.

Emerson, R. "Power-Dependence Relations." *American Sociological Review* 27 (1962): 31–41.

Fama, E.F. "Agency Problems and the Theory of the Firm." *Journal of Political Economies* 88 (1980): 288–305.

Fatehi-Sedeh, K., and Safizadeh, M.H. "The Association between Political Instability and Flow of Foreign Direct Investment." *Management International Review* 29, no. 4 (1989): 4–13.

Fisher, R., and Ury, W. *Getting to YES: Negotiating Agreement without Giving*. New York: Penguin Books, 1981.

Flamholtz, E.G., Das, T.K., and Tsui, A.S., "Toward an Integrative Framework of Organizational Control." *Accounting Organizations and Society* 10, no. 1 (1985): 35–50.

Fox, R. "Agency Theory: A New Perspective." *Management Accounting* 62, no. 2 (1984): 36–38.

Franko, L.G. *Joint Venture Survival in Multinational Corporations*. New York: Praeger Publishers, 1971.

Galaskiewicz, J. "Inter-organizational Relations." *Annual Review of Sociology* 11 (1985): 281–304.

Geringer, J.M., Beamish, P.W., and daCosta, R.C. "Diversification Strategy and Internationalization: Implications for MNC Performance." *Strategic Management Journal* 10, no. 2 (1989): 109–19.

Geringer, J.M., and Hebert, L. "Control and Performance of International Joint Ventures." *Journal of International Business Studies* 20, no. 2 (1989): 235–54.

Goerzen, A., and Beamish, P.W. "Geographic Scope and Multinational Enterprise Performance." *Strategic Management Journal* 24, no. 13 (2003): 1289–1306.

Gomes, L., and Ramaswamy, K. "An Empirical Examination of the Form of the Relationship between Multinationality and Performance." *Journal of International Business Studies* 30, no. 1 (1999): 173–88.

Grant, R.M. "Multi-nationality and among British Manufacturing Companies." *Journal of International Business Studies* 18, no. 1 (1987): 79–89.

Gray, B., and Yan, A. "The Formation and Evolution of International Joint Ventures: Examples from U.S.-Chinese Partnerships." In *Cooperative Strategies: Asian Perspectives*, ed. Beamish, P.W., and Killing, J.P., 57–88. San Francisco, CA: New Lexington Press, 1997.

Hamel, G., and Prahalad, C.K. "Do You Really Have a Global Strategy?" *Harvard Business Review* 63, no. 4 (1985): 139–48.

Hannan, M.T., and Freeman, J. *Organizational Ecology.* Cambridge, MA: Harvard University Press, 1989.

Harzing, A.W., and Noorderhaven, N. "Knowledge Flows in MNCs: An Empirical Test and Extension of Gupta and Govindarajan's Typology of Subsidiary Roles." *International Business Review* 15, no. 3 (2006): 195–214.

Hennart, J. "A Transaction Cost Theory of Equity Joint Ventures." *Strategic Management Journal* 9, no. 3 (1988): 361–74.

Hill, C.W.L. "National Institutional Structures, Transaction Cost Economizing and Competitive Advantage: The Case of Japan." *Organizational Science* 6 (1995): 119–31.

Hill, C.W.L., and Hoskisson, R.E. "Strategy and Structure in the Multi-product Firm." *Academy of Management Review* 87, no. 12 (1987): 331–41.

Hofstede, G. *Cultural Consequences: International Differences in Work Related Values.* Beverly Hills, CA: Sage Publications, 1980.

———. "Problems Remain, but Theories Will Change: The Universal and the Specific in 21st-Century Global Management." *Organizational Dynamics* 28, no. 1 (1999): 34–44.

Hoskisson, R.E., Hill, C.W., and Kim, H. "The Multidivisional Structure: Organizational Fossil or Source of Value?" *Journal of Management* 19, no. 2 (1993): 269–98.

Hymer, S.H. *A Study of Direct Foreign Investment.* Cambridge, MA: MIT Press, 1976.

Inkpen, A.C., and Beamish, P.W. "Knowledge, Bargaining Power and International Joint Venture Instability." *Academy of Management Review* 22, no. 1 (1997): 177–202.

Jacobson, R. "Distinguishing among Competing Theories of the Market Share Effect." *Journal of Marketing* 52, no. 4 (1988): 68–80.

Jensen, M.C., and Meckling, W.H. "Theory of the Firm: Managerial Behavior, Agency Costs, and Ownership Structure." *Journal of Financial Economics* 3, no. 4 (1976): 305–60.

Johanson, J., and Vahlne, J.E. "The Internationalization Process of the Firm—A Model of Knowledge Development and Increasing Foreign Market Commitments." *Journal of International Business Studies* 8, no. 1 (1977): 23–32.

Killing, J.P. *Strategies for Joint Venture Success*. New York: Praeger, 1983.

Kim, W.C., and Hwang, P. "Global Strategy and Multinationals' Entry Mode Choice." *Journal of International Business Studies* 23, no. 1 (1992): 29–54.

Kim, W.C., Hwang, P., and Burgers, W.P. "Global Diversification Strategy and Corporate Profit Performance." *Strategic Management Journal* 10, no. 1 (1989): 45–57.

Kogut, B. "Normative Observations on the International Value-Added Chain and Strategic Groups." *Journal of International Business Studies* 15, no. 2 (1984): 151–67.

———. "Designing Global Strategies: Profiting from Operational Flexibility." *Sloan Management Review* 27, no. 1 (1985): 27–38.

Kogut, B., and Singh, H. "The Effect of National Culture on the Choice of Entry Mode." *Journal of International Business Studies* 19, no. 3 (1988): 411–33.

Kostova, T., and Roth, K. "Adoption of an Organizational Practice by Subsidiaries of Multinational Corporations: Institutional and Relational Effects." *Academy of Management Journal* 45, no. 1 (2002): 215–33.

Kostova, T., and Zaheer, S. "Organizational Legitimacy under Conditions of Complexity: The Case of the Multinational Enterprise." *Academy of Management Review* 24, no. 1 (1999): 64–81.

Lax, D.A., and Sebenius, J.K. *The Manager as Negotiator*. New York: Free Press, 1986.

Lecraw, D.J. "Performance of Transnational Corporations in Less Developed Countries." *Journal of International Business Studies* 14, no. 1 (1983): 15–34.

Lee, Y., and Cavusgil, T., "Enhancing Alliance Performance: The Effects of Contractual-Based versus Relational-Based Governance." *Journal of Business Research* 59, no. 8 (2006): 896–905.

Lessard, D.R. "Finance and Global Competition: Exploiting Financial Scope and Coping with Volatile Exchange Rates." In *Competition in Global Industries*, ed. Porter, M.E., 147–84. Boston: Harvard University Press, 1986.

Lewicki, R.J., and Bunker, B.B. "Trust in Relationships: A Model of Development and Decline." In *Conflict, Cooperation and Justice: Essays Inspired by the Work of Morton Deutsch*, ed. Bunker, B.B., and Rubin, J.Z. San Francisco, CA: Jossey-Bass, 1995. 133–73.

Lewis, J.D., and Weigert, A. "Trust as a Social Reality." *Sociology Forces* 63 (1985): 967–85.

Li, J.T. "Foreign Entry and Survival: Effects of Strategic Choices on Performance in International Markets." *Strategic Management Journal* 16, no. 5 (1995): 333–51.

Li, J.T., Khatri, N., and Lam, K. "Changing Strategic Postures of Overseas Chinese Firms in Asian Emerging Markets." *Management Decision* 37, no. 5/6 (1999): 445–56.

Lieberman, M.B., and Montgomery, D.B. "First Mover Advantages: Retrospective and Link with Resource-Based View." *Strategic Management Journal* 19, no. 12 (1988): 319–32.

Loree, D.W., and Guisinger, S.E. "Policy and Non-policy Determinants of U.S. Equity Foreign Direct Investment." *Journal of International Business Studies* 26, no. 2 (1995): 281–99.

Luo, Y. "Business Strategy, Market Structure, and Performance of International Joint Ventures: The Case of Joint Ventures in China." *Management International Review* 35, no. 3 (1995): 241–64.

Luo, Y., and Peng, M.W. "First Mover Advantages in Investing in Transitional Economies." *Thunderbird International Business Review* 40, no. 2 (1998): 141–63.

Lyles, M.A., and Salk, J.E. "Knowledge Acquisition from Foreign Parents in International Joint Ventures: An Empirical Examination in the Hungarian Context." *Journal of International Business Studies* 27, no. 5 (1997): 877–903.

Mainela, T. "Types and Functions of Social Relationships in the Organizing of an International Joint Venture." *Industrial Marketing Management* 36, no. 1 (2007): 87–98.

Makino, S., and Delios, A. "Local Knowledge Transfer and Performance: Implications for Alliance Formation in Asia." *Journal of International Business Studies* 26, no. 5 (1996): 905–27.

Martinez, R.J., and Dacin, M.T. "Efficiency Motives and Normative Forces: Combining Transaction Cost and Institutional Logic." *Journal of Management* 25, no. 1 (1999): 75–96.

McDougall, P.P., and Oviatt, B.M. "New Venture Internationalization, Strategic Change, and Performance: A Follow-Up Study." *Journal of Business Venturing* 11, no. 1 (1996): 23–40.

Millar, C.C.J.M., Eldomiaty, T.I., Chong, J.C., and Hilton, B. "Corporate Governance and Institutional Transparency in Emerging Markets." *Journal of Business Ethics* 59, no. 1/2 (2005): 163–74.

Mishra, C.S., and Gobeli, D.H. "Managerial Incentives, Internalization, and Market Valuation of Multinational Firms." *Journal of International Business Studies* 29, no. 3 (1998): 583–97.

Mjoen, H., and Tallman, S. "Control and Performance in International Joint Ventures." *Organization Science* 8, no. 3 (1997): 257–74.

Mohr, A.T., "A Multiple Constituency Approach to IJV Performance Measurement." *Journal of World Business* 41, no. 3 (2006): 247–60.

Mohr, J., and Spekman, R. "Characteristics of Partnership Success: Partnership Attributes, Communication Behavior, and Conflict-Resolution Techniques." *Strategic Management Journal* 15, no. 2 (1994): 135–52.

Montgomery, C.A., and Porter, M.E. *Strategy: Seeking and Securing Competitive Advantage.* Boston: Harvard Business School, 1991.

Nooteboom, B., Berger, H., and Noorderhaven, N.G. "Effects of Trust and Governance on Relational Risk." *Academy of Management Journal* 40, no. 2 (1997): 308–38.

North, D.C. *Structure and Change in Economic History.* New York: Norton, 1981.

O'Clock, P., and Devine, K. "The Role of Strategy and Culture in the Performance Evaluation of International Strategic Business Units." *Management Accounting Quarterly Winter* (2003): 65–72.

O'Connor, N.G., Deng, J., and Luo, Y., "Political Constraints, Organization Design and Performance Measurements in China's State-Owned Enterprises." *Accounting, Organizations and Society* 31 (2006): 157–77.

Osborn, R.N., and Baughn, CC. "Forms of Inter-organizational Governance for Multinational Alliances." *Academy of Management Journal* 33, no. 3 (1990): 503–19.

Osland, G.E., and Cavusgil, S.T. "Performance Issues in US—China Joint Ventures." *Californian Management Review* 38, no. 2 (1996): 106–30.

Pan, Y. "Environmental Risk and Foreign Equity Ownership in Joint Ventures in China." *Journal of Asia-Pacific Business* 2, no. 2 (1997): 23–41.

Pan, Y., and Chi, P.S. "Financial Performance and Survival of Multinational Corporations in China." *Strategic Management Journal* 20, no. 4 (1999): 359–74.

Parkhe, A. "Interfirm Diversity, Organizational Learning, and Longevity in Global Strategic Alliances." *Journal of International Business Studies* 22, no. 4 (1991): 579–601.

Peteraf, M. "The Cornerstones of Competitive Advantage: A Resource-Based View." *Strategic Management Journal* 14, no. 3 (1993): 179–91.

Pfeffer, I., and Nowak, P. "Joint Ventures and Interorganizational Interdependence." *Administrative Science Quarterly* 21, no. 3 (1976): 398–418.

Porter, M.E. *Competitive Advantage.* New York: Free Press, 1985.

———. *The Competitive Advantage of Nations.* New York: Free Press, 1990.

———. "Towards a Dynamic Theory of Strategy." *Strategic Management Journal* 12 (1991): 95–117.

Prescott, J.E., Kohli, A.J., and Ventkatraman, N. "The Market Share-Profitability Relationship: An Empirical Assessment of Major Assertions and Contradictions." *Strategic Management Journal* 7, no. 4 (1986): 377–94.

Puffer, M. "A Riddle Wrapped in an Enigma: Demystifying Russian Managerial Motivation." *European Management Journal* 11 (1993): 473–80.

Ramaswamy, K. "Multi-nationality and Performance: An Empirical Examination of the Moderating Effect of Configuration." *Proceedings of the Academy of Management* (1993): 142–46.

Ring, P.S., and Van de Ven, A.H. "Structuring Cooperative Relationships between Organizations." *Strategic Management Journal* 13, no. 7 (1992): 483–98.

———. "Developmental Processes of Cooperative Inter-organizational Relationships." *Academy of Management Review* 19, no. 1 (1994): 90–118.

Rugman, A.M. "Risk Reduction by International Diversification." *Journal of International Business Studies* 7, no. 2 (1976): 75–80.

Rumelt, R.P. "How Much Does Industry Matter?" *Strategic Management Journal* 12, no. 3 (1991): 167–85.

Rumelt, R.P., and Wensley, R. "In Search of the Market Share Effect," proceedings of the Academy of Management National Meeting, August 2–6, 1981.

Saxton, T. "The Affects of Partner and Relationship Characteristics on Alliance Outcomes." *Academy of Management Journal* 40, no. 2 (1997): 443–61.

Shuman, J.C., and Seeger, J.A. "The Theory and Practice of Strategic Management in Smaller Rapid Growth Companies." *American Journal of Small Business* 11, no. 1 (1986): 7–18.

Singh, J.V., House, R.J., and Tucker, D.J. "Organizational Change and Organizational Mortality." *Administrative Science Quarterly* 31, no. 4 (1986): 587–611.

Sohn, S.Y., Kim, H.S., and Moon, T.H. "Predicting the Financial Performance Index of Technology Fund for SME Using Structural Equation Model." *Expert Systems with Applications* 32, no. 3 (2007): 890–98.

Stinchcombe, A.L. "Social Structure and Organizations." In *Handbook of Organizations*, ed. March, J., 142–93. Chicago: Rand McNally, 1965.

Strauss, A., and Corbin, J. *Basics of Qualitative Research: Grounded Theory Procedures and Techniques.* Thousand Oaks, CA: Sage Publications, 1990.

———. *Basics of Qualitative Research: Techniques and Procedures for Developing Grounded Theory.* Thousand Oaks, CA: Sage Publications, 1998.

Stuart, T.E., and Hoang, H., and Hybels, R.C. "Inter-organizational Endorsements and the Performance of Entrepreneurial Ventures." *Administrative Science Quarterly* 44, no. 2 (1999): 315–49.

Subramaniam, M., and Watson, S. "How Interdependence Affects Subsidiary Performance." *Journal of Business Research* 59, no. 8 (2006): 916–24.

Sullivan, D. "Measuring the Degree of Internationalization of a Firm." *Journal of International Business Studies* 25, no. 2 (1994): 325–42.

Sundaram, A.K., and Black, J.S. "The Environment and Internal Organization of Multinational Enterprises." *Academy of Management Review* 17, no. 4 (1992): 729–57.

Teece, D.J. "Profiting from Technological Innovation: Implications for Integration, Collaboration, Licensing and Public Policy." *Research Policy* 15 (1986): 285–305.

Terpstra, V., and Yu, C. "Determinants of Foreign Investment of U.S. Advertising Agencies." *Journal of International Business Studies* 19, no. 1 (1988): 33–47.

Thompson, J.D. *Organizations in Action.* New York: McGraw-Hill, 1967.

Tomkins, C., and Groves, R. "The Everyday Accountant and Researching His Reality." *Accounting, Organizations and Society* 8, no. 4 (1983): 361–74.

Tomlinson, J.W.C. *The Joint Venture Process in International Business: India and Pakistan.* Cambridge, MA: MIT Press, 1970.

Tung, R.L. "US-China Trade Negotiations: Practices, Procedures and Outcomes." *Journal of International Business Studies* (Fall 1982): 23–37.

Veugelers, R. "Locational Determinants and Ranking of Host Countries: An Empirical Assessment." *KYKLOS International Review of Social Science* 44 (1991): 363–82.

Wahlstrom, G. "Worrying about Accepting New Measurements: The Case of Swedish Bankers and Operational Risk." *Critical Perspectives on Accounting* 17 (2006): 493–522.

Welsh, D.H.B., Alon, I., and Falbe, C.M. "An Examination of International Retail Franchising in Emerging Markets." *Journal of Small Business Management* 44, no. 1 (2006): 130–49.

Wernerfelt, B., and Montgomery, C.A. "Tobin's Q and the Importance of Focus in Firm Performance." *The American Economic Review* 78, no. 1 (1988): 246–50.

Williamson, O.E. *Markets and Hierarchies, Analysis and Antitrust Implications: A Study in the Economics of Internal Organization.* New York: Free Press, 1975.

———. "Calculativeness, Trust and Economic Organization." *Journal of Law and Economics* 30 (1993): 131–45.

Yan, A., and Gray, B. "Bargaining Power, Management Control, and Performance in United States-China Joint Ventures: A Comparative Case Study." *Academy of Management Journal* 37 (1994): 1478–1517.

Yan, A., and Luo, Y. *International Joint Ventures: Theory and Practice.* New York: M.E. Sharpe, 2001.

Yin, R. *Case Study Research Design and Methods.* Thousand Oaks, CA: Sage Publications, 1994.

Yip, G.S. *The Role of Strategic Planning in Consumer-Marketing Businesses.* Report No. 84–103. Cambridge, MA: Marketing Science Institute, 1984.

Yunker, P.J. "A Survey Study of Subsidiary Autonomy, Performance Evaluation and Transfer Pricing in Multinational Corporations." *Columbia Journal of World Business* 18, no. 3 (1983): 51–64.

Zaheer, A., and Venkatraman, N. "Relational Governance as an Interorganizational Strategy: An Empirical Test of the Role of Trust in Economic Exchange." *Strategic Management Journal* 16, no. 5 (1995): 373–92.

Zajac, E., and Olsen, C.P. "From Transaction Cost to Transactional Value Analysis: Implications for the Study of Inter-organizational Strategies." *Journal of Management Studies* 30, no. 1 (1993): 131–45.

Chapter 10

Two Case Studies

Harnessing Knowledge Capabilities in Emerging Markets: Offshoring and the Experience of MAC & Co.

Ajay Bhalla

This chapter illustrates the experience of MAC & Co., a large consulting firm that recently set up internal offshore research operations in India. The experience suggests that successful offshoring depends not only on how much can be gained by performing the same activities offshore versus local, but also on developing the right and compatible offshoring options. Specifically, the objectives of the case are to (1) provide insight into the process of setting up an offshore operation that is driven by the forces of globalization and the realities of competition; and (2) raise awareness of the issues that lead such firms to select India or other emerging markets as an offshore destination for research functions.

Introduction

In August 1997, Rohit Goel, Managing Director of MAC & Co., waited in the airport lounge in Sydney. He had been attending the firm's fourth annual Practice Olympics, an annual firm-wide competition to produce new ideas and approaches for its clients. The work was completely driven by teams made up of junior consultants and support staff, with partners participating only as coaches. It was one of the several initiatives he had launched to institutionalize and provide a better leverage for the knowledge base of MAC employees in light of his belief that *knowledge is the lifeblood of MAC*.

MAC was going through a phase of dynamic growth, and Goel's challenge was to maintain and further the prestigious brand of the company. The brand stood for the firm's capability to bring the best intellectual minds to resolve the most critical and challenging problems faced by its clients.

As Goel settled down in the flight, he began to ponder over the internal memo he had sent to the senior partners prior to a recent partners' meeting held in London. The aim of the meeting was to discuss the recommendations of an internal strategy initiative launched to define and develop MAC's strategy for the future. Goel had mentioned,

> I worry that we are losing our sense of village as we compartmentalize our activities and divide into specializations. The power of information technology (IT) has sometimes led our consultants to information overload. The risk is that the more resources we spend on searching for the right document and the ideal framework for conducting basic analysis, the less time we spend on thinking about the problem. I worry that as we increase the science, we might lose the craft of what we actually do.

During the lunch at this meeting, he had conversation with Anil Verma, senior partner at the Kuala Lumpur office, who had mentioned that the solution existed in setting up a regional knowledge center, as part of MAC's strategy for the future. The proposition was to create a critical mass of support staff in a low-cost location such as India that would conduct research and provide information to consultants much faster and at costs much lower than the current model that relied on the local support staff. By way of example, Verma had pointed out that consultants from anywhere in the Asia Pacific region could send in a request for general or specific information or analysis via email or phone, and the staff in India would turn it around within 24 hours. The center will be open 24 hours, five days a week. Verma's proposal fitted well with Goel's vision of building capabilities and infrastructure.

Recognition of Knowledge as a Core Competence

Founded in Atlanta in 1926 by John Mac, MAC & Co. was for many years the unchallenged leader in consulting. Many of its alumni went on to head leading companies, often their former clients, generating further business for the firm. With the world economy in flux, the 1970s proved to be the most challenging decade for the firm. For a decade, demand for consulting services declined while the company faced new aggressive competitors such as the Boston Consulting Group (BCG).

Having conducted an internal analysis, the firm recognized that building knowledge was crucial to pursue growth in the coming decades, so it had to make substantial investments to develop and reuse intellectual knowledge. That commitment led Ron Daniel, the managing director during the 1970s, to hand over the mandate to Fred Peters to launch initiatives that stimulated the intellectual environment within the firm. Peters was a director at the New York office and had joined the firm from Bell Labs, where he had led similar knowledge-building initiatives. Throughout the 1980s, Peters was instrumental in launching a number of initiatives such as the creation of 15 Centers of Competence built around areas of management expertise, including strategy, change management, and marketing. He also promoted and disseminated these new insights by publishing articles in the company's newly launched publication *MAC Quarterly*.

Technological developments enabled the firm to pursue its agenda to codify knowledge and to make it accessible across the firm globally. In 1987, to pursue its *mantra* of one global firm, it launched three initiatives: Firm Practice Information System (FPIS), Practice Development Network (PDNet), and Knowledge Resource Directory (KRD). FPIS was a computerized database of clients accessible to all employees of the company. Not only did it enable the company to organize and store historical data on clients' projects but also captured information on lessons learned, which acted as a benchmark for future projects. PDNet was also a computerized system but aimed at capturing the knowledge that had accumulated in the core practices of the company. Although initially both these initiatives faced difficulties due to the efforts required from individual consultants to upload the information, it was a significant success because the KRD served as a yellow pages directory that enabled the consultants to find coworkers with expertise in specific areas.

Background to the Research and Information Center

Peters was also instrumental in transforming the company's key consulting unit by splitting it into two parts: Engagement Team that focused on delivering short-term client assignments; and the Client Service Team that focused on uniting a core of individuals, particularly at partner level for long-term value creation for the client. However, the Research and Information (R&I) function, which involved supplying consulting engagement teams with facts and customized insights on specific issues relating to the work, remained decentralized. MAC had about 800 researchers at its R&I centers spread across its 80 offices and several practices. None of the offices had sufficient specialist researchers for each Practice Group, whereas the smaller offices did not have enough critical mass even amongst the nonspecialists. This combined with the fact that the demand from consultants had peaks and troughs meant that researchers often found themselves overworked or that consultants ended up spending significant time on gathering and analyzing publicly available information. On the other hand, by working together over time, consultants and R&I staff had often built up a good rapport. Typically, the consultants would know which R&I staff they needed to call upon when struggling with filling gaps in their data, proving or disproving hypotheses, analyzing industry trends, or creating a clear picture of a competitive landscape.

From Research and Information Functions to Knowledge Center

Verma had also discussed the idea of setting up the center (initially proposed as the Quick Information Center) with another enthusiast of remote services—Amit Bhatia, the newly appointed consulting partner for the MAC India office. Verma explained to Goel that he and Bhatia had proposed the idea at a meeting with Asia Pacific managers in March 1997, but it was met with resistance. The other managers pointed out that there would be problems of language differences, database incompatibilities, and the absence of rapport with consultants.

Following the lunch, Goel called up Roger Ferguson, who was the worldwide R&I director for the company. Ferguson supported the proposal and mentioned to Goel that he had been following several companies that had taken advantage of emerging markets such as India, The Philippines, and China in setting up global business processing centers. India and China were especially attractive not only because of their low labor costs and stable economic and political systems, but also because of the fast growing home markets. Characterized by the relative high pace of economic development, both India and China were part of BRIC (Brazil, Russia, India, and China) economies, which were predicted by Goldman Sachs—a leading investment bank—to comprise a 40 percent share of world growth by 2025.

Some prominent firms selected the locations very quickly, for example, GE Capital (India, China and Ireland), American Express

(India and the Philippines), Bank of America (India and the Philippines), Citigroup (India, the Philippines, Malaysia, Taiwan, and Singapore), and HSBC (India and China). Ferguson held several meetings with both Verma and Bhatia to discuss the proposal in detail. One of the challenges was to select a suitable location. As he sat down with Verma and Bhatia to choose the location, Ferguson started the discussion by drawing up three criteria on the whiteboard: (1) availability of skilled manpower—availability of top quality talent, requisite language skills, cumulative knowledge services experience in the market, and attrition rates; (2) financial structure of the country—tax and regulatory costs, infrastructure costs such as telecommunication systems, and labor costs; and (3) business environment—presence of other multinational firms, availability of real estate, IT infrastructure, investor and analyst rating of overall business and political environment, cultural adaptability, and security of intellectual property.

The team then quantified the attributes and assigned weights to each of the three factors using industry and internal proprietary data. Subject matter experts within the firm, and public bodies such as United Nations Conference on Trade and Development (UNCTD), validated the findings from the data. Because MAC needed to set up knowledge-intensive research and analysis functions that required top quality talent, the availability of skilled manpower was assigned a weighting of 40 percent. The other two factors were assigned an equal weighting of 30 percent each. The team then ranked each of the five locations under consideration on a scale of one to five on each of the three factors: China, India, Malaysia, the Philippines, and Singapore. Overall, India scored the highest. Following further deliberations, the team agreed that India was the ideal location for setting up a pilot knowledge services center.

As the idea of setting up remote services, known as the MAC Knowledge Center (MKC), got accepted, the proposal gained momentum and began to find guardian angels for the project. Soon a list of owners was drawn. Kirkland, Verma, and Neeraj Bhargava, a partner from the Mumbai office, became members of an advisory council to drive the MKC idea, while Bhatia continued to be in charge of the operations. Verma took the task of getting the approval of senior firm members worldwide, while Kirkland lobbied with R&I managers in various countries, and Bhargava worked with Bhatia to get the details of the plan in place.

One of the constructive suggestions to make the plan workable was to lower the bar of the services that MKC was proposing to support the MAC's high-end practices. This was lowered. A new plan suggested that the center would first cater to quick information needs, and once that gained momentum, it would move to provide information support to practices. With a sound plan in place, it was only a matter of getting approval. In March 1998, armed with the proposal that had passed through many hands and was backed by a team of partners and directors, the MKC board went to Goel. Goel, who had earlier heard of Verma's proposal at the Strategy for Future Initiative briefing meeting, approved the plan, and the center was incorporated in November 1998.

Creation of an Internal Buy-in for MKC

MKC had attained partner-level support but did not have any internal customers. Offices did not see the value in participating; the local R&I staff was naturally insecure. MKC identified the London and Sydney offices as its pilot customers. These offices supported the idea as there was a niche that MKC could fill. These were large offices whose local R&I teams were not able to meet the demand. Their R&I teams were less insecure about giving up some of their work, because they were overworked and looked forward to getting some work off their back.

Demand took some time to build up. The first few months were extremely slack, with staff seizing any work that came their way. MKC decided to pull work its way. With specific requests from the Sydney and London offices, which gradually began to siphon work to India, what sustained the initial trickle was the quality of output that the team delivered. Within six months, volume ceased to be an issue.

As consultants began to go directly to MKC to circumvent their local R&Is, MKC had to respond to the local teams—after all these were the people whose jobs were being affected. At an operational level, and to gain buy-in, MKC started to respond to the consultants' queries with a copy to the local office, thereby, keeping them in the loop. At a managerial level, Kirkland called an R&I managers' meeting, where the MKC team openly proclaimed, "We are starting with only 10 to 12 people. There is no threat because this will be your back office. We will see how to help it grow after piloting the service for the next six to 12 months."

Building Momentum

In February 2000, Verma, Fredrickson, and Greg Sykes, the newly appointed manager of MKC, sat to review the first year performance of MKC. They were elated with the success. The center had moved from servicing the Sydney and London offices to servicing almost 60 offices. It had planned a 10-member team; it ended up requiring 45 members. Whereas it had planned to do low-end, quick information work, the center had ended up providing significant customized information and analysis support. Sykes asked Verma, "What do you think is the key factor in MAC's success?" "People," Verma responded. Sykes nodded in agreement and continued, "In the Western hemisphere offices, MBAs were consultants, while librarians were R&I, and there was a divide in the middle. In India, you guys have sought to put MBAs on either side." Verma reflected on Sykes comments and explained,

> This was something which I knew was only possible in India with its range of MBA schools, people's willingness to work in shifts, and lower wages. We looked for second- and third-tier MBA graduates who were ready to prove that they were as good as or better than the first-tier MBAs. We hired the first batch of ten people, handpicked from 5,000 resumes generated by the MKC appointment advertisement.

The Current Position of MKC

Today, the firm has three knowledge centers—one in Gurgaon, India, one outside Boston, and another in Brussels. These provide services as knowledge hubs for the three regions and the world. The knowledge centers provide extensive support to consultants and practices. The local R&I offices are very lean. MAC Knowledge Center India Private Limited is the largest hub of knowledge management professionals within MAC (table 10.1). The center has three distinct knowledge capability groups that work with consulting teams to provide solutions to their research and analysis needs. The capabilities were (1) the knowledge-on-call service specializes in addressing low- to medium-level complexity, the English language, business research requests that do not require deep sector, functional, or geographic expertise; (2) the practice research group supports MAC's global industry and functional practices; and (3) the analysis group supplements consulting teams with additional analysts (on site/remote), and helps solve complex analytical problems by leveraging its capabilities in risk modeling, optimization, marketing analysis, building databases, and model building.

This configuration is fairly close to the regional plan first proposed almost ten years ago in the final version of Strategy for Future

Table 10.1   MAC India

	Start	End of first year	Now
Team (India office) customers	10 people pilot to support	45 people	More than 300 people
	2 offices: London and Sydney	60 offices (almost 50% European, 15% U.S., 10% Indian)	All MAC offices
Work	Low-end quick research information	Customized information and analysis support	Support center to practice

Source: Company press releases.

Initiative. It has Goel's *one firm* philosophy embedded across the board. Recently, the company has expanded the MKC concept. In addition to knowledge services, the center also houses the firm's IT India team, which supports the global IT function. The hub in India provides application support, infrastructure support, survey development, and financial application support.

Future Positioning of MKC

Goel briefed Ian Davis, the incoming MAC managing director in 2005; Davis pondered over the opportunities and challenges MKC faced. India had become the global technology and knowledge services hub over the last ten years. As a result, a growing number of international companies had started using it as a software development location, and as a center for equity, financial, and insurance research. GE, with 9,000 employees in its Indian outsourcing operation, had reaped the benefits in excess of US$340 million—largely from reduced labor costs. In 2003, India had provided US$3.5 billion worth of Business Process Outsourcing (BPO) and Knowledge Process Outsourcing (KPO) services. This figure was expected to grow to US$30 billion by 2010. Although the firm was able to attract talent, the competition for the right talent was tough. Not only did MKC face competition in attracting and retaining talent from these fortune 500 firms, they also had to compete for talent with competitors such as AT Kearney, BCG, KPMG, and Bain who had also set up knowledge processing centers in New Delhi, India.

AT Kearney, for instance, opened a Global Research Center (GRC) in India with over 45 employees that undertook activities such as research, database search, report preparation, editing and formatting client reports and presentations, and other knowledge management related activities. In 1973, Bain and Company, a direct competitor of MAC & Co., opened a research capability center in India. It was a prominent management-consulting firm.

In 2004, almost six years after MAC opened its knowledge center, Bain also opened the Bain Capability Center (BCC) in Gurgaon, India, which served as a remote center to support Bain's global consulting operations. Modeled on MKC, BCC was also staffed with a team of analysts with significant functional and industry expertise, who provided knowledge, research, and analytic support to its global staff. It provided two services. First, it played a critical role in the codification of knowledge for Bain's Practice Areas, strengthening Bain's world-class knowledge management capabilities. Second, it provided critical industry, company, and financial analysis along with Bain's global case teams, delivering results for clients. However, Bain had gone a step further than MAC by integrating the R&I function into the client facing consulting engagement team. BCC teams were staffed by experts who had experience in the Indian market and were thus able to define the capability offering advisory services to Bain clients in building pan-Asian strategies and offshoring or outsourcing solutions. By locating in Gurgaon, it served as a point of introduction for firms to meet potential outsourcing partners and see the offshore operations first hand.

Furthermore, a new breed of third-party knowledge process outsourcing specialists such as Evalueserve, Office Tiger, Copal Partners, and Pipal Research, offering research services to their clients, had emerged in India. These firms offered services around knowledge-intensive business processes such as market research, data analysis, investment research, and financial modeling that required significant domain expertise, analytic skills and judgment, and decision-making capabilities. Of these, Evalueserve was modeled on the MAC Knowledge Center. Set up by Marc Vollenweider, who had helped set up the MAC Knowledge Center in India, Evalueserve had grown at an exponential rate. It had recruited several senior level employees from MAC Knowledge Center and IBM and had extended its capability from research to consulting.

As Davis evaluated the growth opportunities offered by the fast growing emerging markets and the challenges in recruiting and retaining talent that MKC faced from the Bain Capability Center and third-party providers such as Evalueserve, he pondered whether MAC should look at other emerging markets to set up similar service centers. He also wondered if he should broaden the scope of the center not only to exploit opportunities offered by the growth of the local Indian market, but also to provide career growth opportunities for the MKC staff.

Change Management
in MAST Africa Limited

Peter M. Lewa

This case describes the evolution and operations of MAST East
Africa Limited. It describes how change, brought about by liberalization, affected the company significantly. Liberalization increased competition in the market and forced the company to address the issue of
change management. This case demonstrates how MAST managed
change. The key learning objectives of the case are to (1) understand
the key issues in change management; (2) demonstrate the importance of developing a strategy that will allow a firm to survive and
continue to grow in a dynamic and hostile environment; (3) learn
how to institutionalize change management; (4) give the readers an
opportunity to conduct a Strength, Weakness, Opportunities and
Threats analysis; and (5) learn how MAST actually managed change
and learnt from the experience.

Introduction

Change management can be described as the tool that prepares us for
the uncertain future by enabling us to create and empower organizations to take responsibility for their future. Change management can
be defined either as the task of managing change, or as an area of professional practice where change is planned, or as a body of knowledge
where the content or subject matter such as models, methods and
techniques, tools, skills, and other forms of *change knowledge* are
studied. Change is a reality that we need to be comfortable with
because we have little or no control over it.

Many authors describe change management as an organization's
attempt to develop and apply some strategic management to both
inevitable and desired organizational changes (Ansoff, 1990; Kotter,
1996). Nobody knows what the future holds, and what happened

yesterday is gone; we only have today to shape it into what we want. The opportunity is there for vision to be actualized and for a corporation to meet the market needs as well as to increase shareholders' value. For a change to be successful, the change managers should not only know what they want to do in the future but also have the right organizational structure to support the process. They should also have a strategy that manages information, people, and procedures and keeps the goals in sight.

Senge (1994) set the standard for change management in his book *The Fifth Discipline* by observing that a particular vision has the capacity to be continually enhanced if the capabilities match with what the organization wants to be in the future. An organization's culture must be supportive of the change, have a positive learning climate, encourage teamwork use their strategy creatively, and be committed to the change. The pace of organizational change is fast. Pressures of all types, from economical to social to political to technological, are on management to come up with new approaches so that they can stay competitive and ahead of their competition.

Organizations have been forced to think about the strategic imperatives of the moment, the changing demands of the people, and the environment. Organizations need a sustainable competitive edge in order to achieve their goals and satisfy their customers. A change facilitator is in charge of managing people and the change management strategy. The communications plans and the know-how on how to manage inherent resistance to change are important. Change can be planned and managed in a systematic way, where the goal is to implement new methods and systems in an organization, or it can be a response to changes where the organization has little or no control over the actions of the competitors or the shifting economic events. This is the reactive approach whereas the former is more anticipative because the change lies within and is controlled by the organization. The change process can be viewed as a problem-solving template where a solution is sought. The main goal is to empower the organization to take responsibility for their future.

Change starts with the *how* question, for instance, how do we get people to be more creative and responsible? Or, how do we raise more effective barriers to our competitors' market entry? The initial formulation of a change problem is centered on the goal. We then have the *what* question; for instance, what are we trying to accomplish? Or, what are the necessary changes? Finally, we have the *why* question, for instance, why do people need to be more creative? Or, why do we have to change the way we do things?

It is important for the scale and scope of the change to be at a moderate pace to match with what most people consider ideal, because every facet of the organization has people with different concerns and adaptation levels. Another consideration is the structure of the organization and how the functions and the people are placed and coordinated so they can complement each other in the organization.

The Process of Change

The process of change has been characterized as having three stages: unfreezing, changing, and refreezing. Unfreezing is the creation of motivation to change by devising ways to reduce barriers to change. It involves the creation of a situation in which employees are dissatisfied with the status quo, thus creating the desire to change. The basic assumption is that change will not occur unless there is a motivation to change. Changing involves developing new behaviors and attitudes and adopting them through employee training, education, facilitation, and support activities. Refreezing occurs when change is stabilized and individuals help integrate the changed behaviors and attitudes into their normal way of doing things. The assumption is that an effective change requires reinforcing new behaviors and organizational practices.

There are five basic skills that ensure that change is successful: political, analytical, people, system, and business skills. Organizations are social systems and political in nature. Analytical skills play a part in change management because guesswork is not effective. Although the insight is good, it cannot be defended. Thus, a lucid, rational, well-argued analysis is useful for both operational and financial systems. People skills are equally important in communications. To be effective, an organization needs to be able to listen actively and clarify any matter of concern. It is important to understand how a business works before any attempts are made to change it.

Bennis et al. (1976) offer four basic strategies for change management. First is the rational-empirical strategy, where people are rational and follow their self-interest. The change is based on the communication of information and the proffering of incentives. Second is the normative-reductive strategy, where people are social beings and adhere to cultural norms and values and develop commitments to new ones. Third is the power-coercive strategy, where people are basically compliant and will generally do what they are told to do or can be made to do. The change is based on the exercise of authority and the imposition of sanctions. Fourth is the environmental-adaptive strategy, where people oppose loss and disruption but adapt readily to new circumstances. The change is based on building a new organization and gradually transferring people from the old system to the new one. We prefer the last strategy because it has characteristics from the first two strategies.

Strategy Selection for Change Management

Several factors should be considered before selecting a strategy; for example, the degree of resistance, the target population, the stakes, the time frame available, the expertise available to handle the change, and the dependency levels on the capability of the management. Because change is mostly turbulent and chaotic in nature, there is no set way to manage it; it is more a matter of leadership ability than management skills. The organization has to start with a clear mission or purpose. Next, a team with the right skills and energy levels should be built in accordance with the new structure and rules. An action feedback model should also be set up and led by the team leader.

Resistance to change is one of the problems faced by organizations. Poor communication or employees putting their own welfare first can cause resistance. When the employees are uncommitted to change, problems occur. Sometimes different assessments of the situation or people may lead to a low tolerance for change.

Ansoff (1990) has defined resistance to organizational change as a multifaceted phenomenon that introduces unanticipated delays, costs, and instabilities into the process of strategic change. This results in unforeseen implementation delays and inefficiencies that slow down the change. Performance lags if sabotage occurs or if employees try to make efforts to go back to the prechange status by striking or by being absent. To overcome this problem, management must educate and communicate with the staff and let them participate in the change process. Further, management should negotiate to reach a consensus or agreement on how the change will be and get help from those supporting the change to influence the resisting ones and offer support at all times. Above all, management should lead the change by creating a shared need for the change, shaping the vision, mobilizing commitment, changing the systems and structure as needed, monitoring progress, and giving continuous feedback to ensure that the change lasts.

Kotter (1996) states that change often fails because the change does not alter behavior and management tries to *manage* the change instead of *leading* it. He further identifies the eight common errors: (1) allowing too much complacency; (2) failing to create a sufficiently powerful guiding coalition; (3) underestimating the power of vision; (4) undercommunicating the new vision; (5) permitting obstacles to block the new vision; (6) failing to create short-term wins; (7) declaring victory too soon; and (8) neglecting to anchor changes firmly in the corporate culture.

As a result of these errors, new strategies are not well implemented, acquisitions do not achieve expected synergies, reengineering takes too long and costs too much, downsizing does not get costs under control, and quality programs do not deliver promised results. Kotter then created an eight-stage process for creating major positive changes within an organization. The following are the stages: (1) establishing a sense of urgency; (2) creating the guiding coalition, developing a vision and strategy; (3) communicating the change vision; (4) empowering broad-based action; (5) generating short-term wins; (6) consolidating wins; (7) producing more change; and finally (8) anchoring new approaches in the culture. The following sections explain how MAST managed change brought about by the late 1980s liberalization and the 1990s growth of Kenya's economy.

Change Management in MAST Africa Limited

MAST Africa was founded before the economic liberalization in Kenya. Since independence in 1963 to the late 1980s, Kenya had a state-controlled economy in which major decisions relating to the operations of firms were made by the state without much regard to what the firms felt. This state of affairs insulated many firms that had direct access to politicians and key decision makers. Their operating environment was certain and predictable at the time. Most businesses operated on the basis of traditional management styles, with historically entrenched company values, attitudes, and beliefs. Under such circumstances, MAST Africa Ltd had a ready market and could not satisfy the demand even for vehicles, as was evident from the automobiles dealers' long waiting lists of customers.

A dramatic change occurred in the late 1980s when the government of Kenya agreed to liberalize the economy due to the pressure from Bretton Woods institutions and other agencies. Liberalization opened the floodgates in the automobile industry, leading to increased competition. This competition caused change. The importation of new vehicles, used vehicles, parts, and accessories was decontrolled. MAST Africa Ltd had to start managing change because the traditional organizational structure with its hierarchical top-down approach and historically entrenched values of stability and security proved unworkable under a liberalized environment. Structures, systems, and values, which formed the bedrock for past successes in times of government control, began to threaten the very existence of MAST. They had to respond to these challenges strategically for their survival and had to start working on institutionalizing change.

The motor industry in Kenya during the controlled period was dominated largely by major companies, which included household names such as Coopers Motor Corporation Ltd., Lonhro Motors East Africa Ltd., DT Dobie Ltd., and Marshalls East Africa Ltd. There were other medium-sized companies such as Kenya Motor Corporation, Colt Motors, Simba Motors, Ryce Motors, Mashariki Motors, and Amazon Motors Ltd. According to the Kenya Motor Industry Association, these companies offered a variety of products and services such as new cars, service, parts, and accessories, including a limited range of used cars. Within the industry, *Jua Kali* (Swahili for hot sun, *Jua Kali* is the local name given to people who work in the metal and wood sector. It is a micro enterprise and is recognized by the Government of Kenya as a sector of an industry) offered repairs, services, and sales of used cars on a smaller scale. The motor industry has two vehicle assembly companies: Associated Vehicle Assemblers and Kenya Motor Vehicle Manufacturers Ltd., located in Mombasa city and Thika town, respectively.

The MAST family, who were a second generation of the early colonial settlers in Kenya, established MAST Africa Ltd. in 1950. MAST changed ownership in the early 1980s when the Pemule family acquired its majority shareholding. It changed hands again in the early 1990s when its majority shareholding was acquired by the Down group of companies. MAST is a public limited company quoted in the stock exchange. It is the third largest motor company in the region. MAST commanded 30 percent of the market share of the medium saloon vehicles according to their annual report. MAST is an exclusive franchisee of Peugeot whose sales constitute 90 percent of its total sales. It also holds the Tata franchise for light and heavy-duty trucks. Its main source of vehicle parts is Automobile Peugeot of France and Tata exporters limited in India.

MAST has the largest motor vehicle branch network in Kenya. During the controlled economy, MAST registered growth in volumes, revenue and profit, and net assets. The only constraint to its growth then, as in the case of other motor vehicle companies, was the shortage of foreign currency to pay for imports. Foreign exchange was controlled by the Central Bank of Kenya and was allocated to various industrial sectors in the economy on a priority basis.

Following the liberalization of the economy, MAST business, like others, started to experience a major decline in sales, although the impact of the liberalization was not felt immediately due to the large number of outstanding orders. Tables 10.2, 10.3, and 10.4 provide useful data on some aspects of the industry. Data in the tables show a general growth in imports and sales of new vehicles. This growth is due to the additional competitors in the marketplace.

Table 10.2   Used vehicles imports (1992–2000)

Type/Year	1992	1993	1994	1995	1996	1997	1998	1999	2000
Passenger cars	6292	7936	7442	7992	7243	6603	4895	9420	10123
Buses/trucks	1261	1020	1097	1678	1780	917	927	1884	2204
Chassis engine	1	0	17	148	196	43	18	319	657
Total	7554	8956	8556	9818	9219	7563	5840	11623	12984

Source: Compiled from Government of Kenya—Economic Surveys (various volumes).

Table 10.3   New vehicles sold in Kenya (1996–2000)

Sales of new vehicles by category	1996	1997	1998	1999	2000
Passenger cars	2586	2556	2749	8466	4802
Pickups	1719	1890	2029	6304	3945
Light trucks	1130	1120	1144	1150	2363
Heavy trucks	417	450	477	1223	1561
4WD estates	364	374	688	837	1856
Other buses	472	475	483	340	377
Minibus	894	748	602	298	559
Total	7582	7613	8172	18618	15463

Source: Compiled from Government of Kenya—Economic Surveys (various volumes).

Table 10.4   Imports of tires and tubes and materials of rubber (1991–2000)

in '000 tones	1991	1992	1993	1994	1995	1996	1997	1998	1999	2000
Tires and tubes	155	211	314	313	358	361	248	275	636	839
Materials of rubber	844	767	963	767	906	923	417	464	1024	1224
Total	999	978	1277	1080	1264	1284	665	739	1660	2063

Source: Compiled from Government of Kenya—Economic Surveys (various volumes).

The early 1990s saw competition and opportunities in the automobile industry. Before 1980, MAST was very successful; it enjoyed a close relationship with the government and had its protection too. In such an environment, the company only needed to maintain a strong presence in government decision-making circles and have expertise in its work, but it did not need a strong marketing focus. The traditional management style tended to be paternalistic and bureaucratic; the organization was conservative with a compliant middle management. The company's focus was on government patronage for survival. Although the senior executives communicated effectively with each other, very little information was passed down to the hierarchical organizational structure.

By the early 1990s, it became necessary to effect significant changes to the organizational structure. The new structure emphasized the customer divisions as the *drivers of business*, while functional divisions such as system design, engineering, and supply divisions now operated in support of the different customer divisions. The focus was no longer solely on engineering and production but on serving the customer better. The overriding imperative was to create a *felt need for change* for everybody else; management needed to instill dissatisfaction with the status quo in order to rally an organizational change.

It was easier said than done. Although a crisis threatened the survival of the organization, it was not a compelling motivator. The change was not widely understood or appreciated. The management, therefore, decided to carry out a *medical treatment* that identified the internal problems and external threats and opportunities. This was an effective means of focusing the stakeholders' attention on issues central to the organization's future. This succeeded in highlighting the gap between the present reality and potential future state; hence, a tension was created that was the first stage of change management.

A clearly articulated vision was needed to explain to the workforce so they could strive to achieve it. The message was simple, direct, understandable, and acceptable to all the key stakeholders. The organization was ready for change. They had a shared vision. The management pushed with a sense of urgency and showed a commitment to change. Large-scale organizational change cannot take place without *magic leaders* who energize the change, envision the future state, and enable the members of the organization to carry out the change. Magic members alone cannot implement and sustain the change. That is why they needed the support of everyone in the organization. Thus, MAST formed coalitions of key constituents across the organization and had them act as messengers and exemplars of the change process. This helped cascade the vision down to everybody else.

It was also important to manage the rate of change as a means of overcoming resistance to the new patterns of organizing and managing the day-to-day affairs. The management did not force change, it instead allowed each business unit to form its own agenda and pace of implementation. Reinforcement and institutionalization represented the final steps in implementing the change. The aim was to develop the mechanisms that would support a long-term capacity for continual adaptation and learning. Integral to this was the establishment of enabling structures that represented the new work arrangements and reporting requirements. The change measures had been communicated consistently and repeatedly up, down, and across the organization with openness and honesty; the management expected the same kind of feedback.

Further, the workforce was significantly reduced. The aim of this restructuring was to create a more responsive, more competitive, and less internally focused organization that was attuned to the needs of the marketplace. However, the rapidly changing external environment found the organization initially to be less prepared than expected. The question was, how to move this new *customer first* agenda into the very competitive environment in which the government could not offer protection. The top management sought to use the marketing imperative as a catalyst for change. They charted out the future direction and goals of the company and set up a framework for narrowing the gap between where they were and where they wanted to be.

To put this in motion, they reformulated their mission statement and established a strategic plan simultaneously. Inability to change fast was a key factor contributing to their failure, as the top managers lacked a unity of purpose and had little respect for customers— because during controlled regime the demand was too high for the too few cars available for sale, so the seller and not the buyer was king. They needed to review their progress. This led to a recasting of the company's change strategy. The executives now recognized that telling people to change was pointless if they did not understand what they must change and what new skills and competencies were required to behave differently.

Two major change initiatives were implemented to overcome the obstacle. A mission statement was drawn up that articulated in clear terms what MAST must commit to; a "leading change" program was developed to equip leaders through the organization with the skills and knowledge to work differently and to give them the tools to cascade these new behaviors into their business areas. In addition to the mission statement, the executive management developed a clearer vision statement to articulate what the company must aim to achieve. The vision statement had been in several drafts as management sought to produce a clear and simple message that the employees could easily understand and identify with.

The aim was to establish clearly what MAST was committed to doing and to communicate in a way that everybody in the organization could relate to. The statements sought to answer the *why* questions such as why the organization needed to change and provide a dynamic analysis of where the organization stood, its current and future goals, and the processes and behaviors that were essential to achieving these goals. They underlined the importance of relationships both inside and outside the company and also vowed to recognize and reward the creativity and skills of its own people.

The target for leading change was the representation of all senior and middle management; nearly all people at this level attended the class that ran for six months. It concentrated on challenging existing organizational attitudes and ways of thinking. The traditionally compliant and unquestioning attitude of the managers was one of the key behaviors patterns that had to change. The benefits of adopting new ways of learning and working together were clearly outlined by explaining the change and by developing new mental tools that challenged the traditional mindset. The company's traditional internal engineering and product focus was shifted to viewing the customers as partners and providing them with value-added solutions. A plan also to redesign the work processes, systems, and structures and to foster an environment that encouraged participation was put in place. Information sharing pushed decision making further down the organization. The implications of these commitments were also clearly outlined and customers were interviewed and assessments done to improve both relationships.

Finally, the organizational attitudes and assumptions were challenged and everyone was encouraged to consider new ways of thinking. This changed the relationships, the focus of the business, the accountability in the organization, the network, the quality of service, and the people's relation to each other. The modified behaviors and work processes changed the culture of MAST, a key factor in their success.

Conclusion

In conclusion, organizations are faced with many unforeseen forces that drive the need for change because the environment is uncertain.

As MAST found out, the ability to understand the source of change is as critical as how fast the adaptation process will be. Their success is largely attributed to timely organizational changes and strategic plans. Due to the effective management in 2007, MAST is equipped to adapt quickly to changes and to withstand fierce competition.

Acknowledgments

The contributions of Sarah M. Mutuku, B.Sc. (Business), MBA (USA), and Miriam M. Mutuku, B.Sc. (International Business), MBA (USA) in the writing of the case are gratefully acknowledged.

References

Ansoff, I., and McDonnell E. *Implanting Strategic Management*. New York: Prentice, 1990.

Bennis, W., Benne K., and Chin R. *The Planning of Change*. New York: Holt, Rinehart and Winston, 1976.

Kotter, J. *Leading Change*. Boston: Harvard Business Press, 1996.

Senge, P. *The Fifth Discipline: The Art and Practice of the Learning Organization*. New York: Doubleday, 1994.

Chapter 11

Conclusion

Satyendra Singh

Indeed, it is not safe to assume that what is true of one country is equally true of other countries, nor it is possible to capture the different reflections of businesses in emerging markets from a single reality perspective. Thus, the chapters in this book have different conclusion for different studies in different emerging markets. The study in Kenya indicates the extent to which political interest groups have shaped government policy through their incredible influence. And that explains why Kenyan government actions relating to the economy have not been consistent with the theory of economics. In fact, economic policies have been influenced by the initial policies and have been modified to suit the existing political situation. Initially, the colonial government created an economy that was based on the political system. Following independence from the United Kingdom, the independent Kenyan government continued the policies of the past to benefit powerful political interest groups such as politicians, bureaucrats, and large-scale African farmers. Thus, politics became an important element in the creation of institutions, and a convenient channel for attaining power using political positions. Creation of institutions in the economy and state appointments to positions of influence had been used to secure benefits from the various exchanges in the markets. Thus, politics has been used to generate, protect, and redistribute wealth through the patron-client system of Kenya to reward those who supported the political regime and to punish those who protested it.

With the reform of Kenya's economy, a change in the marketplace is noticeable, as the government set in motion the reform process even though it came under pressure from some of the vested interests groups—nationally or internationally. At first, government control of marketing activities, intended to correct market failure, resulted in marketing inefficiencies because the marketing function was constrained and many organizations failed to explore the function fully. Production activities, pricing, promotion, and distribution functions were adversely affected. However, with the passage of time, the economic reform policies forced firms to take the challenge and conduct business in a professional way. The increased competition led firms to be competitive, innovative, and market oriented. Firms began to develop products and markets and pursue quality in a bid to deliver value to customers. The future is bright for market-oriented firms; however, firms must train their personnel, apply modern technology, be quality conscious, and implement continually strategic planning in their operations.

Similarly, in India, the transformation of a planned economy to a market economy has attracted a multitude of foreign firms, forcing local firms to compete with foreign firms. This produced a change in the existing business practices—marketing, social, and economic—all relating to business orientation of firms. Further, the role of brand image became very prominent as consumers began to buy foreign products to label themselves as Westerners. Indeed, brand image influenced consumer behavior and mediated the relationship between business orientation and business performance.

Results of the study indicated links between marketing orientation and brand image, economic orientation and business performance, and brand image and business performance in foreign firms; however, Indian firms exhibited a positive and significant link *only* between brand image and business performance. Further, it was discovered that foreign managers were more likely to practice business-oriented activities than their Indian counterparts on items such as creation of wealth by generating information and offering services, and customization of products and production processes. However, both sets of managers were significantly business oriented in treating their markets as multicultural and in targeting their consumers via relationship marketing. Surprisingly, despite the arrival of Internet technology, both foreign and Indian managers still perceived Indian society as hierarchical. Most importantly, both sets of managers were almost neutral on the following four items: nature of society (inherited/ individualistic); media (controlled/free access); consumers (passive/ active); and business activities (covert/overt).

Clearly, managers need to understand the extent to which the Western trend is present in India. The practices identified in this chapter can be utilized for the assessment of existing trends. Managers should track the nature of evolving markets closely to be able to adapt and implement a suitable business strategy. For example, as perceived by both sets of managers, our study found that India's markets were multicultural and consumers were relationship oriented. So, it may be recommended that managers understand the structure of culture, which calls for being more interactive with consumers, possibly on a one-to-one basis. Managers may like to develop a personal form of marketing that recognizes, acknowledges, appreciates, and serves consumers through conscious and planned business practices.

In general, it is concluded that the key to success is an image-oriented product—a factor that would compel firms to offer products beyond its functional values. As Indian society tends to be Western and individualistic, consumers seek self-identity through the consumption of products or services that offer them self-expression through different images associated with brands. Indeed, the time is right to transfer the Western market–oriented knowledge to the Indian market. It can be achieved by modifying the Western techniques, particularly in communications, to suit the growing consumerism.

Admittedly, ethical orientation of businesses can also be hypothesized to have an impact on profitability, particularly in emerging markets that often have a tainted image of being corrupt. Thus, to test the assertion, the study examines the effects of two moral philosophies—deontological (based on rules) and teleological (based on consequences)—on profitability in the context of India. After controlling for firm size and industry type, the findings indicated that there were no significant differences between deontological and teleological philosophies on Corporate Ethical Values (CEV), and that CEV is nonlinearly (U-shaped) related to profitability. The profitability is initially negative but turns positive with higher levels of ethical orientation due to the acquisition of competitive advantage, irrespective of the moral philosophy adopted. Thus, managers should resist their initial temptations to make short-term profit at the expense of CEV. Although long-term benefits of leveraging ethical orientation create efficiencies and build tacit knowledge in a firm, it also imposes a cost. Therefore, managers must either reduce those costs or ensure that the benefits gained from practicing CEV more than offset the costs. Further, training materials in ethics in various formats—printed versus visual—should be useful to train future managers. Indeed, social responsibility and profitability can be compatible.

In conclusion, managers can command a premium price for their products, if consumers perceived them to be ethical. The fact that no particular moral philosophy contributes to CEV suggests that managers can adopt a combination of the two moral philosophies that negate their effects on each other and optimize outcome with available resources. Clearly, no dominant moral philosophy is yet crystallized in Indian corporate culture. So, a balanced ethical practice—a tradeoff between the two philosophies—should be a part of the corporate culture for the moral development of employees. The simultaneous use of the philosophies would allow firms to serve their customers in valuable and unique ways that are difficult to imitate, thereby, developing and sustaining a competitive advantage. In several states in India, for example, the South Indian states, firms may be able to position themselves solely on moral issues and be profitable. But having an ethical platform in poor states such as Bihar, Orissa, or Uttar Pradesh may be less effective than the rest of India. Therefore, managers need to understand the appropriateness of stressing ethics to their customers because these states suffer from resource shortages, population growth, and poverty.

For moral development within firms, managers can use the differential association theory that assumes that unethical behavior is learned in the process of interacting with intimate personal groups or role sets. Therefore, the onus is on the managers to create an environment conducive to forming groups of employees who believe in moral philosophies. Further, employees who perceive that corporate management in their organizations support ethical behavior may also perceive their organization as being just to its employees. Regardless of moral philosophies used to practice CEV, it is important that employees have high ethical standards.

The concept of ethics in Nigeria is somewhat new, though it is crucial to the development of ethical businesses and the creation of value in society. Managers should take responsibility to promote ethics and accountability while generating profit for their firms. Inadequate pay, poor working conditions, job insecurity, and bleak prospects create unethical practices. Naturally, those who have insufficient salaries may resort to immoral means. Thus, salary with retirement benefits, and healthcare services for workers and families, is important. Sanctions against corrupt practices are not effective unless a person's basic needs are met. Managers need to reward ethical employees. The mere enforcement of laws may not be sufficient to deal with unethical practices; sanctions may turn people to be more careful, play safe, and eventually become more sophisticated in unethical practices.

Establishing coalitions of business associations, professional groups, and civil society to explore and combat unethical practices is useful. These professional bodies have ethical standards. Mass campaigns to educate people on unethical practices and corruption are needed.

Systematic and impartial prosecution of unethical people is crucial. We need to look at work ethics vis-à-vis business ethics. Work ethics may precede business ethics, or complement each other. For example, in a society where people do not attach much value to honest work, quality work, and punctuality, among others, business ethics may not thrive.

Therefore, training at work and business ethics is paramount. Management in organizations should employ a full-time ethics officer who will give advice on ethical issues to top management, disseminate information on ethical values, investigate ethic violations, advise the board of directors on ethics, and oversee ethics-related training programs. This should be a training ground for corporate leaders who should be able to make positive changes in their societies and in the international community.

Performance appraisal processes, promotion, salary increases, and other incentive schemes in firms should be securely anchored in ethical values. These have the potential of promoting high ethical standards among employees who may wish to reciprocate the good intentions of management. Attempts by top management to create an ethical atmosphere may have little effect on the ethical attitude and behavior of employees if management does not practice what it preaches. Therefore, top management should fully support an ethics program. The expectations of top management and efforts related to ethical issues should be publicized in the organization handbook, newspapers, television, and radio commercials.

Emerging markets not only forced firms to be market oriented and ethical due to the competition brought by the foreign investments and firms but also changed consumer lifestyle and behavior. Drinking wine is one of them, the premise being today's consumers are more informed and knowledgeable about wine. Changes are evident in distribution (retail consolidation), technology (grape harvesting), marketing (market orientation), and lifestyle. Further, wine is a sophisticated product and requires sophisticated marketing, because wine purchasing is a behavioral process that involves choices and preferences based on attitude. The attitude is conceptualized as a three-component model—affective (feelings), behavioral (response tendencies), and cognitive (beliefs). It is proposed that the behavioral component is the most significant predictor of consumers' *choices*, followed by cognitive and affective components. Further, the attitude model was tested to predict the consumer's choice—drinking wine for pleasure or prescription.

Results indicated that the behavioral component contributed most to determining consumers' choice, followed by the cognitive and affective components. Intuitively, managers may assume that all attitude components are equally important, but in practice, it may not be the case. Thus, the implication for managers is that the emphasis should be on assessing the intention of consumers to change their behavior (i.e., tendency to respond) rather than on merely trying to change behavior that may have only transitory effects on consumers. Using the attitude model, managers should be able to assess the effectiveness of the components of attitude, market the product in Indian context, and position wine accordingly in the market. Understanding the pattern of the consumer choice process for each segment can contribute to positioning a wine brand and to maximizing profit by achieving efficiencies and effectiveness in advertising and promotion. Thus, informed consumers would be able to trade up between price-points for brands and labels that offer superior value Marketing managers can design and implement strategies to target these additional segmentations after understanding how Indian consumers make choices about purchasing wine.

Another challenge for foreign managers is to create advertisements that are compatible with the culture of emerging markets. Often advertisements are prepared in Western countries and applied to emerging markets elsewhere. This straight translation of advertisements is usually not effective; advertisements need modifications. Thus we conducted a comparison of creative aspects of advertising of perfumes between the United Kingdom and the United Arab Emirates. Findings suggested that the British creative directors encountered cultural limitations as impediments to the creative process of perfume advertising in the UAE. Although there might be creative talents in the UAE, advertisements for most of the major brands of perfumes were brought from Western countries. Only a few advertisements were made in the UAE. Creative directors based in the UAE should consider cultural values when conceiving ideas for advertising, even if there was little scope to maneuver in the area of creativity. The message of perfume advertising is like selling a sort of illusion of style and glamour, so it may be difficult to conceive an idea that sells glamour without showing glamour. These cultural limitations may hamper the creative process of advertising as the main creative theme. Indeed, machismo, femininity, and feminine allure may not always be displayed in the advertisement. All these sensitivities, censors, and perceptions of the target audience may impede the creative process of advertising in the UAE.

Implication for managers is that they can no longer rely on female allure when conveying creativity in advertisements in non-Western cultures. Instead, focus of the advertisement should be on the product and its utility only, because the creative process has relevance to social values, beliefs, and culture. Findings suggested that national culture influenced the creativity of advertisements, and that Western advertisers were creative by using female allure whereas non-Western advertisers were creative by using graphical designs. Therefore, when a female model is being used to advertise perfumes in the UAE, the focus of the advertisement should be on the product and its utility. Use of female allure to attract readers should be avoided, even if machismo and feminine allure are relevant to almost every culture. It is important to acknowledge the cultural subtleties and allow those kinds of latitudes that accept cultural differences. It is important that advertisers are sensitive to the cultural implications of their creative strategies. In this regard, advertising and marketing practitioners need to appreciate individual country differences in historical values and religious practices that may serve to form customer impressions and perceptions about advertising. In general, creative directors cannot apply universal standard perfume advertisements to the UAE market.

In Ghana, a former British colony, a similar pattern emerged—foreign firms perceived marketing functions to be more important and tended to perform more marketing activities than domestic firms. An attempt was made to determine marketing functions and to distinguish between foreign and local firms in their actual performance of marketing activities. Due to economic reforms in Ghana, although marketing practice is on the rise, foreign firms tend to outperform domestic firms in all areas. This portends long-term anxieties for indigenous firms that need to maintain a competitive edge in order to survive. These results may stem from the fact that domestic managers still do not *fully* appreciate the benefits of certain marketing functions, as evidenced in the scores for analyzing competitors' prices, providing discounts for different categories of buyers, and utilizing personal selling and sales promotion tools. Given the highly competitive environment, this issue is crucial because effective marketing activities will become increasingly important for the survival or maintenance of a competitive advantage. Indeed, there is a pressing need for the transfer of marketing knowledge to emerging markets. New forms of marketing could also be developed through the modification of Western techniques and adaptation of these tools to suit the country's culture. Both managers and employees can benefit from these transfers through more formal educational procedures that lead to the attainment of academic qualifications. In this context, tertiary institutions that serve as the primary agents of such transfers and provision of educational funding for these purposes should be seriously considered.

Evidence from this study suggested that domestic and foreign executives who tended to adopt marketing principles wholeheartedly did so because of the perceived importance of these activities to the firms. The differences in perceived importance and actual performance scores indicated that managerial perceptions were not matched by actual performance. However, in general, it is accepted that effective marketing practice results in higher performance. So it is important for managers to fully understand the benefits associated with marketing activities in order to perform them effectively. This calls for procedures to formalize marketing programs with an aim of redressing the apparent ad hoc approach that generally characterizes certain aspects of marketing practices, particularly among indigenous businesses.

In China, over the last two decades, the volume of transactions between parent organization and its international joint ventures (IJVs) operating in emerging markets has increased exponentially, creating a need to measure, recognize, and reward performance and achievements. Two factors are commonly used for this purpose—financial and nonfinancial. The *financial* factor is based on comparisons between expected and actual monetary returns such as sales, return on investments (e.g., share capital, long-term loans, etc.), and net profit, among others. Any variance leads the parents to reward or punish the IJVs. For the *nonfinancial* factor, the study has identified two sources—internal and external. The internal source includes five elements: agency relationship, the extent of control, strategy, technology, and transaction costs. The elements of the external sources are: culture and society, economy and market size, government and politics, industrial structure, and resources. Each of the elements affects performance and growth of IJVs.

Findings of the study suggested that firms used both financial and nonfinancial factors for performance measurement. These factors when used simultaneously ensure that the parent assesses the performance on a holistic basis, rather than solely on a particular element or factor. This avoids undue bias toward a particular IJV. Further, it is suggested that the basis of evaluation should be transparent among the IJVs, and that any changes to the basis should be communicated to the IJVs with justifications. This provides the IJVs with the opportunities to adjust to the new standard of performance. Variance in targets should be investigated and adjusted. IJVs should understand that new measurement tools are for comparison purposes due to the changes in the business environment. IJVs should not be prosecuted due to uncontrollable elements. Therefore, the elements of the measuring formula should be reviewed and calibrated regularly. Indeed, performance measurement is an important method to motivate and set targets for the players because what gets measured gets done. The continual change in measurement processes has implications and ramifications for mangers, parent organizations, IJVs, and stakeholders.

In the context of India, the case study of MAC & Co. describes how globalization enables firms to split their knowledge functions such as research and development in emerging markets to take advantage of low cost wages and high-quality personnel to improve business performance. In 1987, the firm pursued its mantra of one global firm and launched three initiatives: Firm Practice Information System (FPIS), Practice Development Network (PDNet), and Knowledge Resource Directory (KRD). FPIS was a computerized database of client engagements accessible to all employees of the firm. It enabled the firm to organize and store historical data on client projects. It also captured information relating to lessons learned, which acted as a benchmark for future projects. PDNet was also a computerized system but aimed at capturing the knowledge that had accumulated in the core practices of the firm. This was, however, a challenging task, as it required individual consultant to upload and use the information. Whereas both these initiatives faced difficulties early on due to the efforts required by individual consultants to upload the information, KRD, which served as a yellow pages directory assisting the consultants with finding coworkers with expertise in specific areas, was a huge success.

Certainly, firms apply certain criteria when locating research/ knowledge-driven functions in India or in other emerging markets. By creating a mass of support staff in a low-cost location, the firm allows the research and information staff to give consultants information faster and at a lower cost than before. For instance, consultants from anywhere in the Asia Pacific region could send in a request for general or specific information or analysis via email or phone, and staff in India would turn it around within 24 hours. The center was open five days a week around the clock. Indeed, MAC & Co. built capabilities and infrastructure across the globe.

The forces of globalization have produced change in business practices, particularly in emerging markets that were immune to competition in the past. Being no longer the case, another case study in Kenya describes the evolution and operations of MAST East Africa Limited. It describes how the liberalization affected the company, increased competition in the market, and forced the company to address the issue of change management. The case demonstrates how MAST managed change.

MAST Africa Ltd. faced change due to the economic liberalization in Kenya in the early 1980s. The main aim of change management is to build a new organizational capability to enable the organization to fulfill its objectives and mission. Organizational capability, as defined in the case, is the collective skill of the organization that combines structure, culture, and process. To build capability, the initial point is the recognition of the need for change, followed by the will to change. An organization must develop and perfect the art of managing strategic change. Strategic change requires strategic competence as it contributes to the success of an organization.

This case further demonstrates that managers must see change management as strategy implementation. It is about managing the change to take the organization to the next level while trying to assure employees that the changes are for the better, keeping their morale high and motivating them to move along with the change. To have a smooth transition, managers should exercise leadership quality and management skills and drive the changes in the systems, culture, organization, and the inherent processes. Leadership is used to influence people to move positively toward the new desired state, whereas management is about coordinating the various tasks and activities inherent in the change management process. Change leadership must begin with communicating the vision for the new direction. Employees must subscribe to the vision. People's hearts and minds must be won before managers can exercise management, which involves planning, organizing, directing, staffing, control, coordination, budgeting, and activities.

Thus, it is important that managers prepare employees for change. Change takes place smoothly if it is articulated to staff as to how the change will benefit them and why a new strategy is necessary under the changed circumstances. The managers must strive to change the firm's culture to support the new strategy. Everybody must be involved. The case concludes that organizations are faced with unforeseen forces that drive a need for change because the environment is subject to change. As MAST found out, the ability to understand the source of the change is as critical as how fast the adaptation process will be. Their success is largely attributed to timely organizational change and strategic plan implementation. Now MAST is equipped to adapt quickly to changes and to withstand fierce competition.

Index